D1167950

Cold War Summits

NEW APPROACHES TO INTERNATIONAL HISTORY

Series Editor: Thomas Zeiler, Professor of American Diplomatic and U.S. Economic History, University of Colorado at Boulder

New Approaches to International History covers international history during the twentieth and twenty-first centuries and across the globe. The series incorporates new developments in the field, such as the cultural turn and transnationalism, as well as the classical high politics of state-centric policymaking and diplomatic relations. Written with upper level undergraduate and postgraduate students in mind, texts in the series provide an accessible overview of international diplomatic and transnational issues, events, and actors.

Published:

Decolonization and the Cold War, edited by Leslie James and Elisabeth Leake

Forthcoming:

Latin American Nationalism, James F. Siekmeier
The History of United States Cultural Diplomacy, Michael L. Krenn
The United Nations in International History, Amy Sayward

Cold War Summits

A History, from Potsdam to Malta

CHRIS TUDDA

Bloomsbury Academic
An imprint of Bloomsbury Publishing Plc

BLOOMSBURY
LONDON · NEW DELHI · NEW YORK · SYDNEY

Bloomsbury Academic

An imprint of Bloomsbury Publishing Plc

50 Bedford Square   1385 Broadway

London   New York

WC1B 3DP   NY 10018

UK   USA

www.bloomsbury.com

BLOOMSBURY and the Diana logo are trademarks of Bloomsbury Publishing Plc

First published 2015

© Chris Tudda, 2015

Chris Tudda has asserted his right under the Copyright,
Designs and Patents Act, 1988, to be identified as Author of this work.

All rights reserved. No part of this publication may be reproduced or
transmitted in any form or by any means, electronic or mechanical,
including photocopying, recording, or any information storage or retrieval system,
without prior permission in writing from the publishers.

No responsibility for loss caused to any individual or organization acting on
or refraining from action as a result of the material in this publication can be
accepted by Bloomsbury or the author.

British Library Cataloguing-in-Publication Data
A catalogue record for this book is available from the British Library.

ISBN: HB: 978-1-4725-3227-5
PB: 978-1-4725-2958-9
ePDF: 978-1-4725-2974-9
ePub: 978-1-4725-3425-5

Library of Congress Cataloging-in-Publication Data
A catalog record for this book is available from the Library of Congress.

Series: New Approaches to International History

Typeset by Integra Software Services Pvt. Ltd.

CONTENTS

LIST OF ILLUSTRATIONS

SERIES EDITOR'S PREFACE

New Approaches to International History takes the entire world as its stage for exploring the history of diplomacy, broadly conceived theoretically and thematically, and writ large across the span of the globe, during the twentieth century. This series goes beyond the single goal of explaining encounters in the world. Our aspiration is that these books provide both an introduction for researchers new to a topic, and supplemental and essential reading in classrooms. Thus, *New Approaches* serves a dual purpose that is unique from other large-scale treatments of international history; it applies to scholarly agendas and pedagogy. In addition, it does so against the backdrop of a century of enormous change, conflict, and progress that informed global history but also continues to reflect on our own times.

The series offers the old and new diplomatic history to address a range of topics that shaped the twentieth century. Engaging in international history (including but not especially focusing on global or world history), these books will appeal to a range of scholars and teachers situated in the humanities and social sciences, including those in history, international relations, cultural studies, politics, and economics. We have in mind scholars, both novice and veteran, who require an entrée into a topic, trend, or technique that can benefit their own research or education into a new field of study by crossing boundaries in a variety of ways.

By its broad and inclusive coverage, *New Approaches to International History* is also unique because it makes accessible to students current research, methodology, and themes. Incorporating cutting-edge scholarship that reflects trends in international history, as well as addressing the classical high politics of state-centric policymaking and diplomatic relations, these books are designed to bring alive the myriad of approaches for digestion by advanced undergraduates and graduate students. In preparation for the *New Approaches* series, Bloomsbury surveyed courses and faculty around the world to gauge interest and reveal core themes of relevance for their classroom use. The polling yielded a host of topics, from war and peace to the environment; from empire to economic integration; and from migration to nuclear arms. The effort proved that there is a much-needed place for studies that connect scholars and students alike to international history, and books that are especially relevant to the teaching missions of faculty around the world.

We hope readers find this series to be appealing, challenging, and thought-provoking. Whether the history is viewed through older or newer lenses, *New Approaches to International History* allows students to peer into the twentieth century's complex relations among nations, people, and events to draw their own conclusions about the tumultuous, interconnected past.

Thomas Zeiler, University of Colorado Boulder, USA

ACKNOWLEDGMENTS

The views presented here are my own and do not necessarily reflect those of the US Department of State or the United States government.

Many people helped me produce this book. First, I would like to thank Thomas W. Zeiler, the editor of Bloomsbury's New Approaches to International History, for asking me to contribute to this new and exciting series. Claire Lipscomb of Bloomsbury believed in my proposal, and she and Emma Goode shepherded it to publication.

Many of my current and former colleagues at the Office of the Historian at the Department of State either read individual chapters or encouraged me to write the book. Kristin L. Ahlberg read the Glassboro chapter, Tiffany Cabrera read the Bandung chapter, Seth Center read the Potsdam chapter and helped me shape the introduction, David Zierler read the Beijing and Vienna chapters, and James Wilson read the Malta chapter and made important suggestions for the introduction. Tiffany Cabrera, Renée Goings, David Herschler, Kerry Hite, Susan Holly, and Dean Weatherhead did their usual best to keep me focused on important things like sports and television shows when I needed down time.

I wrote most of the Glassboro and Vienna chapters during the fall 2013 semester, when I had the good fortune and honor to be the Stanley Kaplan Visiting Professor of Foreign Policy at Williams College. Thanks to Steven Randolph, the Historian of the Department of State, for allowing me a leave of absence to teach at Williams. Thanks especially to James McAllister, professor of political science at Williams, who not only bestowed this incredible honor on me but also helped me shape my arguments in the Potsdam chapter. Yafeng Xia helped me shape my arguments about both Bandung and Beijing. And last but not least, thanks to my mother Barbara, brother Mike, sister Corinne, brother-in-law Corey, and my one-of-a-kind nephew and best friend, Jake, for making my stay in Vermont even more fun than I expected.

This book is dedicated to all my students, who make me realize that I'm still learning all the time.

ABBREVIATIONS

ABM	Anti-Ballistic Missile
Bulletin	Department of State *Bulletin*
CCP	Chinese Communist Party
CFE	Conventional Forces in Europe
CF	Country Files
CWIHP	Cold War International History Project
DAC	Diary of Anatoly Chernyaev
DBPO	*Documents on British Policy Overseas*
DMZ	Demilitarized Zone
DOSCF	Department of State Central Files
DRV	Democratic Republic of Vietnam
EDC	European Defense Community
EOB	Executive Office Building
FD, LOC	*Frontline Diplomacy*, Library of Congress
FAH	*From a Head, Through a Head, to a Head*
FRUS	*Foreign Relations of the United States*
HD	*Haldeman Diaries*
INF	Intermediate Nuclear Forces
MAD	Mutually Assured Destruction
MFN	Most-Favored Nation
MIRV	Multiple Independently-Targeted Re-entry Vehicle
NA	National Archives, College Park, MD
NATO	North Atlantic Treaty Organization
NSC	National Security Council
NPL	Richard Nixon Presidential Library and Museum
NPT	Non-Proliferation Treaty
NSA	National Security Archive
OSI	On-Site Inspections
PPP	*Public Papers of the President*
PRC	People's Republic of China
RD	*Reagan Diaries*
SALT	Strategic Arms Limitation Talks
SDI	Strategic Defense Initiative
SEATO	Southeast Asian Treaty Organization
START	Strategic Arms Reduction Talks
SWJN	*Selected Works of Jawaharlal Nehru*

TTBT	Threshold Test Ban Treaty
TYP	*Tehran, Yalta, and Potsdam Conferences*
UKNA	United Kingdom National Archives
UN	United Nations
UNGA	United Nations General Assembly
WHT	White House Tape

Introduction

This book grew out of the numerous lectures and exchanges I have had with my students at The George Washington University over the past eight years. I had begun teaching courses on US foreign policy since 1945, and then a few years ago I also started teaching a course called "The International History of the Cold War." I began to realize that an analysis of the various summits that occurred during the Cold War had become a key component of all my courses. My students were repeatedly struck by the importance of the more "famous" (infamous?) summits such as Yalta, Vienna, and Moscow, and as I began to focus more on the interplay between Cold War leaders they encouraged me to include more discussion of the less well-known summits such as Glassboro in class.

A few years ago I discovered David Reynolds' 2007 book *Summits: Six Meetings that Shaped the Twentieth Century*, and I was impressed with not only the depth and breadth of his research, but also his coverage of forty years of the Cold War. I began assigning individual chapters of the book based on the needs of my courses and began to do my own research into the summits that he did not examine. Serendipitously, my students asked "why don't you write about the other summits, especially Bandung?" As I began to explain that Bandung wasn't really a "summit," or at least the way I had been taught to think about the term, I realized that, actually, Bandung did belong in this book. Indeed, as Reynolds notes in the introduction to the book, the word "summit," coined by British Prime Minister Winston Churchill in 1950, denoted meetings "at the highest level."[1] In other words, they consisted of face-to-face meetings between presidents, prime ministers, and general secretaries aimed at resolving tensions that could not be resolved at the ambassadorial or foreign minister levels. Other, less known summits such as the 1979 Vienna meeting had either not been covered in great detail by other scholars or had occurred so recently that documentation had only recently become available. At the same time, I could include my own assessments of other famous summits such as Potsdam and Beijing. As I conducted more research, I realized that summits such as Glassboro and Malta proved important in and of themselves, as venues where leaders with opposing ideologies could personally meet to dispel misconceptions, myths, and misunderstandings. Summits, famous or not, often penetrated the public consciousness, and until the last days of the Cold War, they served as bellwethers for the state of Cold War tensions.

To be sure, former policymakers and political scientists had examined Cold War summitry before the publication of Reynolds' book. In 1976, former Under Secretary of State George Ball, who had served under presidents John F. Kennedy and Lyndon Baines Johnson, criticized summitry for "tend[ing] to create an illusion of understanding where none really exists." Moreover, he dismissed as a "myth" the "sentimental conceit that men of different countries can understand one another better through direct conversation than when their exchange of views and ideas is filtered through experts sensitive to the nuances that derive from different cultures." Highly critical of President Richard M. Nixon's February 1972 visit to Beijing—which I discuss in great detail below in Chapter Four—as well as Nixon's three summits with Soviet leader Leonid Brezhnev and other Cold War summits, Ball argued "there is nothing more dangerous than to rest the relations between states too heavily on the capricious interaction of diverse personalities." A reliance on interpreters, especially by "monolingual" American presidents, often led to "mischief" when leaders misunderstood what their foreign interlocutors said or promised during these personal conversations.[2]

G. H. Berridge has, for the most part, accepted Ball's criticism of summitry. Although he concedes that sometimes summitry can be useful as long as "it is employed judiciously," Berridge contends that leaders "may conclude agreements which are inconsistent with or irrelevant to national interests, or conclude no agreement at all, out of ignorance of the detail of the issue under discussion." The public relations stakes, instead, often make it impossible for leaders (as opposed to diplomats) "to contemplate bringing a negotiation to an end without something substantial to show for it."[3]

Most scholars, however, see both advantages and disadvantages in high-level summitry. In his examination of the American president and summit diplomacy, Elmer Plischke argues that, on the plus side, summits often lead to the establishment of a good personal relationship between allies and adversaries (one of the key claims of this book). The president's interlocutors, he notes, "may rest assured that they are dealing with the center of U.S. governmental power and responsibility" rather than a diplomat who may have exceeded their instructions. On the minus side, presidents may become so enamored with personal, summit diplomacy that "it may become an addiction, and that it tends to create a seductive and proliferating precedent." All the pomp and circumstance of summit meetings, meanwhile, could "inhibit unhurried judgment as well as careful consideration and negotiation."[4]

David H. Dunn also discusses the downsides of summitry and highlights the increased chances for miscommunication, cultural differences between foreign leaders, excessive like or dislike of an interlocutor, leaders' overestimation of their own abilities, or simple mistakes due to a lack of expertise. At the same time, he acknowledges one of the key claims of my book: that high-level summits can be useful for information gathering, sizing up the leader of another country—allies as well as adversaries—and for "breaking down the barriers of mutual suspicion which inevitably exist between two parties who are unfamiliar with each other." The establishment of a good personal relationship, he admits, also can have political and diplomatic benefits.[5]

Keith Hamilton and Richard Langhorne have, like Dunn, analyzed both the advantages and disadvantages of summitry. The former include what they call the "educative function in so far as they compel political leaders to turn their attention from the domestic to the international implications of their policies." Hamilton and Langhorne, however, also place special emphasis on the symbolism of summitry and conclude that it has helped leaders conclude lasting agreements. Summits can signal new policies to allies and adversaries alike, give added momentum to negotiations already underway, and allow leaders in democracies to "respond to the requirements of democratic politics." The downsides include playing to popular sentiment, a leader's "desire for a personal triumph," which may lead him or her to make a bad deal instead of preserving or advancing national interests, and raising expectations that can be dashed during the actual meetings.[6]

While these scholars have done some good work in pointing out the pros and cons of summitry, their analyses are flawed for two reasons. First, for the most part, they only analyze Western leaders. The Cold War, however, was a multipolar phenomenon, and recent historiography has demonstrated that Soviet and Chinese leaders faced significant domestic opposition of their own. While they may not have been subject to the vicissitudes of public opinion, they still had to contend with bureaucratic opposition, in particular from the military, which remained skeptical of talks with the West. Second, these political scientists do not use documents, especially from behind the Iron Curtain. So they are only speculating about whether or not promises were made or not made, in particular by Western leaders, and they rely mainly on public reporting, memoirs, and the like on which to base their analyses. They also rarely take into account the beliefs of Soviet, Chinese, and other non-Western leaders.

In this book, like Reynolds, I will try to "internationalize" summitry by using, when possible, non-US sources. Almost all of the American documents are readily available to scholars either in published form or on the internet in the *Foreign Relations of the United States* (FRUS) series, while some are now available on the various Presidential Libraries websites and other websites such as the National Security Archive. Other US documents are open at the National Archives in College Park, Maryland and at the Presidential Libraries. I also use British, Chinese, Indian, Soviet, and other international sources—many available on the internet, in particular at the

Cold War International History Project's website—to explain the competing priorities of the leaders engaging in these high-level talks.

In the summer of 1945, approximately two months after Germany's surrender, the new US president, Harry S. Truman, Churchill and his successor, Clement Atlee, and Soviet premier Josef Stalin, came to Potsdam, a suburb of war-ravaged Berlin, to try to end the Second World War and create a postwar order. Topics included whether or when the Soviets would enter the war against Japan, the disposition of defeated Germany, Poland's new western frontiers, and the hot-button issue of German reparations. Late in the conference, Truman learned that the United States had successfully tested an atomic weapon. Historians remain divided over whether Potsdam represented the beginning of the Cold War or whether prospects for postwar cooperation remained. I argue that, despite their disagreements about these key issues, in the end they compromised. Each leader expected another "peace conference" to occur afterwards where they could settle the Polish borders, the actual amount of reparations the Soviet Union would receive, and the like. That this peace conference did not occur is due to events that occurred between 1946 and 1948. I contend, therefore, that the Cold War did not begin at Potsdam, nor was it inevitable. I have nevertheless called the book *Cold War Summits* because I know I will not have the last word about this historiographical controversy.

In April 1955, some twenty-nine nations met at the Asian-African Conference in Bandung, Indonesia. I have included Bandung because it announced that the developing world had arrived on the world stage. The Cold War was a far more complex phenomenon than some historians and scholars have portrayed. The consensus that emerged from Bandung, that the developing world should concentrate on its own economic development, that imperialism of both the left and the right should be condemned and eradicated, and that the emerging nations should remain neutral in the Cold War helped define what Odd Arne Westad has called "the global cold war."[7] Despite this consensus, the Bandung Conference also exposed the fissures within the developing world, as "neutralists" such as Indian President Jawaharlal Nehru clashed with leaders such as Filipino delegate Carlos Romulo, who condemned the Soviet Union's new colonialism and sided with the United States. Meanwhile, the premier of the People's Republic of China (PRC), Zhou Enlai, argued that Communist China belonged with the nations of the developing world in spite of its friendship with the Soviet Union and its support of "continuous revolution."

June 1967 was a time of increased tensions between the United States and the Soviet Union. President Lyndon Johnson and Premier Alexei Kosygin met at Glassboro State College in New Jersey to try to mend the relationship. Relations between the two superpowers had been hurt by the US war in Vietnam, the Soviet decision to undergo a massive nuclear arms buildup, and the Six-Day War between Israel and the Arab states that had erupted earlier in the month. Not much has been written on Glassboro with the exception of a few pages in a few monographs; most scholars consider Glassboro to be a well-intentioned and relatively inconsequential footnote in the Cold War. I will demonstrate, however, that the summit jump-started important arms control negotiations such as Non-Proliferation (NPT) and the Strategic Arms Limitations Talks (SALT) between the two nations and also signaled that neither side wanted to be dragged into a proxy war in the Third World. This will be the first thorough examination of the goals, discussions, and outcome of the Glassboro summit.

The 1972 Beijing summit, on the other hand, has been considered one of the crowning successes of Cold War summitry. The meeting between US President Richard Nixon and PRC Communist Party Chairman Mao Zedong, and Nixon's subsequent meetings with Chinese Premier Zhou Enlai, has been dubbed "the week that changed the world." Indeed, this summit represented a turning point in the Cold War, as the Americans and the Chinese buried two decades of animosity and began to alter their strategic relationship. The Nixon strategy of "détente," or the relaxation of tensions between adversaries, received a huge boost after this meeting.

Vienna seemed to be the last achievement of the détente era. The United States, led by President Jimmy Carter, and the Soviet Union, led by General Secretary Leonid Brezhnev, met in Central Europe in June 1979 to sign the SALT II Treaty. However, the signing of the treaty masked a deepening freeze in the US–Soviet relationship. The Carter administration was alarmed by the Soviet, Cuban, and East German intervention in the Horn of Africa, the discovery of a Soviet combat brigade in Cuba, and Moscow's refusal to allow Soviet Jews and other dissidents to emigrate from the Soviet Union. Moscow, in turn, was angered by Carter's demands that it respect human rights, and grew frustrated that the president's national security team seemed to want to repudiate the agreements that Brezhnev had made with President Gerald R. Ford in 1974. Brezhnev's declining health and Carter's troubles with Congress also hampered US–Soviet relations in 1979. Thanks to the recent release of documents, this will be the first thorough examination of the goals, discussions, and outcome of the Vienna summit.

US President George H. W. Bush and Soviet General Secretary Mikhail Gorbachev met in Malta in December 1989, only a few short weeks after the peaceful fall of the Berlin Wall. Many observers were stunned when Gorbachev decided not to intervene to prevent East Germany's dissolution. The Malta Summit represented Bush's attempt to manage the end of the Cold War and to work with Gorbachev to insure against a conservative backlash within the Soviet Union against Eastern Europe's rapidly changing strategic, political, economic, and social conditions. Gorbachev's declaration that the Soviet Union and the United States were "not inherently enemies" signaled that the Cold War had ended.

Each chapter also contains a historical narrative and an analysis of some—but not all—of the seminal events that led to and followed each summit. The chapters that analyze the four "superpower" summits—Potsdam, Glassboro, Vienna, and Malta—focus on the most important conflicts in the US–Soviet (and sometimes British) relationship. The Bandung and Beijing chapters, on the other hand, focus on the events that occurred in the Third World such as decolonization, revolutions, and, in particular, the conflicts that arose between the United States and the PRC.

CHAPTER ONE

The Potsdam Conference: The Beginning of the Cold War?

The alliance that opposed Germany, Italy, and Japan during the Second World War was always one of convenience among three nations with different national ambitions and interests. Great Britain was a capitalist, constitutional monarchy and a colonial empire. In 1938, the prime minister, Neville Chamberlain, unsuccessfully attempted to "appease" German dictator Adolf Hitler by allowing Hitler to annex the German-speaking areas of Czechoslovakia in return for "peace in our time." After Germany invaded Poland on September 1, 1939, Britain and France declared war on Germany on September 3. Chamberlain resigned in May 1940 and was succeeded by Winston Churchill, who had opposed Chamberlain's German policy. After the fall of France on June 22, 1940, Britain became the sole holdout against Germany in Europe, which necessitated arms shipments from the United States. Churchill also looked to Washington to help preserve the Empire.[1]

The Soviet Union, on the other hand, was a totalitarian communist dictatorship led by Josef Stalin that was dedicated to world revolution and the overthrow of capitalism. On August 23, 1939, in order to forestall a potential German attack, Soviet foreign minister Vyacheslav Molotov and German foreign minister Joachim von Ribbentrop signed a treaty agreeing to not attack the other nor aid the enemy of the other. Secretly, the two nations agreed to divide the Baltic States, Finland, and Poland between themselves. Only two weeks after Germany invaded western Poland, the Soviet Union invaded eastern Poland. The treaty lasted until June 22, 1941, when Germany invaded the Soviet Union. Over the next four years, the two belligerents fought some of the bloodiest battles in human history and committed terrible atrocities in the East.

The United States had a very different experience, and very different goals. A capitalist democracy, it was closely allied with Britain. However, the United States had once been a British colony, and had fought the world's first successful anticolonial revolution. Its twin devotion to anticolonialism and capitalism put it at odds with both the British and the Soviets.

For the first two years of the war, President Franklin Delano Roosevelt officially adopted a policy of neutrality between the belligerents. This position was, in reality, anti-German. On September 2, 1940, US Secretary of State Cordell Hull signed the "destroyers for bases" agreement, which transferred 50 aging US destroyers to Britain in exchange for ninety-nine-year leases of land for air and naval bases in British possessions in the Western Hemisphere. On March 11, 1941, Roosevelt signed the Lend-Lease Act, which authorized him to sell, transfer, lend, or lease arms and other "defense articles" to any country. He quickly began to transfer weapons and other material to Britain and, in October, to the Soviet Union.

Lend-Lease came with conditions to which Churchill, desperate to maintain the US supply lines, agreed. He and Roosevelt met for the first time off the coast of Newfoundland in August 1941 and agreed to the Atlantic Charter, a joint statement that established the principles envisioned by the two leaders. One is particularly important for this study: the two nations publicly agreed that all peoples had the right to self-determination. Although Churchill later said that it only applied to German-occupied territories, Roosevelt considered it universally applicable.

Despite Washington's increasingly close alliance with London, it did not join the war in Europe. But its policy toward Japan ultimately brought it into the Second World War. Japan, which had invaded and occupied Manchuria, a mineral- and coal-rich region of China, in 1931 and attacked and occupied the Chinese mainland in 1937, had begun to move into Southeast Asia, threatening British, Dutch, and French possessions in the region. In 1940, Japan invaded French Indochina; Roosevelt responded by ending shipments of airplanes, aviation fuel, parts, and machine tools to Japan. In July 1941, he embargoed oil sales to Japan.

The two nations edged toward war during the fall, and Japan began secretly planning an attack against the US and British possessions in Asia. On the morning of December 7, 1941, Japan attacked Pearl Harbor Naval Base in Hawaii. That night, Japan also invaded the British colonies Malaya, Singapore, and Hong Kong, the Philippines, and the Dutch West Indies. A day later, Roosevelt and Churchill declared war on Japan, and on December 11 Germany and Italy declared war on the United States, which the United States reciprocated later that day.

After the Allied landings in Normandy, France, in June 1944 and the Soviet conquest of much of Eastern Europe, the war's end seemed imminent. In October, Churchill met with Stalin in Moscow to discuss postwar Europe. Both men exhibited an interest in postwar cooperation, and arguably a partnership. Indeed, Churchill scribbled on a piece of paper the so-called "percentages deal," which divided British and Soviet influence over certain East-Central and Mediterranean nations into actual percentages.

Four months later, Churchill, Roosevelt, and Stalin (the "Big Three") met on the Crimean coast in the resort city of Yalta. Yalta remains controversial to this day, as many Americans and Europeans accused Roosevelt and Churchill of "selling out" Poland. A visibly ill Roosevelt nonetheless was determined, like Churchill at Moscow, to maintain good relations with Stalin. He wanted Stalin's help against the Japanese as well as his support for a world organization, the United Nations (UN), that he believed could preserve world peace.

Stalin, on the other hand, had different goals. First, he wanted reparations from Germany in order to rebuild his shattered nation and cripple Germany's ability to reconstitute its military. Second, he wanted to establish a buffer zone in Eastern Europe, especially by exerting influence over Poland, in order to prevent another German invasion of his country. Third, he sought access to the Mediterranean through the Turkish-controlled Black Sea Straits. In Northeast Asia, he wanted territorial concessions, in particular access to Manchuria, rail lines, and the restoration of Soviet rights at the naval facilities at Port Arthur (Lushun), China. He also wanted control of the islands north of Japan that Russia had lost after the 1904–5 war with Japan.

Conditions were therefore ripe for the deal that the Big Three struck at Yalta. Roosevelt and Churchill both believed that Soviet cooperation would create a more stable international order once the war ended. Roosevelt, who did not want to leave American troops in Europe, also believed that the Soviets would cooperate in the postwar German occupation.[2]

Churchill and Roosevelt agreed to Stalin's demands that Polish communists determine that unlucky country's future. The two Western leaders demanded, and received, a promise of elections to be held in the

FIGURE 1.1 *Molotov and Stalin confer at Yalta. United States Information Agency.*

spring, but held out little hope that those elections would resemble Western elections. Stalin's army controlled Poland, and short of declaring war on the Soviet Union, there was little Roosevelt and Churchill could do about it. Indeed, Roosevelt lamented to one of his advisors, "It's the best I can do for Poland at this time." They also agreed that Poland's new eastern borders would end at the Curzon Line, allowing the Soviet Union to extend its frontier 200 miles west. Stalin, however, proposed that Poland's new *western* border extend 200 miles west into German territory, at the Oder and Neisse rivers. Churchill and Roosevelt objected, and the final communiqué of the Conference said only that Poland would eventually receive "substantial accessions of territory in the north and west" at another conference. This ambiguous wording would cause trouble at Potsdam.[3]

Stalin agreed to declare war on Japan three months after Germany's surrender and acceded to Roosevelt's UN proposal. At the same time, Churchill and Roosevelt refused to accept Stalin's demands for $20 billion in reparations from Germany. Instead, they only agreed to establish a reparations commission, to be located in Moscow, to study the issue.

On April 12, 1945, Roosevelt died of a cerebral hemorrhage. The vice-president, Harry S. Truman, became president, and at first the former Senator from Missouri felt as if "the moon, the stars, and all the planets had fallen on me." He had been kept completely in the dark about foreign affairs during his time in office. Truman spent days reading the Yalta transcripts in order to understand Roosevelt's commitments. He had never even met the US Ambassador to the Soviet Union, Averell Harriman.[4]

Meanwhile, Harriman lobbied Stalin to send Molotov to the San Francisco Conference at which the first meetings of the UN were to be held. Stalin agreed as long as Truman requested Molotov's presence and agreed to invite the foreign minister to Washington for a meeting. Stalin also made an important request that appears in the Soviet version of the meeting but not in the American record, as shown by Geoffrey Roberts: "Stalin specifically asked if there would be any 'softening' of American policy toward Japan. When Harriman replied that a change of policy was out of the question, Stalin said Soviet policy toward Japan remained as before—based on the agreement at Yalta." That meant that he would declare war on Japan three months after Germany's unconditional surrender. This is very important, because it demonstrates Stalin's concern that the new president might not demand Japan's unconditional surrender.[5]

Truman tendered the invitation, and on April 22 he met with Molotov. He affirmed that he "stood squarely behind all the commitments and agreements taken by our late President." Molotov in turn said Stalin planned to keep his promise to declare war on Japan. On April 23, however, Secretary of State Edwin Stettinius told Truman that Moscow had apparently broken the portion of the Yalta Accords that dealt with Poland. Stalin, Stettinius said, was "insisting on their puppet government in Poland regardless of American opinion." Angered, the president told Molotov during their second meeting that he would not recognize any Polish government unless free elections were held. Molotov warned that further allied cooperation depended on the allies treating each other "as equals." Truman replied that he wanted "friendship with Russia, but Poland was the sore point."[6]

In his memoirs, Truman said that Molotov replied "I have never been talked to like that in my life." Truman supposedly retorted "Carry out your agreements and you won't get talked to like that." Interestingly enough, neither the official American record nor the Soviet record mention this incident. Molotov, for his part, recalled,

At our first meeting with Truman, he began talking to me in such an imperious tone! ...I thought, what kind of president is he? I said "I cannot talk with you if you take such a tone." He stopped short a bit. Rather stupid, to my mind. And he had a very anti-Soviet mind-set. That's why he began in that tone; he wanted to show who was boss. Then he began to talk with us more respectfully and calmly.

Tellingly, despite his bluster, Truman wrote Stalin afterward and conceded the legitimacy of Soviet security interests in Poland.[7]

Two days after the Molotov–Truman meeting, the US and Soviet armies linked up at the Elbe River in a symbolic display of Allied unity. Meanwhile, the Soviets surrounded Berlin, and on April 30 they captured the Reichstag. Hitler committed suicide that same day, and on May 7 Germany unconditionally surrendered to the Allies.

Plans for another meeting of the Big Three began as early as May 6, when Churchill wrote Truman suggesting such a meeting. The prime minister also advised "we should hold firmly to the existing position obtained or being by our armies" in Eastern Europe, and "we must most earnestly consider our attitude towards the Soviets and show them how much we have to offer or withhold." Truman agreed, but said that he preferred that Stalin make the request for such a meeting. Meanwhile, he vowed "to adhere to our interpretation of the Yalta agreements."[8]

Churchill recommended that they invite Stalin "to meet us at some agreed unshattered town in Germany" in July and praised Truman's determination to adhere to "our rightful interpretation" of Yalta. In a second message, the prime minister said they could "only" resolve the Polish "deadlock" through another tripartite meeting. But he warned Truman that "the tide of Russian domination" had likely swept "forward 120 miles on a front of 300 or 400 miles. This would be an event which, if it occurred, would be one of the most melancholy in history." Poland, he feared, would be "completely engulfed and buried deep in Russian-occupied lands." The Soviets would essentially control all of Eastern and Central Europe and threaten Turkey.

Ultimately Truman agreed on May 14 that they should make the invitation. Stalin accepted and insisted they meet in Potsdam, a suburb of

Berlin, in the Soviet-occupied area of conquered Germany. The three leaders agreed that the conference would begin on July 15.[9]

In another indication of his determination to maintain good relations with Stalin, Truman sent one of Roosevelt's most influential advisors, Harry Hopkins, who both Stalin and Molotov knew and respected, to Moscow to meet with the Soviet leader.

In five meetings, Hopkins and Stalin went round and round on Poland and the Far East. On May 26, Hopkins explained that American public opinion toward Moscow had taken a nosedive over the previous six weeks thanks to the controversy over the deal on Poland at Yalta. "[F]riends of Roosevelt's policy and of the Soviet Union," Hopkins claimed, "were alarmed that if present trends continued unchecked the entire structure of world cooperation and relations with the Soviet Union which President Roosevelt and the Marshal had labored so hard to build would be destroyed."

Stalin replied that while the Soviet Union only wanted "a friendly Poland," Churchill wanted "to revive the system of *cordon sanitaire* on the Soviet borders." Hopkins assured Stalin that "neither the Government nor the people of the United States had any such intention." Truman, despite his concerns about Poland, nevertheless had expressed "his desire to continue President Roosevelt's policy of working with the Soviet Union and his intention to carry out in fact as well as in spirit all the arrangements, both formal and informal which President Roosevelt and Marshal Stalin had worked out together."

Hopkins also asked when Stalin would declare war on Japan; Stalin said he would check with his advisers and let him know. On May 28, Stalin said that he would be ready to join the war against Japan "two to three months after the surrender of Germany," when "the Soviet armies would be in a sufficient state of preparedness and in position." The actual date of the declaration, however, depended "on the execution of the agreement made at Yalta concerning Soviet desires" regarding Chinese territorial concessions. If China "should agree to these desires the Soviet Union would be ready to commence operations in August." Hopkins seemed satisfied by this answer.

At the same time, Stalin expressed a far more complex view of international relations than the West realized. He claimed that "he knew little of any Chinese leader but that he felt that Chiang Kai-Shek was the best of the lot and would be the one to undertake the unification of China." Hopkins reported that Stalin said "he saw no other possible leader," nor did he believe "that the Chinese communist leaders were as good or would be able to bring about the unification of China." His nation's national interests, at least at this moment, trumped solidarity with his ostensible communist Chinese allies. Stalin's commitment to the declaration of war, meanwhile, showed that he wanted to maintain good relations with the United States.[10]

Shortly thereafter, Truman sent another close Roosevelt advisor, Joseph Davies, who had been Ambassador to the Soviet Union in the 1930s, to London to meet with Churchill. Davies had pushed for the job, because he believed he could convince the prime minister to "see the light" and begin pursuing a "less confrontational approach" toward Moscow. British foreign secretary Anthony Eden didn't like Davies; he called him "the born appeaser" who possessed "the errors and illusions of Neville C., substituting Russia for Germany."[11]

The prime minister told Davies that "Great Britain might have to do certain things" in its "own interests, but would not oppose the U.S." Davies in turn warned Churchill that "without continued unity of the Big Three there could be no reasonable prospect of Peace. The causes of this dangerous situation were also clear. They were differences over what the agreements arrived at in Yalta actually were." These differences, moreover, had been exacerbated "by and fed by fears, distrusts, and suspicions on both sides." Although he understood Churchill's concern about Stalin's behavior, Davies said Truman would "scrupulously" support "every" agreement made by President Roosevelt. Truman's "paramount objective now must be to conserve peace after victory." Davies also warned that they must dispel any idea that they were ganging up on Stalin.

Churchill initially responded favorably to these concerns. Nevertheless, he "complained bitterly" that Stalin had not upheld their percentages deal in Eastern Europe, and Davies wrote that he "became vehement and even violent in his criticisms of the Soviet Armies and officials in the re-occupied areas." Davies concluded that "he was basically more concerned over preserving England's position in Europe than in preserving Peace." Moreover, he "is bedeviled by the consciousness that his Government no longer occupies its position of power and dominance in the world." This feeling was no doubt exacerbated by the fact that Parliamentary elections had been called, and for the next month Churchill faced the prospect of electoral defeat.[12]

Despite Churchill's complaints about Soviet behavior, on June 23 Truman decided to recognize the new Polish government, now called the Polish Provisional Government of National Unity (PPG). The PPG was dominated by communists, with a few token representatives of the so-called "London Poles" supported by Britain. Undersecretary of State Joseph Grew informed Harriman of the decision and said that the recognition came with the proviso that the PPG "shall be pledged to hold free and unfettered elections on the basis of universal suffrage and secret ballot."

The president informed Churchill that he would publicly recognize the PPG on July 3 because it had been formed "in conformity with the Crimea Decision." He now believed that since "the matter has moved this far forward any further delay would serve no purpose and might even prove embarrassing to both of us. I hope, therefore, you will agree to accord recognition simultaneously with us." Churchill replied "Our position is different from yours" since the "old Polish Government is seated here in London." He also remarked, however, "It is, of course, our intention to recognize the new government, but we should hope that some consideration could be shown to us in meeting difficulties which you, in no way, share." He asked that Truman hold off on recognition until July 4 so he could give the London Poles a 24-hour heads-up. Truman not only agreed to delay recognition, but pushed it back a day so it did not coincide with Independence Day celebrations, which would have been awkward for Washington.[13]

The other issue regarding Poland was its western borders. Now that a government "friendly" to the Soviet Union had been created, Stalin made preparations for Poland's western frontiers to be moved westward into German territory.

The problem was the ominous news from Germany. Robert Murphy, the Political Advisor in Germany, told Grew that he had just raised the issue of fuel supplies for the western zones of Germany with Marshal Georgy Zhukov, the commander of the Soviet zone. Coal was supposed to be provided by mines in Silesia, a region that had been part of Germany for 200 years. But Zhukov announced that the mines "were now in another jurisdiction, i.e. Poland," thus "they were not available." Murphy "expressed surprise, stating that it was my understanding that Silesia formed a part of the Soviet zone of occupation of Germany." He reported that "Zhukov corrected me, saying that Germany did not exist and that everyone knew that the Crimea Conference established the Polish frontier along the Oder and Neisse rivers."[14]

Of course, while Stalin had suggested the Oder-Neisse as Poland's new western frontiers at Yalta, Churchill and Roosevelt had postponed an actual Three-Power decision on the issue for the next conference. Grew thus told Murphy that "we can only comment that he has been misinformed," and that they had only agreed to move the borders "at a subsequent time."[15] Stalin and his people, however, considered it a done deal. This fundamental difference of opinion, and Stalin's unwillingness to settle for anything less, would dominate the Potsdam Conference.

As the conference drew closer, Churchill told the British Ambassador to the United States, Lord Halifax, that he didn't want to hurry the summer conference because Yalta had been "somewhat abruptly curtailed in the Crimea. We have here to try to reach settlements on a great number of questions of the greatest consequence, and to prepare the way for a Peace Conference which presumably will be held later in the year or in the early Spring." This is another indication that Churchill, like Truman, did not expect a cold war with the Soviet Union.

More important, however, Churchill feared that Truman did not see the real challenge that the Soviet Union presented. "I have the impression that the Americans take a rosier view of European prospects than we do," he wrote. "They seem to think that, given the settlement of a few outstanding problems, and the enunciation of general political principles and desiderata Europe can safely be left to look after itself and that it will soon settle down to peaceful and orderly development. Our view, on the contrary, is that unless we all work very hard the situation in Europe will deteriorate rapidly and dangerously." Issues in Germany, including its frontiers, were far from resolved. Moreover, Poland had essentially been lost. At the same time, the Soviets had begun to make "serious demands on the Turks without previous warning to their Allies. The resulting crisis, if not soon resolved, may become hardly less serious than the Polish issue which has so poisoned international relations in recent years."

Halifax, however, reassured Churchill that "the American Delegation from the President downwards fully share your preoccupations and are prepared to tackle the difficulties ahead of us with vigour." Truman and the new Secretary of State, James Byrnes, would "stand up to the Russians with us when necessary." At the same time, he explained that the Americans attached "great importance to securing the full co-operation of the Soviet Union in attempting to solve these difficulties and are reasonably hopeful of securing this co-operation provided the Russians are not made to feel that the Americans or we ourselves start with a fundamental hostility towards them." This is an important point. Halifax correctly understood that Truman put more stock in cooperation than confrontation. Apparently convinced, Eden told Halifax that "His Majesty's Government and United States Government are satisfied that the formation of the Polish Provisional Government of National Unity constitutes a substantial step in the fulfillment of the Yalta agreement on Poland."[16]

British intelligence, meanwhile, did not seem too concerned about Soviet behavior in Germany. To be sure, the Soviets seemed "completely indifferent to the plight of the Germans," food was "very short in Berlin," and they were "now refusing to provide food or coal for the 1,7000,000 Germans in the US/British zones." Soviet troops were also uprooting any type of machinery that could be used to rebuild the Soviet Union's devastated economy and sending them to the Soviet Union as reparations. Still, there was "nothing peculiarly sinister about Russia's policy in her zone. It appears in fact to be a perfectly simple policy of using German industry as a means of rebuilding Russia and of eliminating all possible political opposition in their own territory." Nor did Moscow seem interested in "building up a strong German state in the East" or "sponsoring a strong Communist Party in their zone." The question was "how far the Soviet Government will go in developing a four-power policy for Germany."

The British Ambassador to the Soviet Union, Clark Kerr, also reported that Moscow had "taken the initiative in proposing a return to more normal relations." He pointed to their cooperation during meetings of the Reparations Commission, on policy toward war criminals, and the fact that the issue of the Polish government had been settled. He did make the caveat that "the above list of happy events does not include a single instance in which the Soviet Government have given way substantially on any issue affecting their vital interests." Nonetheless, he noted that while "their methods may still be rough and ill-mannered," one of "the main reasons for the unaccommodating and even hostile attitude previously taken up by the Soviet Government on almost every problem of common concern was their suspicion that their British and American allies were combining to deprive them of some of the fruits of victory." The Hopkins trip, however, had gone "a long way to persuade the Soviet Government that for the present at any rate American policy tended to follow the lines laid down by President Roosevelt."[17]

The other, arguably more controversial, issue was how the war against Japan would be ended, including whether or not the atomic bomb would be available for use, whether or not it should be used, and whether Truman threatened Stalin with the bomb at the conference. In the weeks leading up to the conference, the Western allies operated under two assumptions. First, Japan must unconditionally surrender, whether by conventional means or, if it proved to be operational soon, by the use of the atom bomb. Second, Truman and Churchill (and Atlee thereafter) accepted Stalin's demands that the Soviet receive territorial concessions, in particular from their ostensible ally, China, in return for declaring war on Japan.

In order to coordinate the nation's atomic policy, Truman created the Interim Committee in early May, and named Byrnes his personal representative. Byrnes advocated use of the weapon against Japan because it could allow the United States "to 'dictate terms' " at the end of the war, likely "save the lives of hundreds of thousands of American servicemen preparing to invade the Japanese home islands," and "serve to counterbalance the land-based power of the Soviet Union."

The Chair of the Committee, Secretary of War Henry Stimson, who ran the overall atomic project, which was code-named the Manhattan Project by the Americans and "T.A." (for Tube Alloys) by the British, was more circumspect. Although he conceded that the weapon could give the United States "all the cards," he was actually "appalled" by the potential impact of the bomb because of its massive destructive power, especially against civilians. Backed by many of the scientists working on the bomb as well as General George Marshall, the Chief of Staff of the US Army, Stimson suggested that the United States share its atomic technology with the Soviet Union in return for "political liberalization and a transparent inspection regime" within the Soviet Union. Byrnes, however, rejected cooperation with Moscow as well as the scientists' suggestion that the United States demonstrate the weapon in order to "shock the Japanese into submission." Byrnes worried that if the test failed the Japanese would be emboldened to dig in further, therefore risking more Americans' lives. Instead, he argued the United States should use the weapon against Japan "as soon as possible" and "without prior warning." He did agree with Stimson, however, that the United States should find targets where civilian casualties could be minimized. On June 1, Truman told Byrnes that he "could think of no alternative" than to use the bomb against Japan.[18]

The two Western powers agreed on July 4 that if the nuclear weapon became operational, it would be used against Japan. But they would keep their new weapon a secret from Stalin for as long as possible, even though Stimson said "If nothing was said at this meeting about the T.A. weapon, its subsequent early use might have a serious effect on the relations of frankness between the three great Allies." He hoped that if "mutual frankness on other questions was found to be real and satisfactory, then the President might say that work was being done on the development of atomic fission for war purposes."[19]

What the West didn't realize is that Stalin had his own atomic weapons program, headed by Lavrenti Beria, who also ran the Soviet Secret Police, the People's Commissariat for Internal Affairs (the NKVD, the forerunner to the KGB). Stalin also knew about the bomb because Beria had a ring of spies in the United States that had penetrated the Manhattan Project. One of these spies, Klaus Fuchs, a German physicist who had been in Britain when the war began, joined the T.A. team in 1941, and became a British citizen a year later. In August 1944 he began working at the secret US atomic laboratory in Los Alamos, New Mexico. Fuchs sent a steady stream of intelligence back to Moscow about the progress being made on the bomb. As early as February 1945, Beria not only learned that an atomic bomb was "feasible" but that a successful test would likely occur within two to three months. By June 1945, Fuchs informed Moscow about the expected date of the first test and said the United States planned "to use the bomb against Japan if the test proved successful."[20]

For the moment, the US government assumed that it would have to invade Japan. Marshall predicted that in the first month, US casualties "should not exceed the price we have paid for Luzon," where 31,000 soldiers were killed, wounded, or remained missing. (Admiral William Leahy, however, who headed the US–UK Combined Chiefs of Staff, estimated that the United States could lose 35 percent of its invasion force.) "It is a grim fact," Marshall contended, "that there is not an easy, bloodless way to victory in war." More important, the General said the United States needed the Soviets to either threaten to or attack the enormous Japanese army in Manchuria, which would prevent reinforcements from defending Japan's home islands. Stimson, meanwhile, hoped that the allies could warn Japan of the dire consequences should an invasion occur.[21]

As for Soviet aims in the Far East, Russia had long enjoyed the use of Dairen, a large, ice-free port, built an important railroad that linked Siberia to Dairen, and had used Port Arthur, a naval base, all located in Northeast China. Japan received them as spoils of the 1904–5 Russo-Japanese War. The subsequent 1915 Sino-Japanese Treaty, which China had contested and the United States had never recognized, transferred the leases to Japan for ninety-nine years. The Soviets, the US State Department realized, wanted access to the facilities at the very least, and advised Byrnes, "So long as there is upheld the principle of nondiscrimination in international commercial relations, there would be no reason for the United States to oppose any Russian proposal that Dairen remain a 'free port'." The Department advised, however, that Washington "support China's sovereignty over the Kwantung Lease Territory, including Dairen, as that territory has been regarded as forming a part of Manchuria."

Chinese Foreign Minister T. V. Soong, meanwhile, told Harriman that after talks with Stalin, his government had agreed to allow the Soviet Union access to the two facilities as well as joint operation of the Siberia–Dairen railroad. In return, Stalin had agreed to "satisfactory conditions for the Treaty of Friendship and the Civil Affairs Agreement during the military period in Manchuria, also assurances that he would withhold support from the insurgents in Sinkiang and the Chinese Communist Party." Once again, Stalin had emphasized power politics rather than ideology.[22]

As he prepared to leave for Potsdam, Truman remarked that he "was sure the Russians wanted to be friends. He saw 'no reason why we should not welcome their friendship and give ours to them.' He looked forward to meeting both Stalin and Churchill."[23] After eight days at sea, Truman arrived in Antwerp, Belgium, where he boarded the presidential plane, *The Sacred Cow*, for the three-and-a-half hour flight to Berlin, escorted by fighter jets. After landing at Gatow airfield on a sizzling summer day at around 4:00 p.m., Stimson and a large US delegation met the president; the US Army's Second Armored Division, known as "Hell on Wheels," acted as Honors Guard. The motorcade drove the ten miles to Truman's quarters in Babelsberg.

That evening, Stimson received a telegram from his special assistant for the Manhattan Project, George Harrison. The atomic bomb, Harrison said, had been successfully tested. Stimson quickly informed Truman about the results. The President decided that for the moment he would keep the information to himself and not tell either Churchill or Stalin.[24]

Stalin, who feared flying, traveled the nearly 1,200 miles from Moscow to Berlin by armored train, so the first meetings of the Conference were postponed for a day.[25] While he waited for Stalin, Truman decided to see Berlin. A combat veteran of the First World War, he was nevertheless stunned at the level of destruction. The motorcade, as his biographer David McCullogh has written, "passed miles of ruin and desolation, bomb craters, burned-out buildings, and seemingly endless processions of homeless Germans plodding along beside the highway carrying or dragging bundles of pathetic belongings." Moreover, "in the oppressive heat the smell of death and open sewers was nearly overpowering." Gromyko recalled, "Only some of the smaller houses in the outlying streets remained unscathed...There were bricks, mountains of bricks everywhere." After their arrival, Stalin and his entourage too saw Hitler's Chancery and Bunker, both of which "made an indelible impression on us…I came to the Potsdam conference table with impressions of destruction fresh in my mind."[26]

At noon on July 17, 1945, Truman and Stalin met for the first time. Truman said he had "looked forward for a long time to making his acquaintance." Stalin agreed upon the importance of personal relationships and contacts, to which the president replied that he believed "they would have no difficulty in reaching agreement on the matters which would be before them at the Potsdam Conference." Molotov asked about Poland's western frontiers and, at this point, Stalin admitted that Yalta had not decided the issue.

After a brief discussion about whether or not the allies should recognize Fascist Spain and whether Britain was truly committed to the war in the Far East, Stalin told Truman that his military would be ready to enter the war against Japan by the middle of August. The only possible glitch in that scenario, however, was that "prior to acting they would need to complete their negotiations and reach agreement with the Chinese." Stalin then reported on his talks with Soong, including his desire to practice "noninterference in Chinese internal affairs," as well as the railroads in Manchuria, Dairen, and Port Arthur. Returning to the issue of the Soviet Union's entry into the war against Japan, Stalin said "they would keep their word." Truman, the note taker recorded, "appears to have expressed his confidence that the Soviets would keep their word."

Byrnes raised the question of Chinese territorial concessions again, and said "if the arrangements were in strict accordance with the Yalta agreement, this would be all right, but that if at any point they were in excess of that agreement, this would create difficulties." Stalin replied that his government "did not wish to add in any respect to the Yalta agreement or to deceive the Chinese." However, he said that China "did not understand horse trading; they were very slow and tried to wrangle every little thing. They did not seem to be aware of the big picture." Truman and Byrnes said that as long as Dairen and Port Arthur remained "free" ports, they were satisfied with the current Sino-Soviet treaty provisions.

Truman was thrilled with this first meeting. In his diary he wrote "Most of the big points are settled. He'll be in the Jap War on August 15th. Fini Japs when that comes about. We had lunch, talked socially, put on a real show drinking toasts to everyone, then had pictures made in the back yard. I can deal with Stalin. He is honest—but smart as hell." He also wrote his wife "I've gotten what I came for—Stalin goes to war August 15 with no strings on it…we'll end the war sooner now, and think of the kids who won't be killed! That is the important thing."[27]

The Big Three met for their first plenary session at 5:00 p.m. on July 17 at the former Palace of the German royal family, Cecilienhof, in Potsdam. The courtyard featured a giant red star made from thousands of begonias. Each walked into the conference room through their own designated entrance, and after a photo session for the journalists covering the Conference, they sat down to conduct business.[28]

Stalin opened the meeting by proposing that Truman preside, which Churchill seconded. Following a brief discussion of the agenda, Truman said they should discuss Germany and submitted a document with US proposals about the Control Council. Both Churchill and Stalin said they needed to study the proposals first, and Churchill also said "this was such a wide subject that it was not appropriate for the Foreign Ministers but that the heads of state should study it and then discuss it." Truman then read the "document on the implementation of the Yalta Declaration on Liberated Europe" and noted that since Italy had declared war on Japan, he hoped they could support Italy's entry into the UN. Churchill noted that "their positions were not the same. The British were attacked by Italy in 1940 at the time France was going down which was described by President Roosevelt as 'a stab in the back'." Furthermore, his country had fought the Italians "for some time before the United States came in... We also suffered heavy naval losses in the war with Italy in the Mediterranean." Stalin suggested that the discussion be confined to the agenda, and Truman agreed.

After a discussion of various agenda topics, Stalin raised the issue of the Polish Government, especially the émigrés in London. Churchill "agreed that the question should be discussed and that the winding up of the former London Polish provisional government was part of that question." Moreover, he remarked, "It was important to continue to carry out the Yalta agreement and he, of course, attached great importance to the Polish elections in order that the will of the Polish people would be reflected." Truman remained silent, another indication that while he would have liked to have seen elections, he knew he could not demand elections in a country occupied by the Red Army. After general discussion about the agenda and whether or not China should be represented in the proposed Council of Foreign Ministers (CFM) meetings, Stalin asked, "Why does Churchill refuse to give Russia her share of the German fleet?," most of which had been captured by the British after Germany's surrender in April. Churchill "exclaimed 'Why?' and went on to say that he thought that the fleet should be either destroyed or shared. He observed that weapons of war are horrible things." Stalin replied, "let's divide it. If Mr. Churchill wishes, he can sink his share." In the Soviet version of the meeting, Stalin added "I have no intention of sinking mine." The meeting then adjourned.[29]

Shortly after the plenary's end, Churchill and Stalin met briefly. The Soviet leader said that as his party was leaving Moscow, an unaddressed message was delivered to him through the Japanese ambassador. The Emperor of Japan stated that Japan could not accept suggestions of unconditional surrender. However, "if it was not insisted upon Japan might be prepared to compromise with regard to other terms." Stalin said that he had not mentioned the missive "to anyone except the Prime Minister, but he wanted to bring it up at the next session of the Conference." Churchill suggested Stalin send the president a note on the subject in order to warn him before the next session.

Stalin furthermore said he didn't want Truman "to think that the Soviet Government wanted to act as an intermediary, but he would have no objection if the Prime Minister mentioned it to the President." Churchill agreed to do so, "pointing out that he also did not wish the President to feel that we were not at one with the United States in their aim of achieving complete victory over Japan." But he did acknowledge that some Americans questioned the condition of unconditional surrender. Stalin said, "the Japanese realised our strength and were very frightened. Unconditional surrender in practice could be seen here in Berlin and the rest of Germany."

Churchill also backed off on his position about the German fleet. He opined that "Britain welcomed Russia as a Great Power and in particular as a Naval Power. The more ships that sailed the seas the greater chance there was for better relations." Stalin replied "that he also wanted good relations. As regards Russia's fleet it was still a small one, nevertheless, great or small, it could be of benefit to Great Britain." Like the first Stalin–Truman discussion, this secret conversation reveals the Big Three's intention to compromise on some issues in order to preserve overall good relations among the allies.[30]

That evening, Stimson received more details about the successful atomic test. Armed with this news, Truman decided to inform Churchill. Over lunch on July 18, Truman showed the prime minister both telegrams. In his record of the meeting, Churchill noted that the president wanted to know "what I thought should be done about telling the Russians." Truman, Churchill wrote, "seemed determined to do this, but asked about the timing, and said he thought that the end of the Conference would be best." The prime minister replied that "it might well be better to hang it on to the experiment, which was a new fact on which he and we had only just had knowledge. Therefore he would have a good answer to any question, 'Why did you not tell us this before?'" Truman, Churchill wrote, "seemed impressed with this idea, and will consider it."

Truman changed the subject and asked about the disposition of the German fleet. Churchill, reflecting his change of heart, said, "we should welcome the Russians on to the broad waters and do it in a manner which was wholehearted and gracious...I found it hard to deny the Russians the right to keep their third of the Fleet afloat if they needed it." Moreover, he admitted that his government did not have "any use for our third of the warships." Despite this concession, Churchill urged the president to consider the issue in relation to "the general layout in Central Europe" and whether the "States which had passed into Russian control" would be free and independent or not. "The President attached great importance to this," and said he was determined to press for the "true independence" of East-Central Europe "in accordance with free, full and unfettered elections." Truman, Churchill wrote, "seemed to agree with my point that everything should be settled as a whole, and not piecemeal."

Churchill also lamented "the melancholy position of Great Britain, who had spent more than one-half her foreign investments in the time when we were all alone for the common cause, and now emerged from the War the only nation with a great external debt." After Truman acknowledged the sacrifice his close ally had made, Churchill told him about the recent Japanese offer that had come through Stalin. The prime minister said he worried about the high cost of American and British casualties and wondered whether unconditional surrender "might not be expressed in some other way, so that we got all the essentials for future peace and security, and yet left the Japanese some show of saving their military honour and some assurance of their national existence, after they had complied with all safeguards necessary for the conqueror." Truman countered that "he did not think the Japanese had any military honour after Pearl Harbour." Truman nevertheless became "quite sympathetic, and spoke, as Mr. Stimson had to me two days earlier, of the terrible responsibilities that rested upon him in regard to unlimited effusion of American blood."[31]

Shortly before the second plenary meeting, Truman, Byrnes, Stalin, and Molotov met to discuss the Japanese peace feeler. Stalin asked whether the president should reply. Truman said he had "no respect for the good faith of the Japanese." Stalin pointed out, however, that the Soviet Union was not at war with Japan and "it might be desirable to lull the Japanese to sleep, and possibly a general and unspecific answer might not be returned." Byrnes, meanwhile, "observed that it was possible that this Japanese move had been inspired by fear of what the Soviets intended to do. Molotov said that he was sure the Japanese could guess." Stalin assumed that they had probably observed the movement of Soviet forces in the region. For the moment, Truman decided to ignore the Japanese entreaty.[32]

During their second plenary session, the Big Three first debated what they all meant when they referred to "Germany." Churchill asked whether they meant pre-war Germany. Or did it mean something else now that the allies had decimated the once-powerful nation? Stalin said, "Germany is what she has become after the war. No other Germany existed now. Austria for example was not now a part of Germany." Truman suggested "for this purpose they consider Germany as it existed in 1937." After arguing a bit, Stalin "agreed that from a formal point of view Germany might be considered in this way. He suggested that the Western frontier of Poland be fixed now and that the question would then become clear." Germany now only had "four occupied zones." In the Soviet version of the session, Stalin said, "Take this and define what Germany is. It is a broken country."

Discussion shifted to Poland. Churchill said that his government had to deal with all the practical issues of the London Poles. The British, he contended, must now "persuade as many as possible to return to Poland," but worried that they would end up in Siberia (or worse). Still, he must have seen the writing on the wall, because he "wished to take this occasion to rejoice in the improvement which had developed in the Polish situation and to express the wish for the success for the new Polish Provisional Government." While he admitted that he "had wished for more in the setting up of this Government," he conceded that "the progress made was a splendid example of the collaboration of the great powers." The British government, British documents have shown, wanted to press for the London Poles to be given a stake in the new Provisional Government, but recognized that Truman, just like Roosevelt, had decided to cut a deal on Poland and get the "best deal possible."

Stalin answered that "he appreciated the difficulties of the British Government. They had sheltered the former rulers of Poland and in spite of this these foreign rulers had caused much trouble to them." He wanted to terminate the London Government because "it had means to conduct activities; it had agents and press representatives. This made an unfavorable impression on public opinion in allied nations." Truman "recalled that the Yalta agreement had been reached on the holding of free and secret Polish elections as soon as possible. He hoped that this procedure would be carried out by the Polish Government." Stalin "proposed that the question be referred to the Foreign Secretaries." Churchill and Truman agreed and the meeting ended.[33]

The July 19 and 20 plenary meetings frustrated the three leaders, as nothing was settled. Instead they bickered again about the disposition of the German fleet, whether or not they should recognize Italy and Fascist Spain, and Truman's concern that American oil drilling equipment in Romania had been confiscated by Soviet troops without compensating the American businesses.

Truman in particular grew weary of the conditions in Potsdam and the circular discussions. He wrote his wife, "This is a hell of a place—ruined, dirty, smelly, forlorn people, bedraggled, hangdog look about them. You never saw as completely ruined a city." At the conference, he claimed,

> I reared up on my hind legs to [Churchill and Stalin] at least once a day that so far as this President is concerned Santa Claus is dead and that my first interest is U.S.A., then I want the Jap War won and I want 'em both in it. Then I want peace—world peace and will do what can be done by us to get it. But certainly am not going to set up another [illegible] here in Europe, pay reparations, feed the world, and get nothing for it but a nose thumbing. They are beginning to wake to the fact that I mean business...I'm sick of the whole business—but we'll bring home the bacon.[34]

Much of this letter was typical Truman bluster—like his version of his first meeting with Molotov. But the letter did reflect the fact that Truman wanted to get the best deal he could, yet still preserve the alliance. Nowhere in the documentary record of the two meetings did he threaten to pull out of the talks or express irreconcilable differences with the Soviet Union.

His outlook began to change on July 21. Not surprisingly, this coincided with the fact that he and Stimson had just received more specific information about the atomic test. In his diary, Stimson wrote that Truman was "tremendously pepped up by the news," and "said it gave him an entirely new feeling of confidence." Yet Truman was also sobered by the immense power that the United States had harnessed. He confided in his diary: "We have discovered the most terrible bomb in the history of the world. It may be the fire destruction prophesied in the Euphrates Valley Era, after Noah and his fabulous Ark." He explicitly ordered Stimson, who readily agreed, that the bomb could only be used for "military objectives," and ordered that "soldiers and sailors are the target and not women and children. Even if the Japs are savages, ruthless, merciless and fanatic, we as the leader for the common welfare cannot drop this terrible bomb on the old capital or the new." Furthermore, he suggested they "issue a warning statement asking the Japs to surrender and save lives. Still, the President

FIGURE 1.2 *Churchill, Truman, and Stalin pose for reporters at Potsdam. United States Information Agency.*

remained ambivalent: It seems to be the most terrible thing ever discovered, but it can be made the most useful" if it could end the war as rapidly as possible and save American lives.[35]

Once again, however, Truman waited to inform Stalin. Instead, during the fifth plenary session, he told Stalin that the United States wanted free elections in Poland and pointed out there were six million Poles in the United States. "A free election in Poland reported to the United States by a free press," he said, "would make it much easier to deal with these Polish people." Turning to the implementation of the Yalta Agreement on Liberated Peoples, the president said he wanted Italy and the satellite states treated separately. Stalin said this was acceptable, but only if the West recognized the new, pro-Soviet governments in Romania, Bulgaria, Hungary, and Finland. Truman and Churchill refused to do so unless they "were established on a proper basis," in other words, through free elections.

Truman then raised the issue of Poland's border with Germany, and noted that in their second plenary meeting they had decided to treat Germany's borders as they were in 1937. He complained that "We have already gone back to the zone assigned to us and the British have done the same. It now appears that another occupying government was being assigned a zone. This was being done without consultation. If the Poles were occupying a zone this should have been agreed on." Roosevelt had agreed to only consider moving Poland's borders west at Germany's expense, but the issue had still not been decided. Now it seemed as if the four-power occupation of Germany had become a five-power occupation without any agreement by the West. If Stalin insisted on perverting the Yalta agreements, then "he was unable to see how reparations or other questions could be decided if Germany was carved up."

Truman conceded Stalin's interpretation of the Yalta agreement on Poland's western borders, but he wanted the record to reflect that he didn't like the process by which it had happened. Still, he insisted that he remained "very friendly toward the Polish Provisional Government and it is probable that full agreement could be reached on what the Soviet Government desires, but he wanted consultation." More telling, after Stalin argued that they had indeed agreed to move Poland's borders westward at Yalta, Truman objected and said that the Big Three should eschew settling the issue at Potsdam, and again defer a solution to the problem at a subsequent peace conference. This is yet more evidence that neither Truman nor Churchill—who agreed with the president about the need for a future peace conference—considered the Cold War that occurred in the post-Potsdam years inevitable.[36]

The sixth plenary session, held July 22, began with Stalin's announcement that he had withdrawn his troops from Austria. Churchill and Truman thanked him for keeping his promise, and the discussion again turned to Poland's western frontier. While Truman claimed that he did not "see the urgency of the matter," Churchill disagreed, and argued that the "Poles would be digging themselves in and taking effective steps to make themselves the sole masters of this territory. The longer the problem waited the more difficult it would be to settle it." Even more important than the political fallout was the fact that if Poland's borders moved 200 miles west as Stalin demanded, and the burden of feeding of the millions of refugees moving west would fall upon the British, since their zone had the largest concentration of people and the smallest supply of food than any other zone.

Truman repeated that he did not like "the manner" in which Poland's borders had been moved unilaterally, but Stalin refused to budge. Churchill then turned to Turkey. He accepted Stalin's desire for "the free movement of Russian ships, naval or merchant, through the Black Sea and back" and wanted to revisit the 1936 Montreux Convention, which had declared the Straits of Dardanelles and the Bosporus "an international shipping lane under the effective control of Turkey." The Soviet fleet had been "bottled up" in the Black Sea for centuries, and Stalin, like the Czars before him, wanted concessions from Turkey so that he could move his navy in and out of the Straits in order to access the Mediterranean.[37]

Churchill said he wanted to reach "a friendly agreement" to allow Soviet access but without "alarming Turkey," which likely feared "for the integrity of her empire and her power to defend Constantinople." Molotov replied that the Turks and Soviets had to settle mutual claims. The Soviet Union had lost land in Soviet Armenia and Soviet Georgia, and did not regard the Montreux Convention as a "correct arrangement." For the moment, Truman said "he was not ready to express an opinion and suggested that they defer consideration of the question."[38]

The Big Three revisited the Turkish situation on July 23. This time, Truman weighed in, and endorsed the idea of revising Montreux. But rather than giving the Soviet Union special considerations, he argued that the Straits "should be a free waterway open to the whole world and that they should be guaranteed by all of us." His "long study of history" had convinced him that all the wars of the last 200 years had "originated in the area from the Black Sea to the Baltic and from the last frontier of France to the western frontier of Russia. In the last two instances the peace of the whole world had been overturned." The "business of this Conference and of the coming peace conference," he argued, should be "to see that this did not happen again." Churchill backed the president, and said he wanted Moscow to enjoy "free and unrestricted navigation of the Straits by merchant and war ships alike in peace or war" like all other countries. Stalin did not respond to this offer since he wanted special concessions for the Soviet Union, not international access to the Straits.[39]

The following morning, July 24, Stimson informed Truman that now that they knew the atomic weapon's potential destructive force, they needed to decide on a list of targets, the wording of any ultimatum to the Japanese, and whether or not they should reconsider unconditional surrender. Stimson insisted that Kyoto, the site of important historical significance, be removed from the target list, and argued that Hiroshima, the southern headquarters of the Japanese army and a military supply depot, should be the first target. He also urged that Truman reconsider unconditional surrender because the Japanese could not be expected to disavow their emperor. Instead, he asked Truman to threaten to "prosecute the war until she ceases to exist." Byrnes, however, disagreed, and argued that the American people expected the government to force the Japanese to unconditionally surrender just as Germany had done. A June Gallup poll had found that only 7 percent of Americans believed that the Japanese should be able to keep the emperor, while a third said he should be executed as a war criminal. Truman sided with his Secretary of State when he learned that the weapon would be ready anytime from August 1 onward. This became what Truman called his "day of decision," as he planned to inform Stalin about the bomb.[40]

But first he, Churchill, and Stalin met for the eighth time, this time to discuss the status of Italy and the Eastern European nations now occupied by the Soviet army. The United States and Britain wanted Italy to be able to join the UN, but Stalin continued to point out that Italy had been Nazi Germany's ally and had fought against the allies. Meanwhile, he contended, an "abnormal situation was being created for the other satellite states and an artificial distinction was being drawn between them. It appeared that Rumania, Bulgaria, Hungary, and Finland were being put in the category of leprous states." Stalin interpreted this as an attempt "to discredit the Soviet Union." Italy's "behavior," he contended, "had been worse than that of the others. There was no doubt that Rumania, Bulgaria, Hungary, and Finland had done less harm to the Allies than had Italy." He also noted that Italy had not held elections, which the West had insisted upon in Eastern Europe.

Churchill replied that he and Truman "were in general agreement" on this issue. The president, however, said "he had a different point of view with regard to Rumania, Bulgaria, and Hungary than in Italy. We had not been able to have free access to the former countries and had not been able to get information concerning them. Everybody had free access to Italy." Only when they received access to the three Eastern European countries would the United States recognize them as had been agreed to at Yalta.

They also returned to the Turkish Straits issue. Truman said he would distribute a paper about his inland waterways idea, but Stalin pointed out that it dealt with the Danube and the Rhine, not Turkey and the Straits. He wanted a reply to his proposal on the Black Sea. Churchill said he thought they had agreed on freedom of navigation in the Straits. Molotov asked if the Suez Canal would operate under the same principle. Churchill replied that it had been "open in war and peace to all" for decades. Molotov, knowing that the British and French owned the company that operated the Canal, asked if it would come under international control. When Churchill said that it had been open for decades without complaint, Molotov snapped "there had been a lot of complaints. They should ask Egypt."[41]

The meeting ended at 7:30 p.m., and Truman walked over to Stalin and told him, "we had a new weapon of unusual destructive force. The Russian Premier showed no special interest. All he said was that he was glad to hear it and hoped we would make 'good use of it against the Japanese'." Churchill, watching from across the room, believed that Stalin "had no idea of the significance of what he had been told." Stalin not only knew about the bomb, but as Molotov recalled in his memoirs, he "reacted very calmly, so Truman thought he didn't understand. Truman didn't say 'an atomic bomb,' but we got the point at once...[w]e had been doing research in that area since 1943. I was in charge of it...It was a very good intelligence operation by our Chekists." Stalin pretended not to understand in order to prevent Truman from trying to intimidate him with the new weapon. But after he left Cecilienhof that evening, the Premier fumed that the "Soviet Union is being cheated, Truman doesn't even know the meaning of justice...we were supposed to be allies." Truman's unwillingness to compromise on Eastern Europe and reparations, Stalin charged, could be traced to the new weapon.[42]

Although this interpretation has also been cited by many historians, the atomic bomb stiffened Truman's resolve to prevent Stalin from being able to declare war on Japan in order to receive the territorial spoils he had been demanding in the Far East. However, Truman still wanted postwar cooperation, and he and Churchill—reluctantly, to be sure—acquiesced to Stalin's demands for Poland's expanded western borders, his political control over Eastern Europe, and his right to have the Soviet fleet use the Dardanelles.[43]

Practical, not ideological or political, imperatives, meanwhile, drove the United States and the Britain to limit the amount of reparations Germany would have to provide the Soviet Union. Churchill noted during the July 25 plenary session that since Stalin had insisted that Poland's border be moved westward into German territory, the Poles had begun "evacuating" Germans from an occupational zone. This area was part of the Russian zone and Poles were "driving the Germans out." Stalin replied that this population transfer—what would now be called ethnic cleansing—was justified because Poland had suffered under German occupation since 1939 and was now "taking revenge" on Germany. (Stalin, of course, conveniently left out the suffering his soldiers had inflicted on Poland.) Churchill, however, "pointed out that their revenge took the form of throwing the Germans into the American and British zones to be fed."

Truman agreed that this should not be done and contended that "any Polish zone should come out of the area of Germany already allocated to the Soviet Union." Still, he assured Stalin that he wanted to be "as helpful as he could" and that a new Polish-German border should be fixed at the "peace conference" he expected to occur after Japan's defeat. Thus Stalin's intransigence not only caused the humanitarian crisis resulting from the massive exodus of refugees to the western zones of Germany but cost him the reparations he demanded. But again, it is crucial to note that despite his frustration about the new "Polish zone," Truman repeated his belief that the German-Polish border issue could be resolved at a future peace conference.[44]

The Conference was postponed for a day because Churchill had to fly home to learn the results of the election. By lunch on July 26, he knew that he had lost; the great wartime leader had been replaced by Labour leader Clement Atlee who, along with his new Foreign Minister, Ernest Bevin, returned to Potsdam two days later. While Churchill and Atlee disagreed about domestic policy, on foreign policy Atlee hewed closely to Churchill's desire to stand with Truman on the Polish borders but to also maintain allied unity and good relations with Stalin.[45]

Before Churchill left Potsdam, he, Truman, and Chinese president Jiang Jieshi (by telegram) signed the Potsdam Declaration, the ultimatum to Japan drafted by the US and British delegations. They handed it to Molotov late that evening. Byrnes and Molotov met on July 27 to discuss the Declaration. Molotov was unhappy that neither he nor Stalin had been given the chance to see, let alone sign, the Declaration. The Secretary of State "explained that the President for political reasons had considered it important to issue an immediate appeal to the Japanese to surrender." Moreover, since the Soviets were not at war with Japan, Byrnes said the United States did not wish to "embarrass" the Soviet Union. Byrnes and Truman had just signaled that they were rethinking their need for a Soviet declaration of war on Japan.

Turning to the reparations issue, Byrnes asked if Molotov "had had an opportunity to think over the suggestion which the Secretary had made, namely, that each country would obtain its reparations from its own zone and would exchange goods between the zones." Molotov asked "would not the Secretary's suggestion mean that each country would have a free hand in their own zones and would act entirely independently of the others?" Byrnes replied that it "was true in substance but he had in mind working out arrangements for the exchange of much needed products between the zones, for example, from the Ruhr if the British agreed, machinery and equipment could be removed and exchanged with the Soviet authorities for goods—food and coal—in the Soviet zone." This would be the only way that the United States and the British could feed and keep warm the millions of German refugees that had begun flooding their occupation zones. Otherwise, Byrnes said, "the difficulties would be insurmountable and would be a continued source of disagreement and trouble between our countries." Molotov said removal of capital equipment from the western zones could be done quickly but it would take longer for payment from the eastern zones to be made. Byrnes agreed "and said that was a point of course that would have to be worked out." The outlines of a practical settlement had been set.[46]

Because they had to wait for Atlee's arrival, the new Big Three did not convene again until 10:30 p.m. on July 28. After greeting the new prime minister, Stalin complained that he hadn't been informed of the Potsdam Declaration. But he passed along another peace feeler he had received from the Japanese. They also debated whether or not the Soviet Union deserved reparations from Italy.[47]

The following morning, Truman and Byrnes told Molotov (Stalin was sick and missed the meeting), "if we were able to get an agreement on reparations along the lines of [Byrnes's] proposals to Mr. Molotov that the United States was prepared to go further to meet the Soviet wishes in regard to the Polish western frontier." Molotov replied that under this proposal, the area between the eastern and western Neisse would not come under Polish control. Byrnes replied that "this was true, but that since the final determination of the boundary would await the peace settlement, it did not follow that Poland might not receive this additional area if the peace conference so desired." Truman added that this offer "represented a very large concession on our part and he hoped Mr. Molotov would submit it to Marshal Stalin."

The two diplomats got down to brass tacks. Molotov called the proposal "acceptable in principle" but said he "would like to have clarity on certain points, in particular, the amount of equipment which would be turned over from the Ruhr to the Soviet Union. He said they had spoken of equipment to the amount of two billion dollars or five or six million tons." Byrnes said, "our experts felt that it was impossible to put any specific dollar value or tonnage on the equipment which would be available for reparations from the Ruhr, but that our proposal was to offer the Soviet Union 25% of the total equipment considered as available for reparations from the Ruhr." Molotov replied that "25% of an undetermined figure meant very little and that they wished to have a fixed sum or quantity agreed upon." Byrnes replied that the original demand of $20 billion in reparations "had no relation to reality and that this was a very good illustration of the danger of attempting to fix sums prematurely." Regardless of the specifics, Truman said he wanted "a workable plan for reparations and that he desired to see the Soviet Union receive 50% of the total."

On July 30, Byrnes told Molotov that "in regard to the Polish western frontier, we were prepared as a concession to meet the Soviet desire." Poland's western border would now reach the eastern Neisse. Molotov "expressed his gratification at this proposal," but they still disagreed on the percentages of reparations to which the Soviets were entitled. But things were clearly moving in Stalin's direction. The American position on both Poland and reparations clearly shows Truman's desire to maintain cordial relations with Stalin.

The potential destructive power of the atomic bomb, on the other hand, convinced Truman that he didn't need to roll over for Stalin and give him the territory he wanted, especially from China. When Molotov said Stalin wanted "a formal request to the Soviet Government for its entry into the war," and made its acceptance contingent upon the signing of the Sino-Soviet treaty, Truman said he would simply "examine carefully the Soviet request," which meant he would ignore Stalin and do what he wanted. And given the concessions he had made to Stalin in Europe, Truman didn't need to do any more. By Stalin's own logic, since Japan hadn't attacked the Soviet Union, he didn't really have any right to exact "revenge" the way his country and Poland deserved to extract it from Germany.[48]

The issue of the specific reparations percentages remained the last point of negotiation since it became clear that Truman and Atlee believed that Poland's borders would be finalized at a future peace conference. On July 30, Byrnes, Bevin, and Molotov argued about how much the Soviets deserved in reparations and from which zone they should be provided. At the end of their discussion, Molotov said that only their leaders could hammer out a final deal.[49]

Accordingly, in the eleventh plenary meeting on July 31, Byrnes noted that he and Bevin had agreed that the French, British, and American zones could provide reparations to the Soviet zone. Under this plan, the Soviets "could get a factory from the American zone" or from one of the other zones through the Allied Control Council, an "administrative" body, rather than the Reparations Commission, a "policy making body." This practical arrangement would benefit all the allies. Removal of equipment, meanwhile, should occur over the next two years. The Soviets would have five years to deliver the products in the exchange. Byrnes also promised that "reparations claims of other countries should be met from the western zones of occupation." Stalin accepted these formulae, but convinced Byrnes and Bevin to deliver the equipment within six months.

Only the actual percentage of reparations remained to be settled. Stalin said he "hoped the British and the Americans would meet the Soviet wishes. Mr. Bevin should have in mind that the Russians have lost much equipment. They should receive a small part of it back." Bevin didn't dispute the fact that the Soviets deserved reparations, but he wanted to make sure that Germany retained enough equipment so that it could remain an independent and self-reliant nation.

Stalin argued that France didn't deserve any reparations from Germany since it "had signed an armistice with Hitler and had suffered no real occupation." If need be, it should "be satisfied with a small amount." Bevin said his government "had to satisfy France, Belgium, Czechoslovakia and Holland. The British wanted nothing except some raw materials." Byrnes added that "the American proposal used the language 'other countries entitled to reparations.' He urged that this language be adopted." Stalin agreed to that formulation. Bevin countered that the Soviets were still going to get more than 50 percent of the total amount of reparations from Germany if everything was included from their own zone and the western zones. Stalin disputed this, and claimed he would receive less than 50 percent "and pointed out in addition that they were supplying goods to the equivalent of 15 percent. The Soviet proposal was a minimum. The Soviets received only 10 percent—the others got 90 percent. He agreed to 15 percent and 10 percent and thought it fair. The Americans agreed. He hoped Bevin would support them." Bevin gave up and said, "All right then." A committee was assigned to draw up the final text of the reparations agreement.

Discussion shifted to Poland's borders, and again, Byrnes urged that they be finalized at the peace conference. For the moment, the allies had created "a situation where Poland was administering with Soviet consent a good part of" the German territory that had been assigned to the Soviet zone. Byrnes claimed that they had only agreed to Polish administration "in the interim" so "no further dispute between them in regard to the administration of the area by the Polish Provisional Government" would occur. Bevin asked, "what would happen in this zone now? Would the Poles take over and the Soviet troops withdraw?" Stalin promised "Soviet troops would withdraw if this territory did not constitute a line of communications with their army in Germany." In any event, he claimed "the territory was now actually already administered by Poles. There was no Russian administration." Stalin had not yielded and clearly expected the territory be permanently turned over to Poland.[50]

Truman learned from Stimson on July 31 that the atomic bomb was just about ready and that Tokyo had declared it would "ignore" the Allied ultimatum. Truman, who had "already given the verbal go-ahead for the bomb," ordered that the news "must not break before his departure from Potsdam" on August 2.[51]

The final two meetings occurred on August 1. In the penultimate meeting, Truman made one last "personal request" for Stalin to "yield" on his idea for internationalizing European waterways; Stalin said "Nyet," and then in English for the first time, he repeated, "No, I say no!"[52] In their last meeting, they discussed various amendments to the final communiqué. Truman declared "there was nothing further" to discuss, and said he hoped they could meet again in Washington. Atlee thanked Stalin for the arrangements, Truman for presiding over the deliberations, and hoped that the Conference "would be a milestone on the road the three nations were pursuing together toward permanent peace." Stalin said "this was the Soviet desire" as well.[53]

That day, the Big Three issued a Protocol of the Conference, which, in addition to the agreements on reparations and the movement of Poland's borders, officially announced the division of Germany into four zones of occupation. Despite his complaint that France did not deserve reparations, Stalin agreed that it would control one of the western zones as long as it was carved out of the existing British and US zones. (Berlin had already been divided into three zones of occupation in the September 1944 London Protocol. France would now receive a zone in Berlin.) Each power would treat the German population in its zone with "uniformity," while all of

Germany would be completely disarmed and demilitarized. The Big Three agreed that any organization that attempted "to keep alive the military tradition in Germany, shall be completely and finally abolished in such manner as permanently to prevent the revival or reorganization of German militarism and Nazism." The German people, moreover, would have to accept their "total military defeat" and recognize that "they cannot escape responsibility for what they have brought upon themselves." Germany would also have to accept democratization, while its economy must shift its focus from war production to "the development of agriculture and peaceful domestic industries."[54]

The three leaders seemed pleased by the Conference. Atlee wrote Churchill: "The Conference is ending tonight in a good atmosphere," although the Soviets had insisted on "their pound of flesh" regarding reparations. The West had remained "firm on the need for supplies of food etc. from the Eastern zone for the rest of Germany." On Poland, he conceded that Stalin had "insisted on the Western Neisse and eventually the Americans accepted this. We were, of course, powerless to prevent the course of events in the Russian zone." Ultimately, "Other questions proved soluble when these major matters were disposed of ... I think that the results achieved are not unsatisfactory having regard to the way the course of the war had dealt the cards." Molotov said that "throughout the conference there was a good atmosphere, albeit not without harsh polemics and sharp words. Everyone tried to ensure that all questions were resolved by compromise decisions," and Eastern Europe had become "ours." Truman, for his part, admitted "I like Stalin. He is straightforward," and that he could be "depended upon to keep his word." As with Yalta, the United States and Britain had gotten the best settlement they could.[55]

At approximately noon Pacific time on August 6, just as he sat down to lunch on the *Augusta*, Truman received a telegram from Stimson informing him that the first atomic bomb had been dropped on Hiroshima. The president called the news "the greatest thing in history." His broadcast at 11:00 a.m. Eastern time announced the explosion and his threat to "obliterate more rapidly and completely every productive enterprise the Japanese have above ground in any city" unless they surrendered unconditionally. Although approximately 80,000 Japanese died instantly, the Japanese did not surrender. Three days later, the United States dropped a second bomb on Nagasaki, killing another 70,000, and a million Soviet troops entered Manchuria—Stalin had kept his promise. On August 10, Japan agreed to surrender with the proviso that the Emperor "would remain sovereign." Truman, Atlee, Jiang Jieshi, and eventually, Stalin, agreed to allow the Emperor to stay. Four days later, Japan formally surrendered, and the Second World War had finally ended. On August 12, Soong signed the Sino-Soviet Treaty of Friendship and Mutual Assistance, which granted Soviet military occupation of Port Arthur and privileges on the Changchun Railroad in return for Soviet recognition of Jiang Jieshi's control of the Chinese government and Jiang's right to control Chinese territory that had been occupied by Japan, especially in Manchuria.[56]

Throughout the Potsdam Conference, the Big Three tried to preserve their relationship despite the fact that each had different interests. Truman wanted confirmation that Stalin would keep the promise he had made at Yalta and declare war win on Japan, which would help the United States minimize casualties should it need to invade the Japanese home islands. Churchill and Atlee wanted to preserve the British Empire and achieve a modus vivendi in Europe with the Soviets, since both expected that the United States would quickly withdraw its troops from Western Europe. Stalin, meanwhile, wanted confirmation of his political and military domination of Eastern Europe and territorial concessions in Asia. Each essentially got what he wanted, and each made concessions in Europe and Asia in order to come to the larger agreements about Germany and Japan.

More important, each expected another "peace conference" to occur in the future that would settle the Polish-German border issue and establish a lasting politico-military solution to the "German problem." The two Western powers and the Soviet Union enjoyed good relations, at least at the highest levels, in 1945. The idea that they were doomed to failure reflects what Geoffrey Roberts has called "the later impact of the cold war and the influence exerted by protagonists such as Truman and Churchill who subsequently sought to distance themselves from the co-operative spirit of Yalta and Potsdam."[57]

But as Norman Naimark, Michael Dobbs, and others have noted, while the leaders believed that postwar cooperation could occur, the diplomats and military personnel on the ground in Germany and the Soviet Union found Soviet behavior in Europe to be so difficult to contend with that real cooperation, let alone good relations, did not last. The mass pillaging, plundering, and rapes that occurred in the Soviet zone of Germany offended even the most hardened Westerners. The crisis caused by the Soviet insistence on moving Poland's borders westward became a political, bureaucratic, and humanitarian nightmare for the Americans and the British.[58]

This disconnect between those in Germany and leaders in Washington and London began to evaporate, as a growing number of Truman's advisors, including Harriman, pressed Truman to either abandon hopes for accommodation with Stalin or at least to make accommodations dependent upon Soviet concessions. Suddenly, on February 22, 1946, the longest telegram in State Department history arrived in Washington from the Embassy in Moscow. Written by Harriman's number two, George F. Kennan, the telegram arrived in a Washington now ready to receive and react to its recommendations. The "Long Telegram" argued that Stalin's behavior reflected a unique combination of Russian history and communist ideology. For centuries, Russian leaders had been paranoid about their neighbors, and had historically wished to expand their borders under the guise of

Russian nationalism. That nationalism had now been melded into, and began "operating under the cover of," Marxism, which called for worldwide revolution against imperialism. Unless and until the United States developed a long-term strategy to contend with this existential threat to its security, it would be faced with an unrelenting adversary that could eventually defeat the United States. Shortly thereafter, on March 5, Churchill told a crowd at Westminster College in Fulton, Missouri, that an "iron curtain" had descended over Eastern Europe.[59]

The British, meanwhile, were becoming more and more resigned to the fact that they could not hold their Empire together. On February 21, 1947, they informed the United States that they could no longer guarantee the security of the Eastern Mediterranean. Greece, experiencing a civil war with a communist insurgency, and Turkey, under pressure from Moscow to grant access to the Dardanelles, could only be saved by American guarantees. Accordingly, on March 12, Truman addressed a joint session of Congress and asked for $400 million so the United States could support the "free peoples" of Greece and Turkey from "armed minorities or outside pressure." On April 8, Kennan published an anonymous article in the journal *Foreign Affairs*, which called for the United States to "contain" Soviet expansion over the long haul through the use of "counter-force at a series of shifting geographic and political points." Once the Soviets understood the US commitment to such a strategy, he contended, they would back down. On June 5, Secretary of State George Marshall devoted his Harvard University commencement address (based upon Kennan's ideas) to the new US plan to help Western Europe recover from the Second World War. The United States ultimately provided $13 billion over the next four years in American aid to rebuild the region's shattered economies.[60]

The rivalry between the United States and the Soviet Union only intensified when, on June 24, 1948, Stalin, concerned that the United States, Britain, and France were considering recognizing a separate state in western Germany made up of their occupation zones, blocked Western access to west Berlin, which had been guaranteed at Yalta. Stalin gambled that the allies would allow him to establish his de facto control over all of Berlin much as they had allowed him control of Eastern Europe. Truman and Atlee responded with an airlift of supplies, including food and medicine, to west Berlin. Stalin ultimately called off the blockade on May 12, 1949. The Western powers had shown that they didn't need to go to war to force Stalin to back down but instead use the type of "counter-force" Kennan had recommended.

Meanwhile, the Western allies, concerned about the possibility of Soviet aggression against Western Europe, signed the North Atlantic Treaty on April 4, 1949. The Treaty created a collective security alliance, the North Atlantic Treaty Organization (NATO), that included the United States and Canada. Article V of the Treaty called for each nation to aid of any member attacked by an outside force. On May 23 the western occupied zones were officially established as the Federal Republic of Germany. But not until the Soviet Union successfully tested its own nuclear weapon on August 29, 1949, was the Cold War between the East and the West fully established. This development set the stage for all the summits that followed over the next four decades.

CHAPTER TWO

The Bandung Conference: The Rise of the Developing World

The year 1949 became an even more important one in the history of the Cold War as the political and ideological battleground between capitalism and communism shifted to Asia. This time the combatants were the United States, its Asian allies, and the People's Republic of China (PRC). Mao Zedong founded the new communist nation on October 1 after finally defeating Jiang Jieshi in a civil war that had begun over two decades earlier. Jiang, forced to evacuate his remaining forces offshore to Taiwan, created the Republic of China (ROC). The United States refused to officially recognize the PRC and instead backed Jiang's government, allowing him to represent China in the UN and other international organizations. The Soviet Union, on the other hand, supported Beijing's right to represent China at the UN.

Meanwhile, a new force, neutralism, began to take hold in Asia. Former colonies such as India and Indonesia, concerned that the Cold War rivalry had turned hot in Korea and Indochina, fearing the spread of war to the rest of the region, and angered that white Europeans tried to retain influence over their former colonies, urged that the newly emerging nations concentrate on building their economies and political systems and pursue an independent, neutral foreign policy rather than take sides in the Cold War.[1]

Mao initially wanted to introduce his own unique brand of revolutionary foreign policy to the recently decolonized nations in Asia and Africa. He also recognized, however, that China's alliance with the Soviet Union and his rhetoric of "continuous revolution" worried his Asian neighbors. Chinese Premier Zhou Enlai therefore began to meet with Asian leaders to both ease their fears of communist rebellion and to forge a "united front" against imperialism. He found kindred spirits in Indian prime minister Jawaharlal Nehru, Indonesian president Sukarno, and Burmese prime minister U Nu, who also wanted to establish a new Asian policy that would navigate their region's future between the Eastern and Western blocs.

Mao's victory in China, the February 1950 Sino-Soviet Friendship Treaty, and the Soviet Union's explosion of a nuclear weapon rocked the United States government. In early 1950, the National Security Council (NSC) began a study of US national security strategy known as NSC-68. The Report concluded that the Soviet Union was "hostile" and "animated by a new fanatic faith" against democratic capitalism. The United States had no choice but to embark on a massive conventional and nuclear arms buildup both at home and in conjunction with its allies in order to stop this threat.[2]

Mao, meanwhile, was determined to end what he called China's "century of humiliation" at the hands of colonialism by waging "continuous revolution" against the West, and in particular the United States. Mao wanted, Chen Jian has argued, to reassert "China's central position in the world."[3] The PRC took a major step toward achieving that goal when one of its neighbors began a war that changed the politics of the entire East Asian region.

On June 25, 1950, North Korea, led by the communist dictator Kim Il-sung, invaded South Korea, ostensibly an American ally led by the capitalist strongman Syngman Rhee, in an attempt to unify the country under communist rule. At the end of the Second World War, the United States and the Soviet Union divided the country at the 38th parallel. Both Stalin and Mao began supplying the North Koreans with weapons and other military supplies, and Kim secretly informed Mao that he would attempt to unify Korea during an April visit to China.[4]

The three communist leaders may have assumed that the United States would not intervene to protect the South, since Secretary of State Dean Acheson had excluded both South Korea and Taiwan from the US "defense perimeter" in a January speech. Upon learning of the attack, however, Truman quickly called for an emergency meeting of the UN Security Council to condemn the invasion, and the Security Council approved the creation of a US-led UN force comprising some twenty-one countries to free South Korea. Ironically, the Soviet Ambassador to the UN, Yakov Malik, could not veto the resolution because Stalin had recalled him in protest of Beijing's exclusion from the UN.

After an August counterattack by UN forces, combined with the surprise amphibious landing at Inchon—just north of Seoul, the capital of South Korea—on September 15, 1950, under the command of General Douglas MacArthur, the tide turned. On September 30, Army Chief of Staff George Marshall authorized MacArthur to move north of the 38th parallel. Zhou

Enlai warned the United States that if it did so, China would intervene. MacArthur, however, assured Truman on October 15 that the Chinese were bluffing.

Mao began to prepare for war, not only to save Korea from American "invaders" and protect China's physical security, but to promote a revolution throughout the Far East "following the Chinese model." On October 25, 250,000 Chinese attacked the UN forces. By mid-December the UN forces had been forced back into South Korea, and on January 4, 1951, the Chinese captured Seoul.[5] After dueling counteroffensives, a stalemate was reached. Peace talks began on July 10, 1951 and lasted until 1953, when an armistice restored the division of Korea at the 38th parallel and created a Demilitarized Zone (DMZ) that has lasted to this day. It also called for a future political conference to discuss the withdrawal of all foreign forces from the Korean Peninsula and conclude "a peaceful settlement" of the Korean issue. Although it refused to recognize the PRC, the United States was forced to concede its legitimacy by conducting negotiations with Beijing in order to end the war.

The United States and the PRC also squared off in another hot war in French Indochina, although this time they battled indirectly. In 1945, the Vietnamese nationalist communist revolutionary, Ho Chi Minh, had established the Democratic Republic of Vietnam (DRV) after the Japanese surrendered to the allies. France, which had colonized all of Indochina until the Second World War, returned to the region to reestablish its control. Ho declared war on the French in 1946, and in January 1950 both Stalin and Mao recognized his government. Mao decided to help Ho's forces in order to enhance China's international revolutionary bona fides against Western imperialism as well as its physical security on its southern border. China provided weapons, supplies, training, and military advisors against the French.[6]

The United States, on the other hand, had misgivings about France's return to Indochina. Roosevelt had been strongly committed to decolonization and self-determination. After his death, Truman had initially decided to pursue the same policy. But as the Cold War deepened, he changed his mind, and consented to Paris's return to Southeast Asia. When the revolution in Vietnam began, the United States backed France.

Truman had two reasons to do so. First, the communist victory in China, the war in Korea, and Ho's rebellion validated NSC-68's thesis that communism was bent on world domination.[7] Second, he needed France's cooperation in order to create NATO's fighting force, the European Defense Community (EDC). The EDC, initially proposed by French prime minister René Pleven in 1950, was controversial because it proposed that West German forces be integrated with their neighbors' armies. Truman knew the EDC would be a hard sell to America's allies. France, however, essentially blackmailed Truman by making its support for ratification of the EDC in the French National Assembly dependent upon US material support for its war against the Vietminh. Truman's successor, Dwight D. Eisenhower, and his Secretary of State, John Foster Dulles, were equally determined to help the French in the fight for both Indochina and ratification of the EDC.[8]

The United States and China also tangled over Taiwan. Shortly after he defeated Jiang, Mao planned to invade Taiwan during the summer of 1950. However, the Korean War and Truman's decision to deploy the US Navy's Seventh Fleet to the Taiwan Straits forced him to postpone an invasion until 1951. After China entered the war in Korea in November, Mao canceled the attack. The end of the Korean War allowed Mao to refocus on his campaign to "liberate" Taiwan. Eisenhower and Dulles feared that Mao would eventually invade Taiwan.[9]

Even before the Cold War changed the strategic situation in Asia, another crucial phenomenon impacted Asia, the Middle East, and (North) Africa. The decolonization of European empires across the world, which began after the Second World War, had fatally weakened the European nations. France granted Lebanon independence and withdrew from Syria in 1946, while Britain gave up its control of Jordan. The United States officially granted the Philippines independence that same year. In August 1947, Britain granted India and Pakistan their independence. In the winter of 1948, Burma and Ceylon became independent. After a four-year revolution, the Netherlands recognized the independence of Indonesia in 1949.

In September 1947, Britain announced that its Mandate for Palestine would end at midnight on May 14, 1948; the UN proposed that Palestine be partitioned between a Jewish state, an Arab state, and an internationalized Jerusalem. That afternoon, the State of Israel was announced and quickly recognized by the United States, the Soviet Union, and other nations. A war between the surrounding Arab Nations and Israel resulted in an Israeli victory and the displacement of approximately 700,000 Arabs, many of whom ended up in refugee camps in Jordan-controlled West Bank, Egypt-controlled Gaza and Sinai, Lebanon, and Syria. Although Sub-Saharan Africa, with the exception of South Africa, remained colonized, calls for independence steadily increased.

In 1954, the Cold War and anticolonialism collided in Southeast Asia. For at least a year, the French had been struggling to come up with a strategy that could successfully suppress the Vietnamese. The United States, meanwhile, considered the French fight critical to the West's success in the Cold War. In his January 20, 1953, inaugural address, Eisenhower drew "a direct link between the French soldier killed in Indochina and the American life given in Korea."

What Eisenhower didn't realize was that the French had realized that they could not win the war, but could only "maintain a position of strength from which an honorable settlement could be negotiated." Public opinion had increasingly turned against the war, and the French legislature had begun to pressure the government to negotiate directly with the Vietnamese.

To placate the United States—and to achieve the goal of an "honorable settlement"—the French prime minister Joseph Laniel appointed a new commander in Vietnam, Henri Navarre, who vowed to pursue a more aggressive war against the Vietminh. But the Korean armistice sapped Paris of its desire to pursue the war with the requisite vigor given that its American allies had abandoned their struggle against the communist Chinese.[10]

The British government supported France's attempt to find a diplomatic solution to the war. During a conference of the Four Powers—Britain, France, the Soviet Union, and the United States—in Berlin in January 1954, ostensibly convened to solve the German problem, Eden and Molotov argued that Vietnam could only be solved by an international conference that included the PRC. Dulles initially resisted Eden, as did French foreign minister Georges Bidault. But Bidault also knew that sentiment in his government favored negotiations, and if it could be done through a multilateral negotiation rather than one-on-one with the Vietnamese, he would maintain Washington's goodwill. Dulles, who had already said that he could negotiate with the Chinese to settle outstanding issues arising from Korea, reluctantly acceded to Eden's and Molotov's proposal, as long as the others understood that this did not imply US recognition of the PRC as China's "legal government." In exchange for Dulles's support for a conference, Bidault promised that a vote would be held in the National Assembly on the EDC before the conference began. On February 18, the Four Powers announced that they, along with China, would shortly convene in Geneva to restore peace in Indochina and settle the Korea question.[11]

Withdrawal from Vietnam with honor proved to be easier said than done. Navarre decided that if he could draw the Vietminh forces into a major battle and defeat them through a "strongpoint" defense in a village named Dien Bien Phu, he could strengthen France's position in any future negotiations and placate the American call for aggressive action. Unfortunately, he miscalculated Vietnam's battlefield acumen and its willingness to absorb casualties. The Vietnamese commanding General, Vo Nguyen Giap, decided he could defeat Navarre at Dien Bien Phu because it was isolated and surrounded by mountains, which meant it could only be resupplied by air. Giap planned to attack the outpost in late January but postponed it at the last minute in order to augment his forces and deliver a knock-out blow to the French.[12] On March 13, Giap finally began the attack, and within days the French were on their heels. The strongpoint defense, Bidault recalled, had become "a deadly trap."[13]

The French Military's Chief of Staff, General Paul Ely, traveled to Washington to ask for US intervention. At a March 25 NSC meeting, the president contended that the collapse of Indochina "would produce a chain reaction which would result in the fall of all Southeast Asia to the Communists." On April 4, he repeated this claim in a telegram to

Churchill and argued that a coalition of Western nations should intervene if necessary to help the French. Two days later he publicly articulated this "domino theory" in a press conference. Despite these appeals, Churchill rejected Eisenhower's request, believing joint action would not "salvage the situation for France" and "could take the world to the brink of a major world war." For a number of reasons—the recent Korean war, a belief that the American public would not back intervention, concern that he could be labeled a colonialist, and a desire to preserve the idea of a collective Southeast Asian defense framework—the president decided he could not intervene unilaterally.[14]

France's battlefield problems coincided with the beginning of the Five Power Geneva Conference on April 26. Chaired by Eden and Molotov, the participants, which also included the two Koreas, devoted the first two weeks to Korea. No substantive agreement resulted, mainly because the United States and South Korea wanted the UN to supervise national elections, assuming that free elections would result in a democratic and unified Korea. The North Koreans and the Chinese, reflecting their experience during the Korean War, considered the UN a biased organization and wanted "neutral governments" to supervise the elections. A political stalemate that reflected the military stalemate on the peninsula continued at Geneva.[15]

Only a few days after Zhou arrived in Geneva—which was a media sensation—word came that the PRC and India had signed the "Agreement (with exchange of notes) on trade and intercourse between Tibet Region of China and India," in which New Delhi recognized China's control over Tibet and agreed to withdraw its troops from the area. The treaty has also been called the "Panchsheel" Agreement, for in the preamble they agreed to abide by what they called the Five Principles of Peaceful Coexistence. The principles, which reflected what Ronald Keith has called "a rational, mental outlook which accepted differences of religion and ideology within the unity of the human community," included mutual respect for each other's territorial integrity and sovereignty; non-aggression; non-interference in each other's internal affairs; equality and cooperation for mutual benefit; and peaceful coexistence. Zhou and Nehru believed this framework could serve as "a model for the conduct of Asian international relations" and create a "unified front in Asia" against imperialism.[16] Zhou would employ these principles at Geneva, in subsequent meetings with Nehru and U Nu, and later at Bandung.

Dulles, on the other hand, only stayed until May 3, and his time in Geneva was marred by his alleged refusal to shake Zhou's hand. Although a Chinese historian has contended that there is no documentary evidence to support the allegation, the incident symbolized the gulf that existed between the two adversaries. Ji Chaozhu, Zhou and Mao's translator, has written that China's delegation had heard that Dulles had instructed his entire entourage to avoid shaking hands with "any of us 'goddamned

Chinese reds'." The incident became "a legend in our foreign affairs, poisoning our relations with the United States for nearly two decades."[17]

Dulles also continued to argue with Eden about the merits of Anglo-American air intervention in Vietnam. Eden said such action would have "no decisive effect" on Dien Bien Phu. Instead they should keep the communists "guessing" about their intentions. Dulles conceded that air intervention would not only fail, but draw them deeper into the conflict "on an unsound basis." But he insisted that their problem was more psychological than military or political. The allies needed to "give the French some hope for support," otherwise they would not be able to handle the loss of Dien Bien Phu. It would then become impossible to hold "the rest of Southeast Asia" from communist aggression. All non-communist nations with "vital interests" in the region should therefore create a joint defense organization that could "at least attempt to hold the maximum part of Indochina." Eden agreed to explore the idea but only if "no settlement" were reached at Geneva. A day later, however, he said Britain would not join a collective defense effort that "might commit them to fight in Indochina."[18]

Dulles's departure, however, improved prospects for an agreement. His subordinate, Undersecretary of State Walter Bedell Smith, served in his stead, and seemed more pragmatic. Eden got along well with Smith and the tenor of the Anglo-American relationship improved dramatically. Still, Smith shared Eisenhower's and Dulles's determination to prevent Ho (and Mao) from creating a communist Vietnam under the imprimatur of the Big Powers.[19]

While the talks in Geneva proceeded, the leaders of a group of Southeast Asian nations decided that they would try to, as Disha Jani has written, "create an Asian solution for Asian problems" such as the challenges of post-colonial independence and the Indochina war. The prime ministers of Burma, India, and Pakistan, U Nu, Nehru, and Mohammad Ali, respectively, and President Sukarno traveled to the capital city of Ceylon, Colombo, in late April. Together with Ceylonese prime minister Sir John Kotelawala, they laid the groundwork for the Bandung Conference that would occur a year later.

The "Colombo Powers," and particularly Nehru, wanted to solve the Indochina problem (and any other issue that confronted Asia) by preventing "any incursions into their freedom by an external agency." Since they "represented a vast population and a great area," they expected to "exert considerable influence in the cause of peace." Nehru also condemned the bipolar world that the Cold War represented and instead called for a de-emphasis on ideology. Although he opposed communism, he did not seem bothered by its excesses, and seemed more critical of the Western nations, in particular the United States. This was most apparent in his condemnation of all the fighting by outside forces in Indochina except for China—he believed Beijing had come to the aid of a fellow Asian nation being occupied by Europeans. Most notably, he argued that the PRC should represent the Chinese people at the UN.

Ali, an American ally, disputed Nehru and argued that international communism should be condemned since it threatened Asia far more than democracy. If the choice came down to colonialism or communism, Ali said the "former was less dangerous since it could be persuaded by pressure at world opinion to foster nationalism and would eventually lead to independence." Communist "occupation," on the other hand, "was a means to an end and brought danger to world peace closer to home." He and Kotelawala also made sure that the conference did not condemn the idea of a Southeast Asian defense organization, which they both supported. These arguments foreshadowed the conflicts that would occur at Bandung between the pro-Western Asian governments and the "neutralist" Nehru and Nu.[20]

The Indochina portion of the Geneva Conference began only day after the news arrived from Vietnam that the French had surrendered at Dien Bien Phu on May 7. Bidault tried to put the best face on the military defeat by calling for a ceasefire and security guarantees for both sides. Instead of offering any political solutions, however, he praised the courage of French troops in Vietnam and France's "mission civilisatrice" (civilizing mission) in Indochina. Pham van Dong, the Vietnamese delegate, replied by criticizing Bidault's "outdated colonialist outlook" and called for independence for and free elections in all three Indochinese states and the withdrawal of all foreign troops. Significantly, however, as both Qiang Zhai and Frederik Logevall have noted, he expected Vietnam to be partitioned into a communist North led by Ho and a democratic South led by the French-backed Emperor Bao Dai. Pham knew that Ho had already talked with Molotov and Zhou, and both endorsed partition as the best way to create another communist state in Asia. Partition would also prevent American intervention after France withdrew.[21]

Eden also accepted partition, and when the United States learned in early June that Australia and New Zealand, their close allies in Southeast Asia, also declined to participate in any military action in Indochina, Dulles and Eisenhower decided that the United States would only intervene should China do so. In a June 17 NSC meeting, they concluded that France was "desperately anxious to get themselves out of Indochina" and they should "let them quit."[22]

When Pierre Mendès-France, long a vocal critic of the war, became France's new prime minister—he promised he would end the war within a month or resign—a settlement became not if but when. Zhou took advantage of the new sentiment in France and pledged that China would not intervene in independent Laos and Cambodia as long as the United States was prevented from sending its own forces into the region. On June 26 Dulles conceded that "partition was less objectionable" than national elections, which he and Eisenhower knew Ho would win even after Bao Dai appointed the anticommunist nationalist Ngo Dinh Diem his new prime minister. Diem and Ho, who were not consulted about partition, were angered, because both wanted a unified Vietnam but under their own rule.[23] The United States heartily supported Diem but reluctantly prepared to accept the proposed settlement.

In late June, Zhou Enlai took a break from the conference to travel to India and Burma in pursuit of his united front strategy. Zhou told Nehru that the United States wanted to "obstruct any settlement in the Conference. They are against an agreement. Of course the United States would be in favour of surrender by Ho Chi Minh. But that would not be [an] honourable peace for both sides." Regarding the future of Indochina, Zhou—with Nehru's approval—pledged that China would respect its independence and endorsed free elections in Laos and Cambodia. He also declared that "our policy towards South-East Asia is one of peaceful existence. This is our policy towards India, Burma, Indonesia and even towards Pakistan and Ceylon." The two leaders agreed that if they followed the Five Principles of Peaceful Coexistence, "this would create a large area of peace" free from outside military forces.[24]

Regarding Sino-Indian relations, Nehru and Zhou stressed the need for political and economic cooperation. Although he recognized that they had different political systems, Zhou noted that "our countries have been liberated from imperialism and both our countries have certain common characteristics of oriental civilisation." The Five Principles could therefore "build our self-confidence and also our mutual confidence. This will have a great influence" on the rest of Asia. Moreover, Zhou contended, "we want to construct peace and prevent war. I agree entirely with your Excellency that China and India bear great responsibility in making this effort especially in Asia." In a June 27 press conference, he publicly proclaimed the "non-exportability of revolution."[25]

Zhou next traveled to Burma, which had been the first Asian country to recognize the PRC, for talks with U Nu. After a discussion of the unresolved Korean issue, U Nu complained about the communist insurgency in his country. Noting that Burma did not host any foreign military forces and had stopped receiving American aid, he asked Zhou to pledge that the PRC was not aiding the insurgency. Zhou blamed Taiwanese provocateurs for spreading these false rumors. Rather than dwell on this issue, he argued that the Five Principles should apply to China's relationship with Burma. "We should establish trust between us," he said. China wanted "to see Burma independent with the freedom to choose a system approved by the majority of the people." He wanted "friendly cooperation with Burma. This is the usual policy of the Chinese government, which is reaffirmed by the recent joint statement from China and India."[26]

In their second meeting, U Nu proposed five additional principles of peaceful coexistence that pertained to the Sino-Burmese relationship. One in particular is crucial to this study: "The two countries will solemnly assure that they will do everything within [their] powers to further peace in the world and especially in Southeast Asia." Zhou immediately accepted this additional principle. The other three proposals concerned their border, the question of citizenship for overseas Chinese, and a promise not to engage in "conspiracies" to overthrow each other. U Nu also confessed his nation's "fear" of its "big brother" and hoped Zhou could assuage those fears. Zhou noted that this issue had come up with Nehru, and said "I can personally and frankly tell Prime Minister U Nu that the policy of the new China is the policy of peace" based on the Five Principles of Peaceful Coexistence. Moreover, "China sees India and Burma as the same." Regarding territory, he remarked "China is already a large place with a large population. Our nation's founding policy is to make our own country great. We do not have any territorial ambitions." U Nu praised Zhou for allaying Burma's fears.[27]

On July 21 the Geneva Accords were signed. Mendes-France and Pham agreed that Vietnam would be divided at the Seventeenth Parallel. Like Korea, they established a DMZ, and agreed to hold free elections in July 1956. The winner would get to unify the country under his political system. Neither the United States nor South Vietnam signed the Accords, but Smith said the United States "took note" of the ceasefire and promised to not use force to disturb it.[28]

Despite Zhou's bravura performance and reception at Geneva, Mao remained unhappy that his government had "failed to take the necessary measures and make efforts in military affairs, on the diplomatic front, and also in our propaganda" to liberate Taiwan. Mao thus began a propaganda blitz emphasizing the need to liberate Taiwan and ordered his military to prepare to shell Jinmen, one of Taiwan's offshore islands, and to make plans to land troops on the islands off Zhejiang Province. The propaganda campaign was also aimed at the United States; Mao insisted that Taiwan was not an independent nation but rather a part of China. US support for "Jiang's bandit clique," he charged, signified an American attempt to interfere in "China's internal affairs."[29] Jiang responded by sending nearly 60,000 troops to Jinmen. On September 3, Mao ratcheted up the pressure by unleashing a massive artillery attack on the island.

The bombardment occurred as plans for creating a Southeast Asian defense framework neared completion. Once Dulles realized that he could not convince Eden to agree to a joint intervention in Indochina, he proposed that the Western nations create an Asian security framework modeled on NATO. Eden considered such an arrangement "helpful" and suggested that the five Colombo Powers be invited to join. Eisenhower concurred, and "reaffirmed his anxiety over any arrangement which was confined to the five white nations [the United States, Britain, France, New Zealand, and Australia] and left out the Asian states."[30] Negotiations for such a framework continued throughout August.

The talks took on new urgency after the Taiwan Straits crisis escalated, and on September 8 the five "white" nations, Pakistan, Thailand, and the Philippines signed the Manila Pact, which created the Southeast Asian Treaty Organization (SEATO). Most significant is that India, Burma, and Indonesia refused to join. Nehru denounced the treaty in a September 29 speech to the Indian Parliament, saying SEATO "takes up that area which might be an area of peace and converts it almost into an area of potential war."[31] The creation of this anticommunist, collective security alliance caused much controversy in the months leading up to the Bandung Conference.

The Taiwan Crisis also caused the United States and Taiwan to begin to formalize their relationship. Eisenhower was immediately informed about the September 3 shelling. Although the Joint Chiefs of Staff advised him that the offshore islands were "important but not essential to the defense of Formosa from a military standpoint," they stressed "the psychological effects on the Chinese Nationalist troops and other Asiatic countries inclined to support U.S. policy, of a further loss of territory or troops to the Communists."

From Manila, where he was finalizing SEATO, Dulles concurred with this analysis. But he warned that "committal of US force and prestige might lead to constantly expanding US operations against [the] mainland." In a September 12 NSC meeting, Eisenhower said he was "personally against making too many promises to hold areas around the world and then having to stay there to defend them. In each crisis we should be able to consider what was in the best interests of the U.S. at that time ... If we get our prestige involved anywhere then we can't get out."[32]

Despite this concern, negotiations between the United States and Taiwan about a security treaty intensified, and on October 18 Eisenhower said, "as far as he was concerned, the United States would never tolerate" the offshore islands fall "into unfriendly hands." However, he made one caveat: "once we made a security treaty with Nationalist China covering Formosa and the Pescadores, it would be necessary for them to refrain from offensive operations from their 'privileged sanctuary'." Dulles informed Eden of the administration's plans, and noted that with the "armistices now concluded in Korea and Indochina, necessity arose to make clear to Communists fact that we would not allow the islands to fall into 'unfriendly hands'." As long as it was defensive in nature, Eden seemed to support such a treaty. Ultimately, on December 2 the United States and Taiwan signed the Sino-American Mutual Defense Treaty, which committed the United States to defend Taiwan should the PRC invade the island. Like SEATO, this Treaty also upset many of the Asian powers and became a bone of contention at Bandung.[33]

Shortly after the creation of SEATO, Nehru met with Mao in October to discuss his vision for a united, anti-imperialist Asia. In the course of their four conversations, they examined most of the major issues that would be emphasized at Bandung.

The two leaders got down to business in their first meeting on October 19. After a brief exchange of greetings, Mao said,

> Historically, all of us, people of the East, have been bullied by Western imperialist powers…China was bullied by Western imperialist powers for over one hundred years. Your country was bullied even longer, for more than three hundred years…Therefore, we, people of the East, have instinctive feelings of solidarity and protecting ourselves…In spite of differences in our ideologies and social systems, we have an overriding common point, that is, all of us have to cope with imperialism.

Nehru agreed with Mao's analysis. In order to rectify this historical situation and develop their own independent societies, he argued that the Five Principles should be "applicable not only to the relationship between our two countries, but also to all other countries. If these principles are observed, tense situations can be greatly reduced and every country will be able to pursue development in accordance with its own wisdom." Furthermore, he argued that since "China and India are the largest" countries in Asia, "our two countries should play more important roles in Asia. In any case, the population of our two countries reaches one billion. This will lead to immense influence." Chinese and Indian self-interest could lead to the vibrant development of the entire region.

Mao complained that the United States saw their nations as "small" countries rather than "great powers." Nehru agreed, and said the United States only measured greatness by the amount of money a nation produced. Instead, he considered "the human factor" the most important component of a country's greatness. Mao agreed, and the two leaders devoted much of their discussion to their critiques of the United States. Mao argued that "The alleged US fear is truly excessive. It has advanced its defense lines to South Korea, Taiwan, and Indochina, which are so far away from the United States and so close to us. This makes our sleep unsound." Nehru concurred and said the United States "is not mature. It is very difficult for the United States to understand the many things that it dislikes and, at the same time, are happening in the world." Mao replied, "the United States does not care whether others can tolerate them. For instance, in putting together the Southeast Asian Treaty Organization, it did not bother to consult China and India. There are many countries in Asia, yet it consulted only three countries, Pakistan, Thailand, and the Philippines. The United States does not care whether others can tolerate them." Nehru noted that the United States had invited India to attend the Manila Conference, but he had turned down the invitation. "Yes," he argued, "if the United States is determined to do something, it does not care whether others can tolerate it." The European countries that had joined SEATO, meanwhile, "do not necessarily like it. But they dare not say 'no' under the pressure of the United States."[34]

That evening Nehru and Zhou met for four and a half hours. Zhou denounced the United States for attempting to take advantage of all this "to create a tense situation. This is America's policy of threat. After the Korean armistice and the restoration of peace in Indochina, America wants to expand its aggression, train Jiang Jieshi's troops, and make preparations for expanding the war."

Nehru empathized and asked the Premier if he believed whether Washington wanted to provoke a war with the PRC. Zhou replied "America does not want to instigate a major war right away; rather, they are testing the waters to find out if we are prepared and if we have the strength. At the same time, they are giving Jiang Jieshi's forces a boost." This was a problem for Eisenhower, because this would only embolden Jiang to "instigate a major war. But this conflicts with American intents." Rest assured, he told Nehru, "we are prepared and will not tolerate aggression. We have full justification to liberate Taiwan."

Nehru declared that "Undoubtedly, as far as Taiwan is concerned, both the legal basis and the historic basis are favorable to the Chinese government." Still, he confessed that this "is a rather difficult issue—how to cope with the current situation without triggering a major war." He warned Zhou that some American "warmongers" were trying to goad China into a conflict, and urged him to avoid their "trap." He also lamented that the PRC's admission into the UN had run into procedural roadblocks in the General Assembly.

Zhou reiterated his commitment to the Five Principles, and argued "our policy was aimed at international peace and cooperation. We will do everything we can to fight for peace. We have reiterated that the peace and cooperation we talk about do not exclude any country, even America, as long as these countries have the same wish." But China would not "tolerate any bullying." Since the United States refused to recognize the PRC, "we have to make a call of justice and propose to liberate Taiwan. If America continues provoking and bullying us, we will definitely resist." Nevertheless, he conceded "we have no intent to instigate a world war as it would run counter to our policy stated in the first point. On one hand, we want to liberate Taiwan; on the other hand, we will be very cautious if we were to take any action." Regarding UN admission, he took a realistic view: "as long as America opposes it, we can never get in."

After a discussion of the politics of the UN, Nehru said, "We hope that in the current international environment, India and China can do more promotional work" in spreading the Five Principles around the world. "In this sense," he said, "if America agrees to peaceful coexistence, we will not reject. If America is unwilling to have peaceful coexistence and wants war instead, then we will isolate America."[35]

Nehru immediately raised the Taiwan issue during his second meeting with Zhou on October 20. "Peace cannot be restored in the Far East," he began, "upon the failure to settle the Taiwan issue. The only solution to the

Taiwan issue is to return Taiwan to China. I hope the Chinese government can avoid a large-scale war." He hoped he could assist China in this endeavor. He then criticized Pakistani prime minister Ali for saying that he "does not believe in neutralism and that Pakistan is fully in support of the United States." He also called American policy "very strange."

Zhou called American policy "confusing" and said that it had "aroused Pakistan's fears about nonexistent issues and ha[d] also fueled its expansionism," which convinced Ali to join SEATO. Nehru said, "American policies include two factors or two methods. Firstly, use armed forces, menaces, or money as a means of subordination. Secondly, arouse fears about international communism." Pakistan, meanwhile, used America's military aid and SEATO "simply as a menace against India," not because it feared communism. Zhou agreed that the United States had "aroused and utilized Pakistan's expansionism. I have had several talks with the Pakistani ambassador. I tell him that Pakistan's reliance on the US militarily only works to put itself in the American trap and that it will backfire someday."

After rehashing their discussion from the previous night, Nehru raised the issue of Africa. He lamented that the continent did not play "a big role in international affairs, but it is a dangerous place." Most of North Africa remained "the manor of France, and there are strong nationalist movements. To some extent, Egypt can be regarded as part of Asia, and the other African lands are Africans'." The Asian nations, he contended, "must help Africans in their development, because they will be ruined by others if they are not strong enough, which is harmful to both us and the world at large." Moreover, "India's geographic location makes it connected with Southeast Asia, the Far East, West Asia, and Africa."

This made Indonesian prime minister Ali Sastroamidjojo's recent call for an Afro-Asian Conference, which India supported, even more imperative. But he worried that "the participating countries have contrary policies. At the Colombo Conference, Pakistan had contrary policies…I still believe that Asian and African countries should hold a meeting together. Although there are some disputes, the countries will be influenced" by the need for Afro-Asian unity based on the Five Principles. He noted that in December, Indonesia would host another "Colombo Powers" conference to discuss the Asian-African Conference, which he expected to be held two months thereafter.

Nehru also urged Zhou to fulfill his pledge from June to "regard those overseas Chinese who retain the Chinese nationality as Chinese." He said a pledge from China that "these people should not interfere in the internal affairs of the countries where they live," and a declaration that "overseas Chinese who have obtained the nationalities of the countries where they live are no longer Chinese" would assuage the fears of the entire region.

Zhou asked what the Afro-Asian Conference would entail. Nehru replied that "every Asian country will be invited to attend the conference.

Controversial issues will be avoided at the conference, and no internal affairs of any country will be involved. Otherwise, there will be endless arguments. The issues to be discussed are extensive, for example, colonialism, peace, and the relationship between countries." Zhou said, "We'd like to air our opinions. We are in support of holding the Asian-African Conference proposed by the Indonesian government, and we are also in support of your sponsoring the Asian-African Conference. We are willing to attend the conference because it is striving for Asian peace, African peace, and world peace, so it is helpful to mitigate the tension, and it does not repel other countries."

Regarding the issue of the overseas Chinese, he called it "very easy to explain ... What I have said in Delhi and Rangoon is still effective and will be realized. Speaking specifically, the dual nationality issue of overseas Chinese should be solved." Furthermore, "I also said that this issue would be first settled with Southeast Asian countries which had entered into diplomatic relations with China. In principle, we do not think there should be dual nationality. But as I said just now, dual nationality is a question left over by history." He promised that if U Nu came to China, "I will immediately talk with him about this issue. We are willing to talk with Burma after we talk with Indonesia."[36]

The Five Colombo Powers met again in December, this time in the city of Bogor, Indonesia, to make plans for the Afro-Asian Conference. Despite their political differences over SEATO, they all agreed to accept the Five Principles of Coexistence. They also decided that Sino-US tensions could prevent peace from becoming the norm in Asia. Since they shared a common colonial experience with China, they agreed that if China lived up to its pledge to respect the Five Principles, Asia could be stabilized. Nehru, Sukarno, and U Nu, meanwhile, pushed for a declaration of "neutralism" by the Powers in the Cold War struggle between the United States and the Soviet Union.[37]

On December 29, the Powers issued a communiqué that stated that they would host a conference in Bandung, Indonesia, in April that would "promote goodwill and cooperation among the nations of Asia and Africa; consider economic, social, and cultural problems and relations, as well as problems of special interest to them, including racialism and colonialism; and consider what contribution they can make to the promotion of world peace and understanding." They chose Bandung because it had been a recreation center for Dutch coffee and tea planters, standing 2,400 above sea level, and enjoyed a much milder climate, good facilities and accommodations, and security thanks to a nearby army base.[38]

The Powers began the process of deciding which countries would be invited. Despite Kotelawala's concern about Mao's call for exporting revolution, Nehru "insisted that China be included as part of his foreign policy agenda to foster productive regional relations despite the forced acquisition of neighboring Tibet in China. This move eliminated Taiwan as a possible participant, given the tense Strait Crisis which then remained unsolved." When the question of Taiwan's participation was raised, U Nu threatened to withdraw as co-sponsor. The Powers complied with his objections and did not invite Taiwan. Nehru also wanted Japan to be invited, believing he could "entice Japan away from its alliance with the US."

Ali and Sukarno opposed an invite to Israel, despite U Nu's contention that as a fellow socialist country it should be invited and Kotelawala's support for its participation. Ali and Sukarno's position prevailed. All other "white" nations, including the Southeast Asian nations, Australia and New Zealand, the former colonial powers, the United States, and the Soviet Union, were deliberately left off the list. None of the Powers even considered inviting South Africa because of its apartheid policies. All other African nations were invited, but since only one in Sub-Saharan Africa, the Gold Coast, had become semi-independent (its prime minister, Kwame Nkrumah, accepted the invitation), most of that continent's representatives came from North Africa. The key African invitee was Egyptian president Gamel Abdel Nasser, who had overthrown the British-installed King Farouk in 1952 and successfully forced the British military to withdraw from his country in 1954. Nasser also vehemently opposed the creation of the Central Treaty Organization (CENTO) by Iran, Iraq, Pakistan, Turkey, and Britain in February 1955. This collective security organization modeled after NATO infuriated the nationalist Nasser as much as SEATO angered Nehru, U Nu, and Sukarno.[39]

News of the impending conference distressed the Western powers. Despite his acceptance of Zhou's influence at Geneva, Eden's tolerance for anti-imperialist rhetoric had its limits, and he opposed Chinese participation at the Afro-Asian Conference. In particular, he knew that the two principles on which all attendees would agree were anticolonialism and "racialism," which were powerful rallying forces and the West's greatest weakness. London recognized, however, that the more it denounced anticolonialism, the more attractive the notion became to current members of the British Empire. Indeed, a British diplomat argued that "anti-colonialism is such an obsession with, for example, Nehru, that it might even be unwise to approach him with counsels of moderation." Instead Britain pinned its hopes on the pro-Western Kotelawala, and decided to ask him to promote the fact that Britain favored fostering "self-government by stages" in an "orderly transition of dependent peoples" rather than by granting immediate independence to people unprepared to govern. London also hoped Kotelawala would refrain from issuing invitations to any of Britain's African colonies in order to avoid "embarrass[ment]."[40]

The United States, meanwhile, worried more about the attractiveness of Nehru's call for neutralism. It also faced a dilemma: The more Washington opposed the gathering, the more it would face charges of neo-imperialism. Dulles therefore told his ambassadors in Asia and the Middle East to inform their host nations that "attendance of friendly governments would, on balance, be desirable," provided they sent "the strongest possible delegations" in order to make the case for the Western bloc and against communism. The State Department also warned that "Chinese Communists may be expected exert disproportionate influence and make every effort [to] utilize [the] Conference [to] enhance [its] own prestige and discredit U.S. and its allies in [the] eyes [of] Asian-African nations." It conceded the "Fact so-called Five Principles and others [were] equally important to cause of freedom, including principles UN Charter, have long been observed as standards of conduct by democracies." US ambassadors in Southeast Asia should therefore remind their host governments that they should emphasize that the Manila Pact was necessary to "safeguard Southeast Asia from threatened Communist violation [of] such principles."[41]

News of the upcoming conference of Asian and African Peoples caused a sensation in the developing world and among interested Westerners. The African-American novelist Richard Wright, who had become famous chronicling racism in the United States, immediately applied for press credentials to cover the conference. Wright believed that the nations gathering in Bandung represented a billion people who had been the "despised, the insulted, the hurt, the disposed—in short, the underdogs of the human race." Moreover, "class and racial and religious consciousness" would be displayed "on a global scale," and this "meeting of the rejected was in itself a kind of judgment upon that Western world!"[42]

The conference was deliberately scheduled to begin on April 18, 1955, which, as Roeslan Abdulgani, the Secretary General of the Indonesian Foreign Ministry, noted, was the 180th anniversary of Paul Revere's ride that sparked the American Revolution. Abdulgani recalled that it was "clear that April 18, 1775 was an historic day for the American nation in their struggle against colonialism. Why should we not simply link these two events, the date of which was the same, the spirit of which was the same, only the years were different?" Abdulgani believed the reference would "neutralize American fears." The date also fell in between Ramadan, the Muslim fasting holiday scheduled for the end of the month, and the middle of the month, which were sacred days for Buddhists.[43]

On April 11, the Air India plane *Kashmir Princess* crashed in Indonesian waters after a bomb exploded on board. Zhou was rumored to have been on the plane and some Indonesian officials suspected it was an assassination attempt. Abdulgani also worried that the Indonesian Ambassador to China had been on the plane. Neither man was onboard, but eleven members of China's Delegation, two Chinese journalists, and the three-man Indian flight crew died in the explosion. Although rumors persisted that Taiwanese intelligence agents planted the bomb, Zhou shrugged off the incident and arrived as scheduled on April 16.[44]

That afternoon he met with Nehru and U Nu to go over the conference procedures and to discuss the possibility of creating "permanent political and economic institutions" after the conference's end. Nehru conceded, however, that the "the 29 countries had so many differences in opinion that it was unimaginable how this institution would effectively perform its function." U Nu concurred, and argued that "the only purpose of this conference was to provide an opportunity for the delegations of various countries to meet." A permanent institution "would consist of those countries with concerted views on important issues and could be, consequently, effective. However, the present conference could not make any resolutions on important issues, and even if it set up a permanent institution, this institution would not have any effective ways to implement the resolutions."

Zhou replied that "if the conference could succeed in two matters, it would be of great significance." First, it must adopt the Five Principles. Second, it must set up a permanent institution in such "a way that would not bind the participating countries too tightly, such as a liaison institution." As for U Nu's proposal, Zhou said "it would be better if this conference could issue a document and set up a permanent institution. Thus, we could demonstrate to the world that we didn't discriminate against any Afro-Asian state."

After stating "it was not wise" if the conference did anything to enter into a rivalry with the UN, Nehru said he hadn't listed the Five Principles as an item in his proposed agenda "in order to avoid causing argument." Besides, "the first three of the Five Principles were the most important ones, i.e. mutual respect for sovereignty and territorial integrity, nonaggression and noninterference with each other's internal affairs." These were the three on which all attendees, regardless of their political philosophy, agreed.[45]

At Nehru's suggestion, the leaders of the Colombo Powers held an "informal" meeting consisting of fifty members from twenty-two nations on Sunday morning, April 17, 1955, a day before the official start of the conference. Although Pakistani prime minister Ali had not yet arrived, the meeting proceeded anyway under the assumption he would not object to their findings. Nehru, Abdulgani has written, attempted "to dominate the meeting" by suggesting rules and procedures for the conference. In particular he tried to scuttle the idea of having opening addresses by the Heads of Delegations. They also agreed that "the principle of deliberation and consensus became the basis and guide for seeking and deciding common agreement."

Later that day, Sastroamidjojo held a tea party. Ali learned of the "informal" meeting, got "very angry," and demanded a meeting of his fellow Five Powers. In the meeting he "exploded" and demanded an explanation as to why they didn't wait for him, as one of the co-sponsors, to arrive before making such fundamental decisions. Ali, "without naming Prime Minister Nehru, repeatedly pointed an accusing finger at where Prime Minister Nehru was sitting. Everyone felt that [his] explosion had a background in the widening and deepening controversy between India and Pakistan." Ali declared that he would not be bound by anything agreed to at the informal meeting, especially the prohibition against speeches by the Heads of Delegations. This incident higlighted not only the rift between India and Pakistan but also the one between the forces of neutralism and those who opposed communism.[46]

The conference began on April 18. Crowds packed the streets surrounding the conference building, and as Richard Wright wrote, they stood "in this tropic sun, staring, listening, applauding; it was the first time in their downtrodden lives that they'd seen so many men of their color, race, and nationality arrayed in such aspects of powers, their men keeping order, their Asia and their Africa in control of their destinies." The delegates, meanwhile, "were getting a new sense of themselves, getting used to new roles and new identities. Imperialism was dead here; and, as long as they could maintain their unity, organize and conduct international conferences," it would not return.[47]

Sukarno officially opened the proceedings with a powerful speech that explained why the conference had been organized and the direction its participants wanted to go. He began by noting that this was the "first international conference of coloured people in the history of mankind." He bemoaned "all the tribulations through which many of our peoples have so recently passed, tribulations which have exacted a heavy toll in life, in material things, and in the things of the spirit." For decades, the peoples of Asia and Africa had to travel to other countries if they wanted to meet. But now, imperialism was on the run, and "we are free, sovereign and independent. We are again masters in our own house." The participants were united by "a common detestation of colonialism in whatever form it appears. We are united by a common detestation of racialism."

Moreover, as the irresistible force of decolonization swept the world, "There are new conditions, new concepts, new problems, new ideals abroad in the world. Hurricanes of national awakening and reawakening have swept over the land, shaking it, changing it, changing it for the better." Unfortunately, "we are living in a world of fear. The life of man today is corroded and made bitter by fear. Fear of the future, fear of the hydrogen bomb, fear of ideologies." It was up to the formerly colonized to fix this situation. "We can inject the voice of reason into world affairs," he proclaimed. "We can mobilise what I have called the Moral Violence of Nations in favour of peace."

A perfect example was the way the Five Colombo Powers exerted their influence to end the Indochina War.

Look, the peoples of Asia raised their voices, and the world listened. It was no small victory and no negligible precedent! The five Prime Ministers did not make threats. They issued no ultimatum, they mobilised no troops. Instead they consulted together, pooled their ideas, added together their individual political skills and came forward with sound and reasoned suggestions which formed the basis for a settlement of the long struggle in Indo-China.[48]

Sastroamidjojo followed Sukarno. He rejected the idea that peace meant the hegemony of one power, or "an uneasy balance of power used as a deterrent for war; nor in the sense of cold war as the only possible alternative to hot war," since the "present precarious balance of power may shift in the near future." Like Sukarno, he worried about "fear and suspicion not faith which dominates the world." The atomic age and the arms race between the United States and the Soviet Union signified the desire "to achieve superiority one above the other in order to fulfill the dream of another peace by domination. I call it a dream because at the awakening there would not be another peace by domination but only the total destruction of mankind. We do not want any domination either by force or ideology, no matter from whatever quarter it may come." The nuclear arms race, meanwhile, just created more fear, which in turn fueled the arms race. Only the adoption of the Five Principles of Peaceful Coexistence could save the world.[49]

Zhou reiterated many of the same points in his two April 19 speeches, which not only caused a sensation—the Bandung Conference was essentially his coming-out party to Asians and Africans—but also defied the expectations of many in attendance. Most assumed he would act as he had at Geneva, where, as Filipino Foreign Secretary Carlos Romulo recalled, "he was dealing with Westerners, [and] he chose to be seen

FIGURE 2.1 *Zhou Enlai and an unidentified aide at Bandung. United States Information Agency.*

as arrogant, stern, and aloof." Other Asians, even the neutralists, had wondered if he would parrot Mao's fiery rhetoric about the necessity for world revolution. At Bandung, however, "he was affable of manner, moderate of speech" since he was clearly among "fellow Asians and Africans." Zhou "wanted to appear humble and win his fellow Asians by his affability and congeniality."[50]

In his main speech, Zhou stressed their common experiences, and noted that the peoples of Asia and Africa had "created brilliant ancient civilizations and made tremendous contributions to mankind. But, ever since modern times most of the countries of Asia and Africa in varying degrees have been subjected to colonial plunder and oppression, and have thus been forced to remain in a stagnant state of poverty and backwardness." Now that so many countries had become independent, he argued, "new colonialists are attempting to take the place of old ones," and many in the two regions still bore the brunt of racial discrimination. The only way out of this situation, he argued, was "to eliminate the state of backwardness caused by the rule of colonialism. We need to develop our countries independently with no outside interference and in accordance with the will of the people."

After praising the Colombo Powers for helping end the Indochina war, he attacked the United States for wanting "to create tension in the Taiwan area." In a reference to the recent atomic tests that had occurred in the Pacific, he argued that the United States was "clamouring openly that atomic weapons are conventional arms and are making preparations for an atomic war. The people of Asia shall never forget that the first atomic bomb exploded on Asian soil and that the first man to die from experimental explosion of the hydrogen bomb was an Asian." Zhou also contended that while only a few nations possessed nuclear weapons, the majority of the world's populations wanted an end to the atomic arms race, a reduction in stockpiles, the prohibition of nuclear and other weapons of mass destruction, and believed that atomic energy should only be used for "peaceful" purposes.

In his supplementary speech, Zhou earned more goodwill by stressing that the Chinese delegation had come to Bandung "to seek unity and not to quarrel. We Communists do not hide the fact that we believe in communism and that we consider [the] socialist system a good system." Nevertheless, there was no need "to publicize one's ideology and the political system of one's country, although differences do exist among us ... [we] came here to seek common ground, not to create divergence." However, he did raise "the tension created solely by the United States in the area of Taiwan," and called his government's willingness to liberate "their own territory" Taiwan and the coastal islands "a just one. It is entirely a matter of our internal affairs and the exercise of our sovereignty." Still, he acknowledged that no matter what their ideology, countries in Asia and Africa were led by "nationalists" and no longer under the control of colonists. He also dismissed allegations that the PRC wanted to "interfere in the internal affairs of others."[51]

April 20 featured the first closed session of the conference's Political Committee, which was made up of all Heads of Delegations. The agenda included three subjects: Human Rights and Self-Determination, the Problems of Dependent Peoples, and the Promotion of World Peace and Cooperation. Discussion on the first, Abdulgani recalled, was "smooth enough." Consensus was quickly reached about fundamental human rights in connection with the Charter of the UN, "and the right of every nation to determine its own destiny, as well as about racialism." The Committee focused in particular on the North African nations that still remained under colonialism, especially Algeria and Morocco. The Arab nations and Pakistan, Iran, and Afghanistan sharply criticized and condemned Israel, but India and Burma, who had diplomatic relations with the Jewish state, refused to do so. In fact, Nehru refused to condemn Zionism "as imperialism," but conceded that it "was certainly an aggressive movement." Still he asked the conference to recognize the terror of the Holocaust, which "amongst other things … caused the Jews to need the establishment of the State of Israel." The Arabs, on the other hand, said that the Holocaust had been exaggerated and called its invocation "Zionist propaganda to throw dust in the eyes of the world." Meanwhile, Israel "had conducted terror and unequalled cruelties against the Palestine people. And the acts of Israel and Zionism needed to be condemned."

Zhou Enlai's "attitude," Abdulgani said, "was clearly and without doubt on the side of the Arab countries." All UN resolutions, he argued, must be carried out, "with the additional condition that external forces must not intervene." Essentially Zhou equated "the liberation of Palestine and the liberation of Taiwan." Ultimately the conference "declared its support for the basic rights of the Arab peoples of Palestine" by "peaceful means."[52]

The most contentious meeting of the Political Committee occurred the following day when the participants addressed the issue of self-determination. Many of the attendees spoke of it by referencing, understandably, their shared experience of colonialism. Kotelawala asked permission of the Committee as a whole, and made what Romulo called a "two-fisted attack" on communism as simply another form of imperialism. "Think," he said, "of those satellite states under Communist domination in Central and Eastern Europe … Are not these colonies as much as any of the colonial territories in Africa or Asia? And if we are in opposition to colonialism, should it not be our duty openly to declare opposition to Soviet colonialism as much as to Western imperialism?" Abdulgani said that "all the audience was silent. Not silent because they were calm. But silent due to the pressure of tension. Everyone felt like this was a 'bomb'! All glanced sideways in" Zhou's direction. He rose to speak and asked only that the text of Kotelawala's speech be distributed and that he be allowed to respond the following day. Sastroamidjojo closed the meeting and said this "new problem" would be discussed in the morning.

As the meeting adjourned, Zhou approached Kotelawala, "pointing his finger" and asked "What do you want, Sir John, by proposing a discussion of that Soviet colonialism? Is that to provoke" us? "To split us apart and make the Conference fail?" Sastroamidjojo "tried to calm down the atmosphere," but Kotelawala, "pointing a finger back," replied "Why do you become angry because of my criticism of the Soviet? I did not touch at all upon the relations of the Soviet with China in that question of a new form of colonialism. I mentioned only the relations of the Soviet Union with countries of Eastern Europe."

Zhou was "very wise. He smiled" and said "Very well, I'll think about it till tomorrow morning," shook hands, and left. Nehru, who had been "most startled" by Kotelawala's comments, asked "Why did you do that? Why did you not show me your speech before you gave it?" Abdulgani wrote, "This question...showed his paternalistic attitude toward" Sir John, and he noted that Nehru "often displayed an attitude of 'teaching' the other delegations." Sir John "interrupted" him and said "Why should I? Do you show me yours before you give them?" Nehru was "surprised" by this answer, but then acted like "a gentleman," smiled "broadly," and the two laughed before departing.

Although the atmosphere remained "tense" on the morning of April 22, the Political Committee revisited Kotelawala's remarks. U Nu spoke first and asked "us all to restrain ourselves in discussing this matter of the 'new form of colonialism'." Kotelawala said that he hadn't meant to jeopardize the conference or cause it to "fail." Instead he wanted to give "his own opinion." Zhou in turn said he'd come to Bandung "not to look for points of conflict, but, on the contrary, points of meeting." Nevertheless, he disagreed that communism was just another form of colonialism. Abdulgani recalled, after this discussion "The atmosphere really began to relax," but the CENTO and SEATO powers continued to equate communism with colonialism. Ultimately Sastroamidjojo proposed the formation of a Small Committee "to formulate a consensus about this question." They "reached a compromise formulation": that "Colonialism in all its manifestations is an evil which should be brought to an end."[53]

Nehru took the opportunity to twice respond to Kotelawala's charges. In his first address to the closed session of the Political Committee, he denied that the Eastern Europeans were subjected to a "new colonialism." Instead, he argued that "however much we may oppose what has happened to countries in Eastern Europe and elsewhere, it is not colonialism. It may be an objectionable thing, but the use of the word is incorrect," because they were all represented in the United Nations. Therefore,

It seems to me rather extraordinary that we should discuss nations as such whose people we have recognised in the capacity of sovereign nations and then say that they are colonial territories. It may be—I do not know—that there are minorities and groups; but the fact is that the United Nations recognise these countries as sovereign, independent countries and give them a place within their framework. And for us, this Conference meeting as governments, to challenge the very basis of the recognition of the United Nations of these sovereign independent countries is a most extraordinary position to take up—for anybody, and more especially for representatives of the governments of Asia and Africa.[54]

The subject of Nehru's second speech was peaceful coexistence. It was preceded, however, by a sharp debate about the wisdom of adopting the policy. U Nu opened the discussion and said that "in the present situation in the world, with all the different interests becoming more critical and with all the types of conventional and nuclear weapons, we could do no other than take an attitude of living in tolerance and mutual respect." He concluded that the "alternative to co-existence—if it can be called an alternative—is no existence!" Nasser favored peaceful coexistence but wanted the big powers to "stop their games of power politics, and recognise the right of other countries to conduct their own foreign policies freely, without being disturbed by intervention and interference from outside."

Iraq, Turkey, Pakistan, the Philippines, and Thailand, on the other hand, "were sceptical about the execution of the 5 principles of peaceful coexistence. The sharpest 'spokesman' of this group was Pakistan." Ali argued that "Peaceful coexistence is an effect, not a cause. It can follow only when certain prerequisites of international conduct are universally fulfilled." Instead, he argued that the developing nations should establish "some system of defence against aggression. If not, peace could never be maintained." The Iraqi delegate said that communism "always, at any time and any place whatsoever, conducted infiltration and subversion both through propaganda and also through psycho-ideological war. Communism had its own interpretation of all kinds of terms. They possessed their own jargon. For instance, their definition of 'democracy' and 'people' was very different from ours." Such "slogans," he concluded, would not protect the nations from communism, only CENTO and SEATO could do so. The Turkish delegate called NATO "a system of defence that is defensive and not aggressive... it is very naïve to believe that world peace can be maintained without a system of collective defence like NATO."[55]

Nehru's second speech responded to these critiques and challenged the idea that collective security treaties had contributed to achieving a peaceful world. After proudly stating that he did not belong to either bloc, he asked "What has the reality of the peace that followed the last war led us to? ... This so-called realistic appreciation of the world situation, where has it led us to? It has led us to the brink of war, a third world war." He also indicted the two blocs for embracing ideology to the point where they not only created a fearful atmosphere but exacerbated it. Thanks to the hydrogen bomb, "today two mighty colossuses, neither of whom can put an end to each other," could not only "ruin each other" but "the rest of the world." Their competing ideologies overwhelmed their desire for peaceful relationships. "If I join any of these big groups," he declared, "I lose my identity; I have no identity left, I have no view left. I may express it here and there generally but I have no views left. If all the world were to be divided up between these two big blocs what would be the result? The inevitable result would be war."

He urged the anticommunist delegates to remember that "honourable members" such as U Nu had "laid great stress on moral force. It is with military force that we are dealing now but I submit that moral force counts and the moral force of Asia and Africa must, in spite of the atomic and hydrogen bombs of Russia, the USA or another country, count!" The only option was "to accept the concept of peaceful coexistence. In some countries the very word, peace, is looked upon with horror. It is most amazing. That word is considered dangerous. So I submit, let us consider these matters practically, leaving out ideology." He considered the Pakistanis and the Turks wrong about NATO and CENTO. Rather, "every pact has brought insecurity and not security to the countries which have entered into them. They have brought the danger of atomic bombs and the rest of it nearer to them than would have been the case otherwise. They have not added to the strength of any country." While he conceded that the Five Principles were "not a magic formula which will prevent all the ills of the world," they did meet "the needs of the day. It lessens tension; it does not harm anybody, criticise anybody, condemn anybody." He assured the delegates that both Eisenhower and Churchill agreed with the Principles so the conference should adopt them in its closing platform.[56]

Ali, however, rejected Nehru's characterization of collective defense organizations. Pakistan, he declared, remained "an independent and sovereign country, and all its acts are its own responsibility. It requires justification only from its own people. It does not need it from outsiders." Iraq and Turkey said that they had joined defensive, not aggressive, military pacts and "felt proud to be taking part in those pacts. And they didn't feel any loss of identity or self-respect, as Prime Minister Nehru had said."[57]

The debate resumed the following morning. Romulo began the proceedings by defending his country's decision to join SEATO. The organization, he argued, "did not exist in a vacuum but was the result of a specific and all too recognizable cause: a world which had not yet been made safe from aggression." Manila had acted as a sovereign nation, not as a Western stooge, and he contended that the Philippines "would be the first to move for an end to SEATO once the UN had developed adequate police power and the machinery to ensure a rule of law and justice in the world." He also noted that "India was a big country and so could rely upon itself to defend itself. But nevertheless, India should be careful." The Philippines and Thailand, for example, faced aggressive communist insurgencies. They were not as large as India, so why wouldn't they join defensive pacts? He charged that the pro-West nations now feared "the new empire of

FIGURE 2.2 *Nehru, U Nu, Sukarno, Ali, and Sastroamidjojo at Bandung. Department of State.*

communism on which we know the sun never rises. May your India, Sir, never be caught by the encircling gloom!"[58]

Zhou Enlai followed by granting that the term "peaceful coexistence" caused "misunderstanding" because the anticommunist nations associated it with communism. Instead he suggested they adopt the phrase "peaceful cooperation," which he believed more accurately captured the spirit of the conference. Nonetheless, he averred that China opposed military blocs such as NATO, SEATO, and CENTO, but struck a conciliatory tone by arguing that since "we are meeting here to discuss the issue of collective peace," it made more sense to "not discuss the issue of military blocs because they are already a reality." He offered a practical example of how discussion could lead to understanding. Two days earlier, he had had a conversation with Ali, who assured him that "Pakistan did not join the Manila Pact for the purpose of opposing China, nor does Pakistan suspect China of having aggressive intentions. Just like that, we have obtained mutual understanding." Ali had also assured Zhou that if the United States started a world war, Pakistan would not join in, just as it had refused to join in the UN coalition against North Korea. Zhou said he was "very thankful for the explanation from the prime minister of Pakistan, because it led to mutual understanding and allowed us to know that this treaty does not obstruct us from cooperating and reaching agreements for collective peace."

After rejecting Romulo's and Ali's claims about communist aggression, he reaffirmed China's commitment to the Five Principles. He then offered his most spectacular comments yet:

> As for the relationship between China and the United States, the Chinese people are unwilling to fight with the United States. We are willing to use peaceful methods to resolve international disputes. If everyone is willing to push China and the United States to use peaceful methods to resolve disputes between China and the United States, then it will greatly help ease the tense situation of the Far East and be in the interest of preventing a world war.

The comments, Romulo recalled, "electrified the conference," although he believed they sounded "singularly hollow alongside the intermittent blasts of artillery fire" aimed at Taiwan's offshore islands.[59]

Nehru also had a chance to respond to the anticommunists' charges and to reiterate his support for peaceful coexistence. After praising Zhou's "very important statement," he answered Romulo by pointing out that India's size had not prevented it from being colonized. Now that it was independent, "the quality of the Indian people" rather than its physical size would improve the world. "I want to develop that quality," he claimed, "and I do not want any country in Asia to be lulled into a sense of, shall I say, dependence upon others, because that saps; that undermines the growth of that élan of a nation that spirit of self dependence, of having faith in themselves." Rather, a "feeling of cooperation is obviously right and it is necessary in the world of today."

He too apologized for using the phrase peaceful coexistence, since it "seems to bring up all kinds of frightening pictures before people's minds." Instead, he really meant to use the word "disarmament," or even more accurately, the phrase "lessening of tension. The moment the tension is lessened, disarmament becomes easier." As for Romulo's assertion that SEATO was purely defensive, he noted that the timing of its formation— right after the Geneva Conference—was suspicious. "What was the threat in South-East Asia then and where did it come from?" he asked. "There was not the slightest fear of aggression to any of the countries of South-East Asia. I saw none and see none." Instead, he argued that Geneva had lessened tensions in the region. He could only conclude that SEATO had "seemed to be an angry reaction to what had happened in Geneva. It had made no difference to anybody; it had not strengthened even the military potential or the economic potential of South-East Asia; it had not added to the security even in a military sense." He urged the participants to reject all military blocs and instead accept that the "only way, therefore, open is the way of the Geneva Agreement which is the way of non-alignment and friendly cooperation and peaceful existence."[60]

After the conference broke for the day, Sastroamidjojo held a "political" dinner party in his bungalow, which included Nehru, Kotelawala, Ali, U Nu, Zhou, Wan (Thailand), and Romulo, in an attempt to fix the Taiwan problem. Since Zhou's speech had been made in closed session, Sastroamidjojo wanted him to "make the statement openly...so the American side would hear for itself." If nothing else, he believed tensions in Asia could be reduced once the United States learned that China did not want another war. When he steered the conversation toward Taiwan, however, Zhou called Taiwan "a domestic affair of China. That was a fact of history. Taiwan was an inseparable part of mainland China." It could only be settled between the PRC and Taiwan without "any interference whatsoever from outside." The United States remained the "obstacle" to "direct talks" between the two, and he noted the presence of the US Seventh Fleet in the Taiwan Straits. "Conscious of this reality," he nevertheless told the group that China "was prepared to make contact with America and negotiate peacefully what would be the best way to solve the Taiwan problem." Zhou subsequently issued the statement to the press.[61]

The conference ended on April 24, 1955, after a ringing speech by Nehru in which he argued that they had met "because mighty forces are at work in these great continents, in millions of people, creating a ferment in their minds and irrepressible urges and passions and a desire for change from their present condition. So however big or small we might be, we represented these great forces." And what did they hope to achieve? "The very primary consideration," he said, "is peace. You and I, sitting here in our respective countries, are all passionately eager to advance our countries peacefully. We have been backward. We are backward. We have been left behind in the world race, and now we have got a chance again to make good." The peoples of Asia and Africa no longer accepted domination by outside forces, rejected the idea of joining military blocs, and would concentrate on improving their economies and striving for peace. He concluded, "We came here, consciously and unconsciously, as agents of a historic destiny. And we have made some history here."[62]

The participants issued a Final Communiqué, which summed up their program for economic, social, and political development. These included cooperation among the participants "on the basis of mutual interest and respect for national sovereignty;" a call for the creation of a special UN Fund for Economic Development and a special World Bank aimed at helping Asians and Africans; technical cooperation; the stabilization of commodity trade and international prices; cultural cooperation; the condemnation of "racialism as a means of cultural suppression" and racialism in general; a condemnation of colonialism "in whatever form it may be;" the endorsement of the UN Charter's view of Human Rights and a declaration of "its full support of the principle of self-determination of peoples and nations;" support for Algeria's, Morocco's, and Tunisia's demands for independence and "the rights of the Arab people of Palestine;" and a condemnation of the testing, experimentation, and use of nuclear weapons.[63]

The Bandung Conference demonstrated that the former colonies had clearly arrived on the world stage, and Sukarno correctly pointed out that they could no longer be ignored. Still, it is important to note that the conference also exposed the fissures within the developing world, in particular the divide between the neutralists and the anticommunists. However, this divide actually demonstrates that labeling the participants "the developing world" is imprecise, because the very diversity of opinion exposed by the sharp exchanges proves that these nations could not be labeled with one moniker or another. In this sense, Nehru was correct in calling for each nation to pursue its own path free from the ideological constraints of East or West, democracy or communism. But they could also make their own choices, even if that meant that they chose to side with one or the other, or none, as both Romulo and Kotelawala argued.

Asia, Africa, and the developing world began to become more important in the Great Powers' calculations. In July 1956, Nasser nationalized the Suez Canal—built by British and French interests and owned by them for nearly a century—choking off Israel's trade and water routes. The Eisenhower administration condemned the nationalization of the Canal and empathized with Israel's fear that its economy could be smothered by Egypt, but warned Britain and France not to intervene. Three months later, Israel, Great Britain, and France invaded Egypt in order to return control of the Canal Zone and the Suez Canal Company to its British and French owners. The United States, however, forced the British and French to withdraw their troops from the Zone, a decision made imperative by America's long history of anticolonialism as well as the Soviet Union's suggestion that the two superpowers jointly intervene to end the crisis. For all practical purposes, Eisenhower and Dulles sided with the developing world in this important conflict.

By the end of the war, Israel controlled the Sinai Peninsula, the Gaza Strip, and the Straits of Tiran. Ultimately the United Nations stepped in to mediate and created the UN Emergency Force (UNEF), which oversaw the British and French withdrawal from the Canal Zone and, in 1957, the Israeli withdrawal from Sinai. The Canal and the Straits were reopened to international trade. UNEF remained in Sinai as peacekeepers. Nasser, however, retained the right to remove the UNEF as soon as the UN determined that their peacekeeping mission had succeeded.[64]

More and more African and Middle Eastern countries pressed for their independence from their colonial masters. Morocco, Sudan, and Tunisia became independent in 1956. The bloody Algerian insurrection against France began in 1954 as Paris was extricating itself from its Indochinese colony. The war featured suicide bombings by Algerians and brutal crackdowns on Muslims, including torture, by the French authorities. On

July 2, 1957, then-Senator John F. Kennedy made a famous speech on the floor of US Senate. Kennedy criticized the Algerian war and argued that it "confronts the United States with its most critical diplomatic impasse since the crisis in Indochina—and yet we have not only failed to meet the problem forthrightly and effectively, we have refused to even recognize that it is our problem at all." The war raged until 1962, when France finally granted its long-time colony independence.

Sub-Saharan Africa also began to see at first a trickle, and then ultimately a flood, of newly independent nations. On March 6, 1957, Kwame Nkrumah, who had attended Bandung as the representative of the Gold Coast, declared his country's independence, and its new name became Ghana (or "Warrior King" in English). France granted Guinea its independence in October 1958. British prime minister Harold MacMillan, meanwhile, had rethought his country's position on decolonization. During a visit to South Africa, he made what became arguably the most important speech about decolonization during the post-Second World War era. On February 3, 1960, he declared that the independence movements that had swept through Asia had now reached Africa. MacMillan proclaimed that "the strength of this African national consciousness is happening everywhere. The wind of change is blowing through this continent, and whether we like it or not, this growth of national consciousness is a political fact. We must all accept it as a fact, and our national policies must take account of it." He also criticized South Africa's apartheid policy.[65]

This speech heralded a new era in the developing world, and MacMillan turned his rhetoric into action. Plans to grant Somalia its independence, which predated the speech, took on a new urgency, and the nation became independent on July 1, 1960. Over the next seven years, Britain granted independence to all of its colonies in Sub-Saharan Africa except for Rhodesia, another white-minority government that bordered South Africa. France also granted independence to a number of its colonies during the 1960s. Belgium completely decolonized, but its granting of independence to the Belgian Congo (now called the Democratic Republic of Congo) in the summer of 1960 led to American intervention when the new country's prime minister, Patrice Lumumba, revealed socialist/leftist leanings. The resulting civil war, Lumumba's assassination, and his succession by the dictator Joseph Mobutu led to chaos in the mineral-rich nation.

In September 1961, a "Conference of Heads of State or Government of Non-Aligned Countries" was held in Belgrade, Yugoslavia, hosted by the Yugoslav leader Josip Broz Tito. Nasser, Nehru, Nkrumah, U Nu, Sukarno, and Tito created this "Non-Aligned Movement," based on the Five Principles of Peaceful Coexistence, as a way to informally declare that these nations would not side with the two power blocs. In many ways, the developing world had become an important player in the Cold War.

CHAPTER THREE

The Beginning of Détente: The Glassboro Summit

While the developing countries announced their determination to steer a path between the Western and Eastern blocs, the two nuclear superpowers, the United States and the Soviet Union, began to try to improve their relationship. Only three months after Bandung, Eisenhower, Soviet Premier Nikolai Bulganin (although the real power was in First Secretary Nikita Khrushchev's hands), British prime minister Anthony Eden, and French prime minister Edgar Fauer met in Geneva. The most significant proposal of the summit, Eisenhower's so-called "Open Skies" plan, called for the nuclear powers to allow the other to conduct surveillance flights over their territory in order to verify arms control agreements. Although the Soviets rejected the proposal, the summit created a slow thaw in Soviet-US relations, dubbed the "spirit of Geneva."[1]

Khrushchev continued to consolidate his power, but began to liberalize at home. He freed thousands of political prisoners from the Siberian gulag, and in February 1956, he condemned Stalin's crimes, including his cult of personality, at the Twentieth Party Congress in Moscow. He also suggested that the Soviet-dominated Eastern bloc nations could exercise some independence in their pursuit of socialism. When Hungarians rebelled in October 1956, however, Khrushchev crushed the revolt, showing the limits of his new policy. The United States refused to intervene in Hungary, demonstrating its acceptance of Moscow's domination of Eastern Europe just as Roosevelt and Truman had earlier. In 1957, Khrushchev survived an attempted coup by conservatives in the leadership and the military who objected to his "de-Stalinization" campaign and his desire to cut spending from heavy industry and the military and increase spending on consumer goods and agriculture.

Problems between the two superpowers persisted, however. Khrushchev was angry that Eisenhower installed intermediate range ballistic missiles (IRBMs) in Turkey, which could reach numerous targets within the Soviet Union.[2] In November 1958, he threatened to unilaterally recognize East Germany within six months unless the Western Powers agreed to settle the status of Berlin. Recognition of East Germany as a sovereign state would not only violate the Potsdam agreements but also cement the division of Germany and Berlin.

Despite these controversies, Khrushchev began to pursue a policy of "peaceful coexistence" with the United States. The two nations agreed to establish cultural exchange programs, including the opening of exhibits in each nation. In July 1959, US vice-president Richard M. Nixon visited the Soviet Union. He and Khrushchev engaged in their famous "Kitchen Debate" at the opening of the American National Exhibition in Moscow, where they debated the merits of capitalism versus communism.[3] Two months later, Khrushchev visited the United States and met with Eisenhower at the presidential retreat, Camp David. The boost in prestige he received from meeting with Eisenhower strengthened his position at home and the Berlin issue temporarily faded.

The brief thaw in superpower relations abruptly ended on May 1, 1960, when the Soviets shot down an American U-2 spy plane and captured the pilot just two weeks before a scheduled Four-Power summit in Paris. Khrushchev was stunned, first when the US Government lied about the flights, and second, after Eisenhower refused to apologize. Eisenhower did agree to cease the overflights and renewed his call for Open Skies. Furious, Khrushchev walked out of the summit.[4]

Soviet-American relations continued to deteriorate. In April 1961, US president John F. Kennedy supported an invasion of Cuba at the Bay of Pigs. It failed miserably, and Khrushchev, who considered the Cuban leader, Fidel Castro, the future of international communism, pledged to protect Castro. Kennedy, in turn, instituted Operation Mongoose, a plan to depose or assassinate Castro.[5] In June, Kennedy met with Khrushchev in Vienna, and Khrushchev bullied the new president over Cuba, Berlin, and arms control. Two months later, worried about the "brain drain" caused by the most educated and skilled workers leaving East Germany, East German leader Walter Ulbricht ordered his police and military forces to build the Berlin Wall, which stopped the flood of emigration westward. Kennedy protested but did not take action to remove the wall. Berlin was now divided in violation of the Potsdam Accords. In October, US and Soviet tanks confronted each other at the Brandenburg Gate.[6]

A year later, the Kennedy administration discovered that Khrushchev had secretly shipped IRBMs to and was constructing missile sites in Cuba. If built, the missiles could hit much of the continental United States just like the missiles in Turkey could hit targets in the Soviet Union. The 13-day Cuban Missile Crisis nearly resulted in nuclear war between the two superpowers. The crisis was resolved when Khrushchev publicly agreed to withdraw the missiles from Cuba in exchange for the secret American withdrawal of the missiles from Turkey. The United States also agreed to cease attempts to overthrow Castro, while the Soviets agreed not to station any offensive nuclear weapons or weapons systems in Cuba. This US-Soviet "Understanding" on Cuba governed superpower policy toward Castro for the remainder of the Cold War.[7]

Kennedy and Khrushchev recognized that they had come dangerously close to a nuclear exchange, and over the next year, they worked to improve relations. In November 1962, Khrushchev wrote Kennedy proposing a comprehensive nuclear test ban. In a June 10, 1963 speech at American University, Kennedy called for a test ban, unilaterally suspended atmospheric nuclear tests, and dismissed the inevitability of war. Ten days later, the superpowers signed an agreement setting up a hotline that would establish instant communications between the two governments and hopefully prevent another Missile Crisis. In August, the United States, Britain, and the Soviet Union signed the Limited Test Ban Treaty (LTBT), which prohibited all nuclear tests except for those conducted underground.

A second Kennedy–Khrushchev summit was in the planning stages when on November 22, 1963, Kennedy was assassinated, and Vice-President Lyndon Johnson became president. He vowed to continue his predecessor's desire to improve relations with Moscow. At his first National Security Council (NSC) meeting after Kennedy's assassination, he repeatedly read a statement prepared by National Security Advisor McGeorge Bundy: "The greatest single requirement is that we find a way to ensure the survival of civilization in the nuclear age. A nuclear war would be the death of all our hopes and it is our task to see that it does not happen."[8]

On October 14, 1964, Khrushchev was overthrown by a group of rivals led by Leonid Brezhnev and Alexi Kosygin, who opposed his liberalization at home, worried that Khrushchev's brinksmanship during the Cuban Missile Crisis had damaged Soviet prestige, and worried that the Missile Crisis had exposed the Soviet Union's strategic vulnerabilities. They quickly began to increase the Soviet stockpile of nuclear forces in order to achieve parity with the United States.[9]

Washington's support for the Multilateral Nuclear Force (MLF), which would grant West Germany partial control over nuclear weapons without giving Bonn an independent nuclear force, impacted US-Soviet relations. Soviet officials opposed the MLF, arguing that opening the door even the slightest to West German nuclear aspirations signified West German "revanchism" (military revival).[10]

Despite this disagreement, Johnson told Soviet Ambassador Anatoly Dobrynin, "there was no reason for us to be frightened of each other. He was prepared to go to bed in the same room with the Ambassador without a pistol, and thought the Ambassador felt the same way. The problem was how to get our peoples to understand this." The new

Soviet leadership seemed to agree, and on November 3 it wrote Johnson "we would like to emphasize not those questions on which there are differences of opinion between us, but those areas where there are points of convergence between us."[11]

In his January 4, 1965 State of the Union address, Johnson hoped the new Soviet leadership could visit the United States, and privately, the president wrote, "I believe that such a visit would allow us to have serious and constructive discussions together."[12] On January 14 he suggested that a member of "the Soviet leadership" visit the United States, using that phrase deliberately "to enable the Soviet side to decide on who would actually come." After numerous messages back and forth, Dobrynin recalled that his government decided to invite Johnson to Moscow "because they could not agree which among them should go to Washington." Many of the messages from Moscow were unsigned, so the United States did not know to whom the president's letters should be addressed. This reflected, Dobrynin wrote, "a behind-the-scenes power struggle between Brezhnev and Kosygin as to who was to sign messages to foreign leaders." Kosygin, "as the head of government, believed he was entitled by normal international protocol to send messages to foreign heads of government." But Brezhnev, who "envied Kosygin and disliked him" and was "itching to play a role on the world stage," disagreed. On January 31, the Soviet news agency *Pravda* called the Soviet reaction to the president's statements on Soviet/American contacts "positive."[13]

Any talk of a possible US-Soviet summit was dashed on February 6 when the communist revolutionaries in South Vietnam, the National Liberation Front (NLF or Vietcong), attacked the US air base in Pleiku, killing eight American soldiers, while Bundy was in Saigon meeting with the South Vietnamese. The NSC quickly and unanimously agreed to retaliate with airstrikes on military targets in North Vietnam.[14]

Coincidentally, Kosygin was in Hanoi meeting with North Vietnamese leaders when the airstrikes hit. Dobrynin wrote that Kosygin "bitterly resented the bombing that had taken place while he was in Vietnam and turned against Johnson, although previously he had been more favorably disposed toward him in Kremlin meetings." On February 9, Dobrynin read an oral note from his government that accused the administration of saying on the one hand that it wanted to improve relations with Moscow but, on the other hand, acting provocatively by bombing North Vietnam.[15]

The administration began the sustained bombing of North Vietnam, known as Operating Rolling Thunder, on March 2, 1965, and American combat troops arrived six days later. On March 12, Dobrynin met with Vice-President Hubert Humphrey and excoriated the administration for attacking North Vietnam. He again questioned Johnson's sincerity about wishing to improve US-Soviet relations. While he praised Johnson for supporting the LTBT and international efforts at nuclear non-proliferation, the ambassador confessed "we can't understand why you are testing us now. We are in a quandary. Don't you think your relations with the USSR are of high priority? If you do, then why do you bomb North Vietnam? Why do you test us?"[16]

The issue of US involvement in Vietnam prevented the establishment of good relations between the Soviet Union and the United States during this time. However, it is also important to note that the growing intensity of the Sino-Soviet split exacerbated Moscow's insecurities about the war. The State Department's Policy Planning Council warned Secretary of State Dean Rusk that Moscow was preoccupied by "the Chinese challenge to Soviet influence in the Communist movement ... The imperatives of this struggle, in particular the USSR's need to avoid being outdone in revolutionary fervor, works against rather than for détente with the US." While the Council urged the administration to keep trying to achieve better relations with Moscow, it concluded that the United States should "Harbor no illusions and make no myths about the USSR's intentions."[17]

The prime minister of the United Kingdom, Harold Wilson, also reported Soviet anger about the US intervention in Vietnam. During Wilson's July 1966 visit to Moscow, Kosygin called Johnson "virtually a madman" and compared the president to the Italian fascist dictator Benito Mussolini, who had bombed Ethiopia in the 1930s. Wilson, however, stressed Kosygin's concerns about Chinese intervention in Vietnam, and he told Johnson that the Soviet leadership "sincerely" feared a US–PRC "confrontation" over Vietnam.[18]

Despite the clashes over Vietnam, progress was made in other fields. The two sides remained optimistic that they would sign a civil air agreement and an agreement on the use of outer space. Most important, they discussed the need for arms control negotiations. In the fall of 1966, Rusk and Soviet foreign minister Andrei Gromyko met in New York during the UN General Assembly (UNGA) meetings and discussed the need for a non-proliferation treaty (NPT). Gromyko made the signing of an NPT dependent on the scuttling of the MLF. Dobrynin said that "it frightened us to think of Europeans and especially Germans with their fingers anywhere near a nuclear trigger." Gromyko and Dobrynin continued this theme with Rusk, and said the Soviet Union was ready for negotiations to limit the spread of nuclear weapons. The United States, however, would have to choose between "a nonproliferation agreement or a NATO nuclear force."[19]

For the moment, Rusk dismissed Moscow's attempt to become what he called "the 16th member of NATO with veto power at the NATO table" and assured the Soviets that only the United States could fire any nuclear weapons deployed in Europe. Meanwhile, Johnson issued National Security Action Memorandum 352, which called for "the peaceful settlement of the division of Germany and of Europe." The Memorandum also said the United States should encourage West Germany to move away from the MLF toward a nuclear nonproliferation treaty, which Johnson believed Moscow considered "acceptable." This marked what Frank Costigliola has called Johnson's "shift" in focus "from Cold War to détente."[20]

Johnson continued to demonstrate his seriousness about improving relations with the Soviets. On January 27, 1967, the United States, Britain, and the Soviet Union signed the Outer Space Treaty, which prohibited the placement and testing of nuclear weapons in outer space or in orbit around the earth. On a personal level, Johnson showed his commitment to better relations by nominating Llewellyn "Tommy" Thompson, who had been Kennedy's Ambassador to the Soviet Union, to return to Moscow. The president called reaching "an understanding between us which would curb the strategic arms race" his "first priority."

However, he wrote Kosygin that the United States had discovered that the Soviets had begun to construct a limited Anti-Ballistic Missile (ABM) defense system around Moscow. He not only faced "great pressure" from Congress and the American public to deploy such a system himself "but also to increase greatly our capabilities to penetrate any defensive systems which you might establish." The United States not only began to develop its own ABM system, but also Multiple Independently-Targeted Re-entry Vehicles (MIRVs), missiles that contained multiple warheads that could destroy separate targets, to defeat an ABM system. The Soviets responded by beginning to develop their own MIRV capability.[21]

These developments questioned the validity of the doctrine that had grounded the US-Soviet strategic relationship since the late 1950s. Both sides had adopted Mutually Assured Destruction (MAD), the concept that each possessed sufficient nuclear retaliatory power to destroy the other. Each side assumed that the other was rational enough to eschew a first-strike nuclear attack because they knew that they too would be destroyed in a nuclear counterattack. The development of an ABM system, however, could allow one side to launch a first strike and then prevent the other from retaliating by either shooting down incoming missiles or shielding targets from such an attack.

Dobrynin has written that Kosygin called an ABM necessary to "protect human life, and no negotiations were needed to prove it." However, the Americans, Brezhnev argued, would launch a massive missile attack that would overwhelm such a missile shield and build their own ABM system. Still, it is important to note that Brezhnev refused to scuttle his nation's ABM system. Instead, he believed the Soviet Union must seek "a balanced and a more conclusive response to meet 'the American challenge' diplomatically and militarily." An ABM system could therefore be a diplomatic tool. Dobrynin therefore argued that "Moscow came up with the more realistic idea of combined talks on offensive and defensive weapons. Underlying this was our principle objective of reaching parity with the United States in strategic weapons."[22]

The arguments over offensive and defensive nuclear weapons systems continued to be paralled by the divisions over Vietnam. In February 1967, Kosygin traveled to the United Kingdom to meet with Wilson. During five face-to-face meetings, the prime minister urged Kosygin to convince the North Vietnamese to come to the bargaining table with the United States, but Kosygin replied that this would not happen until the United States stopped its bombing campaigns. He understood that Wilson was "keeping the Americans continuously informed" about the Soviet position, and asked that Wilson "advise" Johnson to accept Hanoi's latest proposals if he truly wanted to end American involvement in the war.

Wilson agreed to be a mediator between Washington and Hanoi. He recalled that during his 1966 visit to Moscow, Kosygin had raised the relationship between China and Vietnam. Hanoi, Kosygin replied, was "deeply concerned" that Beijing would interfere in its affairs and had therefore refused to allow Chinese troops into their country. "They knew," he claimed, "that once Chinese troops had entered Vietnam, they would not be withdrawn easily." Kosygin warned that China wanted to "dominate" not only Vietnam but "the whole of Asia." Soviet aid to Vietnam, on the other hand, was given as "a friend." The bulk of Soviet aid, he insisted, was economic and foodstuffs. Any arms, he insisted, were "for the use against the allies of Britain" and "helped to counteract Chinese pressure." American "aggression" against the Vietnamese, Kosygin concluded, only helped the Chinese, and both men worried that American escalation could result in overt Chinese intervention.

Wilson, nevertheless, stressed that when it came to the war, he was "completely <u>au fait</u> with the United States' position on Vietnam." Kosygin said he understood, but urged Wilson to "stand up to the United States" and resist "the U.S. monopoly" over the Western alliance, otherwise there was little chance for progress on finding a solution to the Vietnam conflict. Wilson replied that "he was certainly not afraid of the United States," opposed all monopolies, and stated that "Britain had a real and considerable influence on the Americans."

The two leaders also debated whether or not Britain and the Soviet Union should jointly call for the United States and North Vietnam to undertake "mutual acts of de-escalation," including a halt to the American bombing and a North Vietnamese pledge to stop introducing new troops into South Vietnam during the Tet (the Vietnamese New Year holiday) truce. The sticking point was that Kosygin insisted that the American bombing halt be publicly declared, while the North Vietnamese concession would be made privately. Wilson seemed amenable to this formulation but he remained concerned about Kosygin's insistence that North Vietnam's troop pullback stay private.[23]

Johnson, for his part, had sent Ho Chi Minh a personal letter on January 8, 1967, proposing direct, but secret, talks between "trusted representatives" of both countries. He offered to halt the bombing and freeze the number of American troops in theater in exchange for an end to North Vietnamese "infiltration" into South Vietnam. As a sign of his goodwill, he decided to halt the bombing during the Tet truce. However, US aerial and naval reconnaissance immediately spotted large-scale movement of North Vietnamese forces southward. One pilot said that the roads were so crowded that they looked like the New Jersey Turnpike.

The president, however, "strongly" doubted that Wilson and Kosygin could successfully mediate a settlement, especially given that Kosygin promised only "vague" talks in exchange for a long-term bombing halt. Johnson told Wilson that a bombing halt would accomplish nothing unless the North Vietnamese "consider seriously the reasonable proposals we are putting before them, which would take us not merely into negotiation but a long step towards peace itself." Indeed, when National Security Advisor Walt Rostow informed Johnon that Wilson had requested a halt in the bombing until after Kosygin had departed London, Johnson initially agreed to do so. However, when Rostow noted that the administration had already told Wilson that "we were going to have to resume" bombing the North in the "restricted area" between the seventeenth and twenty-ninth parallels because Hanoi had used the ceasefire to resupply their troops, Johnson approved the plan. For the time being, therefore, both the Americans and the British remained at loggerheads with the Soviets about how the United States and the North Vietnamese could come together and end the war.[24]

The initial momentum to begin constructive negotiations on arms control also hit a roadblock when Stalin's daughter Svetlana arrived at the US Embassy in New Delhi in March and requested political asylum. Recognizing the potential political bombshell he had on his hands, the Ambassador to India, Chester Bowles, simply issued her a visa to leave the country. Rusk informed Thompson in Moscow that it would be "undesirable for Svetlana to proceed to U.S., both politically and from point of view her security." He hoped that she could seek and receive asylum in another country such as Switzerland, Spain, or Italy, and said he would immediately inform Dobrynin that the situation had been "thrust upon us by circumstances and not of our own seeking."

Initially the Soviets reacted calmly to the incident, but after further thought they changed their tune. Dobrynin read a March 23 note from his leadership, stating "it is completely clear" that American officials had "organized her travel." These activities, Moscow charged, "are saturated with a spirit of open unfriendliness toward our country and are in direct conflict with statements about striving for an improvement in U.S.-U.S.S.R. relations."[25]

Believing that the state of superpowers relations had deteriorated, Secretary of Defense Robert McNamara, having heard from "an individual" that Dobrynin wanted to talk to him, agreed in April to sit down with the

Ambassador. Dobrynin came to McNamara's house, alone, for lunch and the two had "a very frank discussion of the interests of each of the nations," including how they could achieve deterrence "at a lower level of strategic nuclear forces than might otherwise be the case." McNamara came away from their meeting with the sense that Dobrynin favored such talks.

Dobrynin recalled that in this meeting, McNamara said that "in a peculiar way," MAD provided stability, "and what impressed me was McNamara's firm conviction that this balance of terror, as some called it, actually kept the peace." At the same time, McNamara "admitted frankly that America's arsenal exceeded what was necessary" for MAD, and conceded that a reliable ABM system could not be built. Nevertheless, he warned Dobrynin that if the Soviets continued to build its own ABM system, the United States would respond by building more offensive missiles. This cycle would continue, McNamara believed, until the superpowers met and discussed arms limitations.[26]

Things briefly settled down after the Svetlana incident, and on May 19 Johnson wrote Kosygin that despite their disagreements, he believed that "there are two areas of opportunity" where they shared a "common interest and common duty to humanity": an ABM agreement and a non-proliferation treaty. While he noted that the two issues were not necessarily linked, achievement of both could "bring the nuclear arms race under control."[27]

Unfortunately, tensions between the superpowers flared far more ominously on June 5, 1967, when Israel, believing that it had detected a general mobilization of Egyptian and Syrian armed forces, launched a preemptive attack against both nations. Six days later, the war ended, and Israel occupied the West Bank, the Gaza Strip, the Sinai Peninsula, and the Golan Heights, fundamentally changing the politics of the Middle East. The United States and the Soviet Union employed the hotline for the first time during the crisis, which Dobrynin later credited with "preventing each side's perception of the other's intentions from becoming dangerously uncertain to a point that might precipitate rash acts in support of either side."[28]

Another war in the Middle East had been intensifying for some time, as tensions between Israel and its Arab neighbors had continued since an armistice had ended the 1948 war. Interestingly, at this time, both the United States and the Soviet Union recognized the new state, but as time passed, Israeli-Soviet relations soured. By 1956, the Soviets had all but signed a defensive alliance with the Arab states, providing Egypt and Syria with millions of dollars in weapons and other military supplies.

The United States, meanwhile, had an ambivalent relationship with Israel. While it backed Israel's right to exist, it refused to directly sell the Jewish state weapons, fearing that doing so would touch off an arms race between the two sides that could set off another war. Instead the United States provided food aid under Public Law 480 that allowed the Israelis to free up funds so they could purchase planes and weapons from West Germany and France. Eisenhower also worried that the United States could be dragged into a war with the Soviet Union if the Arabs and Israelis went to war again. The United States had not only condemned the British-French-Israel invasion of the Suez Canal Zone in 1956, but essentially sided with Nasser's stand against imperialism. Israeli's pointed exclusion from the Bandung Conference indicated that most of the developing world backed the Palestinians and the Arabs in their dispute with Israel.

Over the next eleven years, the Arab-Israeli dispute continued at a low boil, with occasional moments of high tension. Cross-border incursions from Egypt, Jordan, and Syria by Palestinian guerillas into Israel were routinely followed by Israeli military retaliation. The squalid refugee camps proved to be fertile breeding grounds not only for Palestinian nationalism but also recruiting grounds for the nascent Palestinian guerilla groups. Resentment rose as Palestinians seemed to suffer the most casualties from Israeli military retaliation. Israel and Syria, meanwhile, attempted to divert the Jordan River and tried to exclude the other from using the River for irrigation and other projects.

Although Kennedy reversed Eisenhower's policy and began to sell weapons to Israel, in particular Hawk ground-to-air missiles, he also tried to improve relations with Nasser, especially by selling wheat and other commodities to Egypt. Kennedy also criticized Israel's retaliation policies, its Jordan River projects, and its refusal to allow the repatriation of Palestinian refugees who had fled their homes during the 1948 war. Perhaps most importantly, Kennedy opposed Israel's development of nuclear power, which he feared could produce a nuclear weapon. Ironically, the very Hawk missiles he had sold to Israel were deployed around Israel's nuclear reactor at Dimona in the Negev desert.[29]

Johnson, however, enjoyed warm relations with Israel and its prime minister, Levi Eshkol. As a Senator, he had criticized Eisenhower's handling of the Suez crisis in 1956, consistently supported foreign aid to Israel, and he admired Israel's ability to defend itself from its enemies. A Texan and friend of oil men, he nevertheless refused to tilt toward the Arab states. He and Eshkol also shared an agricultural background, and both men understood the importance of water in an arid climate. When rioters attacked the American embassy in Cairo and Egyptian forces accidentally shot down a plane owned by one of his friends in November 1964, Johnson cut off aid, especially wheat sales, to a defiant Nasser. The Egyptian president, in turn, began to believe that Johnson wanted to assassinate him.

By the spring of 1967, tensions had neared a boiling point. Palestinian guerillas attacked Israeli irrigation pumps and railroad tracks near the Jordanian border. A week later, Israeli tractors tasked with cultivating the DMZ between Israel and Syria were fired upon from the Golan Heights by Syrian guns. The Israeli army retaliated, and in the resulting escalation, Israeli and Syrian fighter jets engaged in a dogfight over Damascus. Cross-border attacks by Palestinian guerillas continued, along with the shelling of Israeli kibbutzim from Lebanon and Syria. The Israelis continued their policy of retaliation as well as the cultivation of the DMZ, while the Soviet Government backed Syria and criticized Israel for acting provocatively.

Eshkol, worried about the possibility of Soviet intervention, asked Johnson to sell Israel Patton tanks and Skyhawk jets. Johnson, however, refused to provide the weapons, especially since Israel still resisted the American demand for on-site inspection of the Dimona nuclear site. On April 29, the Soviets told Egyptian vice-president Anwar Sadat that Israel was planning to invade Syria. Two weeks later, when Israel celebrated the nineteenth anniversary of its independence in West Jerusalem, the Arab world and the UN protested that this was yet another Israeli provocation.[30]

Shortly after hostilities began on June 5, Kosygin contacted Johnson via the hotline, argued that the superpowers had an interest in stopping the fighting, and asked the president to use his influence to restrain Israel. Johnson replied that night that he was "astonished and dismayed" by reports of the fighting. Washington had been "making the maximum effort to prevent this situation." The Israelis, he said, had assured him that they "would not initiate hostilities pending further diplomatic efforts." The United States, Johnson said, wanted the issue brought in front of the UN Security Council. Moscow broke relations with Tel Aviv on June 10.[31]

The hotline and the quick responses by both powers prevented the war from widening into a superpower clash. But Johnson was so concerned about the state of the US-Soviet relationship that when Kosygin announced that he would come to New York to attend an emergency session of the UN on the Middle East, he invited the Premier to meet with him in Washington. The president proposed a formal meeting at the White House, or if Kosygin preferred, they could get away "from the hurly-burly of a big city" and meet at Camp David. The latter "would give the opportunity for relaxed talks in a comfortable and isolated location."

Dobrynin replied that he would immediately transmit the invitation to the Kremlin, but argued with Thompson about who should be blamed for starting the war in the Middle East. Switching topics, he claimed that his government was ready to sign a treaty on nuclear non-proliferation. However, he warned that the American bombing of North Vietnam and Washington's refusal to begin direct talks with the North Vietnamese could prevent the treaty's signing. Thompson replied that the United States would stop the bombing once Hanoi stopped infiltrating troops into South Vietnam. The Johnson administration, he stressed, was "most anxious to resolve the problem either through negotiations or through a tapering off of the use of violence."[32]

It turned out that Kosygin had already arrived in New York, but that did not matter: after consulting with the Politburo back in Moscow, he refused to meet Johnson in Washington. "The Soviet leadership," Dobrynin has written, "especially his rival Brezhnev, reacted in a rather reserved way. While a meeting seemed a possibility, Moscow sent a cable stating that it had to take place 'in New York or in any event in its environs, clearly indicating that Johnson would be coming to visit the Soviet prime minister rather than A.N. Kosygin going to the president for a meeting'." Face demanded that Kosygin not be seen as a supplicant. As Zbigniew Brzezinski, then a member of the Policy Planning Council, argued, Kosygin likely possessed a "sense of humiliation and frustration, brought on by recent events in the Middle East as well as by Soviet inability to deter the United States from bombing North Vietnam." This made it an imperative that Johnson reach out to Kosygin and treat him as an equal.[33]

While the administration tried to arrange a meeting with Kosygin, Johnson told a group of educators on June 19 that "every nation" in the Middle East "has a fundamental right to live, and to have this right respected by its neighbors." At the same time, he said the refugees in the region deserved "justice" and unless and until their plight was settled, "no peace for any party in the Middle East" would occur. He also called for an end to the arms race in the region, noted that US arms shipments had been "limited," and asked all UN members "to report all shipments of all military arms into this area."[34]

That afternoon, Kosygin spoke before UNGA. He rebuked Israel for starting the recent war and for its occupation of the Arab territories, the United States for the war in Vietnam and its "hostile stance" against Cuba, the "harebrained plans" of West Germany to gain "access to weapons of mass destruction," and he accused Washington of creating and "fanning international tensions and precipitate international crises." In particular he said Israel had "enjoyed outside support from certain imperialist circles" that had essentially encouraged it "to commit acts of aggression" against the Arab states. After the speech, he told reporters that he had "not heard anything from President Johnson during my stay. It would be difficult for me to say at this moment whether I will be meeting with him."[35]

Johnson was furious, because he had thrice asked Kosygin for a meeting and had been turned down each time, which made *him* look like the supplicant. "I think it would be phony," he fumed to Senator J. William Fulbright (D-Arkansas), the Chairman of the Senate Foreign Relations Committee, "and I think I can get embarrassed very easily. I got no reason to go" to New York. Johnson, like Brzezinski, believed that the Soviets were "losing all over the world...the Chinese are eating them up, the North Vietnamese won't pay a damn bit of attention to em, they got trouble in their own damned country, Israel with less than 2 million [people] captured over $2 billion worth of their tanks and planes, and got them locked up. He just hadn't got anything to brag about." Fulbright agreed but said that he considered Kosygin "dangerous." The president replied "I know he's dangerous but I think it's a lot more dangerous for him to think I'm slobbering over him...you try to date a girl Bill and if she don't wanna go out with you, you can't do it." As for Kosygin's political style, Johnson said, "I think this fella's just a cold-blooded, hard-hearted, straight, strictly business executive that's a good administrator who doesn't have all the showmanship, dramatics, and the bluff that Khrushchev had."[36]

Johnson, angry that Kosygin had breached protocol by not informing either the White House or the State Department of his arrival, lashed out at press leaks incorrectly stating that the two leaders would meet in New York. He called Julian Goodman, the president of NBC News, to complain:

I don't know whether it's the Central Committee that's got him in problems. I don't know whether it's the Arab world. I don't know whether it's [the] fact that they sent him off her for this job while Brezhnev called the Committee together or whether he's rushing back. I don't know whether he's feared [sic] that China would give him hell for meeting with the United States. But he's not following the normal procedure that a Head would do. A) he didn't notify us he's even coming. [B] He hasn't officially informed us yet that he's here which is never done. And C) he has never been able to work out his plan, he's got under consideration, but he hasn't completely rejected, but he has not accepted it. Now, we do not know what will come out of that. But in view of the fact to just keep building up with our people and with the rest of the world that we're seeking and we are just almost crawling, through our news medium, and we have no, no regulation of him at all, we just can't even guide em when we tell em, I think it's very bad public posture for the United States to be in this situation.

He called NBC's coverage "irresponsible" and said "I don't want us to be responsible for building up the American people to a point where I just fall on my face and they'll say, well, 'Johnson's petulant' or 'he's irritable or he's moody' or something else" that prevented their meeting.[37]

Johnson subsequently suggested that they meet at McGuire Air Force Base in New Jersey. Kosygin, sensitive to the idea that he could be meeting with Johnson on an air base while the US Air Force bombed North Vietnam, refused. Luckily, on June 22, Johnson's friend Richard Hughes, the Governor of New Jersey, suggested Glassboro State College, located in a "small, peaceful college town" approximately halfway between Washington and New York. The president of the college, Thomas Robinson, readily agreed to host the summit and offered Johnson the use of his house, Hollybush. The "invaders" from Washington, as Johnson called his staff members, and Secret Service men (McNamara called them "locusts") descended on the college and installed modern communications systems and, because the weather was unseasonably hot and humid, extra air conditioners needed for the two delegations.[38]

The president's helicopter landed on the college's football field at approximately 10:40 a.m. on June 23. Kosygin's party, stuck in traffic on the New Jersey Turnpike, arrived at 11:22 a.m. to what Dobrynin described as a "huge crowd of local residents, reporters, and other curious folks waiting for us outside the building" who had been awaiting eagerly "to see the event, with vendors selling hot dogs and cold drinks, a typically American picture our prime minister watched with great interest." The two delegations, which included the First Lady and Kosygin's daughter, posed for pictures.[39]

The two leaders sat down at 11:30 in Robinson's study for their first talk with only their interpreters present. Kosygin apologized for all the back-and-forth over the meeting's arrangements and noted that "the recent period of time" called for "a great deal of clarification" so that each could understand the other's actions. While he recognized that they would not "reach all-encompassing global solutions here," it was to their "mutual advantage" to reach agreement on "some problems." Johnson agreed and said that perhaps they had both been "poor communicators." But he knew that the American and Russian people wanted "to live in peace and harmony" and work together "to prevent the holocaust that would come about otherwise."

Kosygin agreed that neither country wanted war and recalled his own experience as a young worker who had survived the Nazi siege of Leningrad. He thus had a "clear understanding" about the "horrors of war." The maintenance of peace was "their greatest duty." Turning to the Middle East, Kosygin said while their hotline communications had been "useful," their discussions had occurred after the cat had been let out of the bag. While Moscow had successfully discouraged their Arab allies from starting a war, the United States had clearly failed to influence Israel to do the same. When Johnson replied that they had both failed since Egypt had closed the Straits of Tiran, Kosygin "was quite emphatic" in saying the Arabs had "heeded his advice."

In his memoirs, Johnson wrote that this was the only time that Kosygin became "heated" and "came close to issuing a threat. Unless we agreed to his formula, there would be a war—'a very great war.' He said the Arabs would fight with arms if they had them and, if not, with bare hands." Johnson replied "If they fight with weapons...we would know where they got them. Then I leaned forward and said slowly and quietly: 'Let us understand one another. I hope there will be no war. If there is a war, I hope it will not be a big war. If they fight, I hope they fight with fists and not with guns'." The president warned Kosygin that if the superpowers were dragged into such a war, "it will be a very serious matter."[40]

Johnson acknowledged that both sides now had weapons that "had permitted them to become that reckless." He hoped that his June 19 call for full disclosure of weapons shipments to all countries in the region would restrain the parties in the future. Kosygin dismissed this idea as unrealistic and complained that their hotline discussions had not led to an actual ceasefire until after Israel had captured the lands of its neighbors.

The president answered that, as in Vietnam, the United States adhered to the "principle of preserving territorial integrity of all countries." But once again he reminded Kosygin that Nasser's closure of the Straits and the Gulf of Aqaba, which Israel interpreted as direct threats to its national security, had led Israel to preemptively strike and ultimately destroy Egypt's air force. That was why he made arms sales proposal.

This last comment allowed him to segue into a discussion of ABMs, and he argued that the $40 or $50 billion that it would cost to build an ABM system could better be spent on the "peaceful development of our country." Surely the two nations could agree to this, as well as ending the war in Vietnam?

Kosygin said that while he too wanted agreement on these issues, the president should realize that "this was not such a simple matter." The Soviet Union, he stressed, simply wanted to help Middle Eastern nations develop their own economies, and foreswore either military involvement in or the reaping of economic benefits from the region. He then demanded that the United States convince Israel to withdraw their forces to their original lines.

First, Johnson replied by reminding Kosygin that his administration had spent the last three years attempting to cooperate with the Soviet Union, and he pointed to the civil air and outer space agreements. He urged Kosygin to join him in pushing for progress on a non-proliferation treaty, again called for an agreement to gain control of the ABM race, and said "he did not like to see one-half of our budget devoted to military expenditures." Indeed, he hoped the Soviets would reduce their military budget as well.

Kosygin agreed with Johnson's concern about high military budgets, but complained that the United States "was being carried away by the military situation, as if driven to it by some force." Moscow had no choice but to respond to American military spending—mainly caused by the Vietnam war—by increasing its own spending. Because of technological advances, Kosygin lamented that weapons were built, became obsolete, and discarded for better, more lethal systems. ABMs, therefore, were not the problem, but the "development beyond reason" of new, more effective offensive weapons systems.

Johnson replied that because the Soviets had begun to build an ABM, he was under "pressure" from many Americans to do likewise. He had brought McNamara with him to Glassboro because the Secretary of Defense wanted to avoid an ABM race. McNamara also recognized how quickly new systems became "junk" and were replaced, which only fueled a never-ending arms race.

Turning to Vietnam, Johnson said that even though North Vietnam continued to infiltrate its soldiers into the South, all he wanted was for this aggression to stop. The United States did not want to conquer the North, which was why "we sent planes" in order "to bomb instead of men to fight." The United States wanted South Vietnam to have free elections and let the people of the South choose their own government without military pressure from the North. After further discussion about the Middle East, they broke for lunch.[41]

During the lunch of roast beef, shrimp, rice pilaf, asparagus, and Cabernet Sauvignon, Johnson asked McNamara to discuss the ABM issue with Kosygin. In his memoirs, Dobrynin claimed that McNamara "was not prepared" for the discussion, mainly because "he had suggested a secret briefing of the two leaders so that his position would not become known in public." McNamara was "confused" and "feverishly began to sort out his papers, tying to select the least secret charts and diagrams from his folder." McNamara regained his composure and told Kosygin that the nuclear arms race between the two superpowers had "already gone beyond all reason." Indeed, he contended that the more each reacted to the other's escalation, the more they had chosen "an insane road to follow."

While he believed that they could not abolish nuclear weapons, limiting the development of both offensive and defensive strategic systems would stabilize US-Soviet relations. Kosygin said that "he did not quite agree with this view" considering that research and development of offensive weapons systems had continued unabated. He also pointed out that McNamara had recently argued in a speech that it was cheaper to develop offensive rather than defensive systems, a view Kosygin considered "immoral." Arms control talks, he contended, had to consider both types of systems.

FIGURE 3.1 *State Department interpreter William Krimer, McNamara, Kosygin, and Johnson talk outside Hollybush on the first day of Glassboro. Gromyko is behind Johnson. White House Photo.*

McNamara conceded that he had not been "clear" in the speech and that he did believe that talks should cover both systems. Kosygin thanked the Secretary for clarifying his position but couldn't resist remarking that he had indeed interpreted the speech correctly.

On the other hand, McNamara recalled that Kosygin said that his government was acting "morally" and simply "protecting the fatherland" by building an ABM system. Kosygin, he argued, "didn't seem to grasp the point that they were pursuing deterrence in their way, and their way ... weakened our deterrent; and we, therefore, were forced to respond with an action which offset their action but advanced neither one of us."[42]

After a thirty-minute break, Johnson and Kosygin met again with only their interpreters. Kosygin told the president that he had just received a communication from Hanoi. If Johnson halted the bombing of North Vietnam, Hanoi would "immediately" come to the conference table. Kosygin said Johnson should accept the offer because it "provided for the first time the opportunity of talking directly with Hanoi at no risk for the United States."

Johnson replied with a question: if the United States immediately began talking to Hanoi, would fighting on the ground continue as it had during the Korean War? Kosygin responded that he had no idea, but said that if Johnson thought that he was fighting China in Vietnam, he was "actually helping" Beijing to achieve "their worst designs." Johnson acknowledged that "China represented the very greatest danger to both countries at present, and that he certainly did not want to do anything that would promote Chinese policy." He explained that if he stopped the bombing and exposed US Marines to the five North Vietnamese divisions that were currently encamped above the DMZ, he would be "crucified" if they suffered casualties. Kosygin replied that direct US-North Vietnamese talks would save more lives "that would otherwise perish in vain."

Johnson twice asked Kosygin if he could "provide assistance at the conference table," because he believed Moscow could help the United States withdraw from the war. Kosygin replied that he couldn't speak for Hanoi. However, he would be happy to transmit Johnson's "views and conditions" to the North.

Switching topics, Johnson said that the confusion over McNamara's position on limiting offensive and defensive weapons was misplaced. Kosygin, however, replied that he was "still shocked" by McNamara's speech. After some back and forth about nonproliferation, Kosygin said "all problems between the two nations could be solved if it were not for the grave problem in Viet-Nam and the new problems which have arisen in the Middle East." Vietnam, he contended, had "destroyed" the chances for US-Soviet cooperation and had allowed China to "raise its head with consequent great danger for the peace of the entire world." Johnson did not reply, and after a brief discussion on the text of a joint public statement, the meeting adjourned.[43]

Although the two leaders admittedly didn't make any real progress during these two meetings—a *New York Times* story quoted Rusk that "serious problems" remained in the Middle East and Johnson that they had at least "explore[d]" Vietnam—the one-on-one, personal meeting reduced the "stiffness" of the previous week, when the two nations had been "pulling and hauling" in their attempts to find an appropriate place to meet. For Johnson, establishing a personal relationship was a key component of his negotiating style. Whether talking to a congressman or the leader of another country, Johnson assumed that he could either charm or bully his opponent. Kosygin, of course, was quite a different character and certainly immune to the Johnson style, but their mutual desire to prevent a nuclear war and their willingness to move toward the signing of a non-proliferation agreement differentiated Glassboro from Khrushchev's "table thumping" histrionics at the Vienna summit.

Both leaders also played the public relations game. After the meeting, Kosygin jumped from his limousine and asked the crowd, estimated to be several thousand, which had gathered around Hollybush, to be silent. With Dobrynin translating, he yelled "I want friendship with the American people and I can assure you we want nothing but peace with the American people" to cheers. Not to be outdone, when Johnson emerged to shouts of "We Want Johnson, we want Johnson" he said "We had a good meeting today and we liked things here so well we're coming here again on Sunday."[44]

Kosygin and his daughter took advantage of the break to visit Niagara Falls on Saturday, and at the beginning of their final meeting on June 25, he told Johnson that "as an expert" in engineering he particularly enjoyed inspecting the site's power station. He bragged that the Soviet Union already had the largest power station in the world and that in 1968 they would begin building an even larger one. Johnson, in turn, talked about the six water projects located on a river near his ranch in Texas.

He then praised Kosygin for making "an excellent impression on the American people" and the American press. Despite their strong anticommunist sentiments, he said that more than anything Americans hoped that the two peoples could "find a way to like each other rather than hate each other." Kosygin's visit had "considerably" helped that cause. Kosygin agreed that the American people he had encountered had been "very friendly and pleasant," but he complained about a recent Johnson speech in which the president said that "tensions would remain" between capitalism and socialism.

The president claimed he had either been "misquoted or else quoted completely out of context" because he had, in reality, mentioned "a new spirit of friendship" that had recently developed between the United States and the Soviet Union. He "earnest[ly]" hoped that they could find "mutually acceptable solutions to outstanding problems." While he had conceded in the speech that one meeting couldn't solve all their problems, "extended talks" could do so, and that's what he wanted.

Kosygin noted that after a brief two-day stopover in Cuba, he would return to Moscow to tackle some difficult budget issues. He was under "great pressure," he claimed, to devote more of his nation's resources to "peaceful pursuits" such as construction and development projects," and had been "hard put to explain why all these requests could not be granted." Johnson interjected that he hoped that both countries could reduce their military budgets so each could devote more money to such peaceful pursuits, and noted that he had tripled the education and health budgets of the US government since he'd become president. This could continue only if he could reduce the US military budget. He noted that he had asked for arms talks for the past three months but "nothing further had been heard" from Moscow. When could McNamara meet with his counterparts in Moscow to begin the discussions?

Kosygin said that his government sought to reduce military spending, but that this "very much depended upon relations with the United States." The United States could not simultaneously reduce its military spending while escalating the war in Vietnam. As long as the United States continued the war, any discussions about reducing military spending "could not be more than academic." Johnson replied that if the Soviet Union reduced or ended its supply of military equipment to the North Vietnam, he could "de-escalate the struggle in South Vietnam" and in turn reduce overall defense spending.

Furthermore, Johnson argued that they could both cut such spending if they could reach an ABM agreement. For the moment, he said that he "had held back authorizing full development of ABM systems in order to provide the opportunity for full exploration of this question with the Soviet Union." Kosygin, however, repeated that "he could not agree" to focusing arms control talks on "defensive systems only." The president "retorted" that he had repeatedly stated that he wanted to explore "all possibilities of reducing expenditures for offensive as well as defensive systems."

Kosygin said that if Johnson "really wanted" such discussion, he would be happy to return with a "delegations of experts," but the prospects for successful arms control talks were dim given US escalation in Vietnam and the fact that the Middle East remained "unsettled." Regarding the latter issue, he accused "3 million Jews who were 20th century people" of attacking and taking the territories of "100 million Arabs who were really people of the 19th century as far as their spiritual development was concerned." Until the Israelis withdrew from those occupied territories, there could be "no peaceful settlement" in the region.

Johnson countered that while he didn't want to get into a numbers game, the issue in the Middle East involved "what was right," and noted that Kosygin had told UNGA that Israel had a right "to a national life." He agreed with that basic tenet, which included free passage through international waterways such as the Straits of Tiran and the Suez Canal, which he assumed Kosygin also supported. Kosygin replied that only after

Israel withdrew its troops to the original armistice lines could they attempt to solve any of the other problems Johnson had raised. If the United States had been invaded, the Premier argued, Johnson would refuse to talk about a settlement while parts of the country remained under foreign control. If the Soviet Union experienced such an attack it would not negotiate until the "aggressor" had withdrawn. He then drew a parallel between Israel's actions toward its neighbors and the US intervention in Vietnam.

Johnson pointed out that the United States had not gone to war with the Soviet Union over Cuba even when the Soviets had installed offensive missiles on the island, which was located only ninety miles from American territory. Kosygin countered that "we [he and Brezhnev] had been instrumental in pressuring Khrushchev" to withdraw the missiles, a promise his country continued to honor. Kosygin contended that because Nasser was in a "difficult position," the two superpowers needed "to find a way out for Nasser" through an Israeli withdrawal of the occupied territories. This would be followed by the opening of the Straits as well as the consideration of "all other issues."

The president replied that Israeli troops could not be withdrawn "without at the same time removing the dangers which had caused the conflict in the first place." The two sides had to "talk and listen to each other." He recognized that Nasser had ignored Moscow's advice and closed the Gulf of Aqaba, and this "pertained to some of our friends too." Neither of the belligerents had listened to them, and he was certain that Kosygin was "too intelligent" to believe that the United States had encouraged Israel to attack Egypt.

The "dangers facing Israel," Johnson continued, had to be removed as well. "Alarming reports" of arms shipments carried by hundreds of ships to the Arab countries after the ceasefire, he complained, had forced the Israelis to ask for arms from the United States because Israel assumed that the Arabs wanted to renew hostilities. His administration had, for the moment, refused to sell Israel any weapons, "in the hope of getting the Soviet Union's agreement to full disclosure of arms shipments."

Kosygin replied "emphatically" that he was "certain" another war would break out if the Israelis refused to withdraw their troops from the occupied territories. He urged Johnson to support a UN Security Council resolution "forcing" Israel to withdraw, with a provision that negotiations on the other issues will begin following the withdrawal. This was "the only way to prevent a new war" in the Middle East. He was sure that the president "knew" that the Straits would have been reopened had the Israelis not attacked. Johnson replied that "both countries" should have taken "immediate steps" to open the Straits after Nasser had closed them. Kosygin dismissed the idea of a "historical review" of the situation, and said the problem was "here and now and the only solution was troop withdrawal."

Johnson repeated his contention that any such resolution would not be heeded by Israel. Nasser had taken these provocative actions, not Israel, and he reminded Kosygin that Nasser "had threatened to liquidate Israel and had concluded a military agreement for that purpose with Syria," which "must have scared Israelis to death." He also argued that the Israeli Cabinet had been "split almost evenly" on how to respond to Egypt. Instead of being concerned about determining "what was right depending upon the numbers of people on each side," they should "remove the fears along with the troops." The two leaders then adjourned for their final private meeting.[45]

After Kosygin urged that they keep this last discussion as "specific" as possible, Johnson agreed, and called the arms race "the controlling question" of the summit. He repeated his desire to embark on discussions about both offensive and defensive strategic systems as well as conventional arms sales to other countries. If he understood Kosygin correctly, the Soviets wanted these discussions, so Kosygin "should give the time and the place they could meet." Even if no results were achieved, it was better to talk than not to talk, because they could at least understand each other's position. Johnson cited McNamara's speech that Kosygin had criticized as an example of how misunderstandings could impact superpower relations.

The Premier responded that if the president really wanted to discuss the arms question, they should begin with the Middle East and Vietnam since they both "had a direct bearing" on arms control. How could the United States, he asked, reduce its armaments while it continued to spend upwards of $20 billion on Vietnam? American intervention in Vietnam, he charged, had forced his country to spend "enormous amounts of money in connection with the situation." Meanwhile, as a result of the Six Day War, reducing arms spending in that region would be impossible as long as that "situation remained unresolved."

FIGURE 3.2 *Kosygin, Soviet interpreter Viktor Sukhodrev, and Johnson talk before their final meeting at Glassboro.*

In response, Johnson noted that in his speech at the UN, Kosygin had asked the United States to join his government in formulating "common language" to deal with the fallout from the war. He suggested that his five points—"territorial integrity, freedom of innocent maritime passage, refugees, arms, etc."—should be used as a basis for any Soviet-American agreement, but added that Kosygin himself had said that he couldn't agree to these points. Nevertheless, the president believed that they could agree on certain things: the withdrawal of forces, Israel's right's to exist as an independent state, the "elimination of the state of belligerency," the reaffirmation of the non-use of force to resolve disputes, freedom of passage through the Straits of Tiran and the Gulf of Aqaba, "intensified social and economic development" of the entire region, the "effective presence of the UN," and the need for mediation. He pointed out that Kosygin had called for some of these conditions in his UN speech, and said that Rusk would discuss these proposals in more detail with Gromyko when they meet in New York.

Kosygin replied that while he had no objection to the talks in New York, "all of the points listed by the President referred to the Arabs and none of them said what Israel, the party guilty of aggression, should do." The Arabs would never accept any of Johnson's proposals. The "only realistic approach" was Moscow's, which called for the "recognition of Israel as the perpetrator of aggression, withdrawal of Israeli forces, and compensation."

Johnson cut in and said he *had* called for withdrawal of Israeli forces from the territories, but Kosygin said that while he "did understand this…the problem was that the point was listed at the end whereas the Soviet Union placed it first." Furthermore, this "was the main question." If Israeli forces did not withdraw, "there would be a new war in the Middle East." The General Assembly, he argued, should recommend withdrawal, after which the Security Council would determine the time frame. If Israel refused to comply, the Security Council could then decide the appropriate sanctions. While he agreed that they should "work on the Arabs to open the Straits," all of Johnson's other questions "were of a long-term nature and could be resolved only through prolonged discussions and debates." For now, the two nations should "concentrate" on withdrawal. If the United States did not agree to his government's plan, Kosygin warned, it seemed "quite clear that the US and the Soviet positions were different."

Johnson replied that the United States "could not agree to a resolution which would deal only with withdrawal and ignore elements of 'common language' that are important and imperative for a solution to the problem." If the General Assembly passed a resolution that only dealt with withdrawal, it "would bring no results."

Kosygin countered that the only way such a resolution could pass was if the United States voted for it, because that would sway "a large group of states under US influence." Some forty non-aligned states would definitely support a withdrawal-only resolution. The United States must understand that it was now a numbers game in UNGA. "Long-term" proposals, such as the refugee problem, he considered a distraction. He claimed that only Israeli withdrawal could reopen the Suez, get the oil flowing again, and resolve all the other issues.

Johnson repeatedly objected to the idea that UNGA should only take up one issue—withdrawal from the territories—while ignoring the other problems in the region. Those issues should instead be debated by the Security Council—in which the Soviet Union, not to mention the United States, had veto power. Kosygin dryly noted that "the situation did not look good as there seemed to be no understanding on this problem."

Kosygin compared the territorial issue in the Middle East to the October 1965 war between India and Pakistan over the state of Jammu and Kashmir (an area on the Indo-Pakistani border, mainly populated by Muslims but ruled by a Hindu). He noted that without the mutual withdrawal of forces—which Moscow had brokered during talks in Tashkent—war would likely still be going on, even though "the problem still remained unresolved."

Kosygin said that the question both at Tashkent and now in the Middle East was one of "principle." Withdrawal had stopped the war between India and Pakistan; in the Middle East, however, "we now have tension and military hostilities could break out any minute." If the United States and the Soviet Union failed to seize this opportunity, he argued, then "a long war would occur, which like the one in Algeria, would last several years. Responsibility for such a war would fall upon those who made a wrong decision; if the United States should make a wrong decision, responsibility would fall upon it." Trying to solve all the issues at the same time, he maintained, "was impossible." Another war would break out, the United States and the Soviet Union would be on opposite sides again, and it would be "illusory" to expect any arms reductions. Mankind "would have to wait for a long time for the solution to these problems. That was why we had to make a decision today."

Johnson repeated that the United States had already suggested a number of proposals. Far from ignoring the Arabs, the United States had been talking and listening to them, and sought "a fair decision which would be acceptable to all parties concerned. "Again, while he conceded that an Israeli withdrawal would help, and "perhaps reduce some fears, it would not resolve the basic problem and the situation would be the same as now."

Kosygin replied that "this was bad; he had hoped the President would support withdrawal," since it would be "a just and fair step to remove the results of aggression. However, the President supported the aggressor. He was apparently under the influence by some Zionist forces, which existed everywhere, and which wished to seize Arab territory." If the Israelis remained in the occupied territories, "Millions of people might perish, the world would be in a state of tension, and Israel would have to return to the previous situation because time had passed when territories could be seized." He warned that "no one, and certainly not the USSR, would permit such seizures."

Johnson said he agreed with Kosygin's last two comments, but claimed "we had a different view" about who had committed aggression. While he refused "to engage in name calling," he contended "we could have held the situation down had it not been for Nasser's threats to liquidate Israel, movement of his troops, and the closure of Aqaba. It was these actions that identified the perpetrator of aggression."

Kosygin said he didn't understand why Israel had attacked Egypt with its Air Force rather than take the closure of Aqaba to the Security Council. Nasser's threat to eliminate Israel, he claimed, had been made only after the Israeli attack on Egypt, "when passions were running high." He assured Johnson that the Soviet Union supported Israel's right to exist and had voted for its establishment in 1948, and "had had diplomatic relations with it" (it had broken relations with Israel on June 10). Moscow, he averred, "did not care if Jews or Arabs lived in that area, all it wanted was peace." But, he warned Johnson, "if the US could not agree to a peaceful settlement, it would incur the wrath of hundred million Arabs, who would remember this for a long time." Moscow, meanwhile, would do all it could "to prevent fighting" in the region and achieve the withdrawal of Israeli forces from the territories.

Johnson, for his part, said the United States was also committed to achieving peace in the region, as long as withdrawal was accompanied by the reopening of Aqaba and Suez as well as the other conditions he had already mentioned. The United States would go to UNGA, and the Security Council, and would "work with all nations concerned." But he reiterated his desire that each nation disclose the amount of arms it supplied to the various nations in the Middle East, which he considered the best way to influence events in the region. However, he warned Kosygin that if Moscow continued to ship arms "to those nations for war, then the US would have to see what it ought to do in the area."

The United States, he noted, gave mainly economic aid to some of the countries in the region. He said he "would like to see the day when we could join with the USSR in seeking solution to such questions as desalinization of water for the area and other economic problems, instead of spending money on arms as both of us, including the US to a certain degree, were now doing."

After a short discussion about whether they should issue a joint statement about the summit, the president said that he had "direct evidence of Cuba's encouragement of guerilla operations in seven Latin American countries. This was a form of aggression and was dangerous to peace in the Hemisphere as well as in the world at large." He noted that Venezuela had twice seized Soviet-manufactured arms in the past year and had arrested at least seven Cubans in the second incident. Johnson "emphasized that he felt strongly that Castro should be convinced to stop what he was doing." The rapporteur recorded that Kosygin simply ignored Johnson.

Turning to Vietnam, Johnson read the text of an oral message that stated that the United States "anticipates that it could stop the bombing" of North Vietnam, and following this, that it could engage in "immediate discussions" with the North. The message proposed that the meetings be held in Geneva, Moscow, Vientiane, "or any other suitable location." Meanwhile, the United States "anticipates that its own and allied forces in the northern provinces of South Viet-nam would not advance to the north" provided that North Vietnamese forces "would not advance to the south." The talks, the United States hoped, would result in "the stabilization of peace in Southeast Asia" and the United States looked forward to Hanoi's reaction to the proposal.[46]

Johnson asked whether he recalled correctly that Kosygin expected that a cessation of bombing would result in the North's agreement to sit down to talks within a day or two. Kosygin replied that this was correct. Johnson then read another statement:

Mr. Chairman, you and I have a very special responsibility on matters involving peace. It is of the greatest importance that you and I not misunderstand each other and that no problems of good faith arise between us. Therefore, I want you personally to know that we are prepared to stop the bombing as a step toward peace. We are not prepared to stop the bombing merely to remove one-half of the war while the other half of the war proceeds without limit. I am accepting very large risks in giving you the message for transmittal to Hanoi which I have just given you. I want you to know that if talks do not lead to peace or if protracted talks are used to achieve one-sided military advantage against us, we shall have to resume full freedom of action. I say this to you and not to Hanoi because I think it is of great importance that you and I fully understand each other. I do not ask you to agree; I am merely asking you to understand what is in my mind.[47]

Kosygin promised to keep the message's confidentiality, transmit it "promptly" to the North Vietnam, and "immediately" notify the White House when the DRV responded. He also said that on the whole, the message "looked alright to him."

The Chairman then thanked Johnson for the opportunity to meet and talk. While he "regretted," through no fault of his government, that they could not reach an agreement on the Middle East, he wanted to assure the president that the Soviet Union wanted peace in the region. In particular, he said that his country "did not wish a confrontation with the US anywhere and the two countries had no conflict in any part of the world." Furthermore, should "an acute situation" occur somewhere, he wanted consultations, not conflict, with the United States. The United

States, he stressed, "should not believe those who are trying to raise questions between our two countries," and singled out the PRC as one such country. Noting that Beijing had "raised a hullabaloo" about his trip and had accused him of being at Glassboro "to sell out someone," Kosygin reminded the president that neither one of them had sold anyone out.

Kosygin recognized that they still had much to discuss, in particular the issue of nuclear explosions, but regretted that time was so short. The two superpowers, he contended, "must remove the hotbeds of war wherever they might occur," and he urged the president to try to convince Israel to "take a more reasonable position" vis-à-vis its Arab neighbors.

Johnson said that he would like their meetings to take place yearly and suggested they "set aside a week every year" right now to discuss all the necessary issues. Kosygin said that they should continue to use the hotline, but Johnson opined that regular meetings would be better than phone calls during crises.

After each repeated their positions on the Middle East, Cuba, and Vietnam, Johnson closed the meeting by saying that he believed Kosygin's contention that he didn't want confrontation or war with the United States "The same was true," he said, "of us," and he vowed to "personally do everything to remove tensions between our two countries and prevent any such development."[48]

Despite their fundamental differences on Vietnam and the Middle East, Johnson correctly said that even it was only "reducing misunderstanding," it was worth it to meet with Kosygin. Such meetings, he admitted, did "not themselves make peace in the world." Still, he noted that "it does help a lot to sit down and look at a man right in the eye and try to reason with him, particularly if he is trying to reason with you." The world, he said, had become "a little less dangerous" after Hollybush.[49]

Détente means a "relaxation of tensions," and the Glassboro summit gave new life to nuclear non-proliferation and strategic arms limitation talks (SALT) between the United States and the Soviet Union.[50] On November 22, despite the deep differences on the Middle East that had been prevalent at Glassboro, when it counted, the US and the Soviet supported UN Security Council Resolution 242, which called for Israel to return all the territories it had ceased during the Six Day War as well as a call for a "lasting peace in the Middle East in which every State in the area can live in security." The Resolution essentially endorsed Israel's right to exist.[51]

On December 5, the United States joined 81 other nations in UNGA in voting for the Treaty of Tlatelolco, which established Latin America as a nuclear-free zone. Vice-President Hubert Humphrey signed Protocol II of the Treaty, which committed the United States not to threaten to use nuclear weapons against any Latin American signatory, on April 1, 1968, in Mexico City.

Events in Vietnam, however, torpedoed Johnson's personal political fortunes. On January 30, 1968, Vietcong and North Vietnamese forces broke the traditional Tet holiday truce and attacked hundreds of cities in South Vietnam. Vietcong forces briefly swarmed the grounds of the US Embassy in Saigon. While the American and South Vietnamese armies beat back the attack within days and essentially destroyed the Vietcong as a fighting force, the political damage was done. On television, Americans saw Vietcong and American troops shooting at each other at the Embassy, after they had been told for the past three years that the United States was winning the war. The famous television news reader Walter Cronkite later remarked to his audience "it seems now more certain than ever that the bloody experience of Vietnam is to end in a stalemate... it is increasingly clear to this reporter that the only rational way out then will be to negotiate, not as victors, but as an honorable people who lived up to their pledge to defend democracy, and did the best they could."[52] Johnson supposedly saw the broadcast and said "If I've lost Cronkite, I've lost the country," although this remark has been disputed.

Even if Johnson never made the comment, the Tet Offensive occurred at the worst possible time for the president. The American presidential primaries were about to begin, and many in the Democratic Party had been protesting the war for the past two years. Senator Eugene McCarthy (D-Minnesota), the antiwar candidate, won 42 percent of the vote to Johnson's 49 percent in the March 12 New Hampshire primary, a stunning rebuke to the incumbent president. Johnson shocked the political world by withdrawing his candidacy on March 31, 1968.

Free from reelection concerns, Johnson continued to push arms control negotiations with the Soviets. On June 22, he wrote Kosygin and proposed that the two nations jointly announce on July 1—the day the NPT would be open for signature in London, Moscow, and Washington—that they would soon hold talks "on the strategic missile problem." Kosygin agreed five days later.[53] At the July 1 signing ceremony, fifty-three additional nations signed the NPT. Later that day Rusk told Dobrynin that Johnson was thinking about meeting with Kosygin again, perhaps at the end of the month.[54]

The two leaders agreed that Johnson would visit the Soviet Union sometime in October, SALT talks would begin in Geneva on September 30, and talks about how and whether nuclear weapons states could conduct "peaceful nuclear explosions" were set for early October. However, the United States canceled all three when the Soviet Union and other Warsaw Pact nations invaded Czechoslovakia on August 20, and Johnson publicly condemned the invasion. A successful SALT agreement and a summit in Moscow would only occur when Johnson's successor, Richard M. Nixon, became president.

CHAPTER FOUR

The 1972 Beijing Conference: Nixon and Mao Change the World

Asia initially experienced a thaw in the Cold War struggle between the United States and the PRC in the wake of Bandung. During the July 1955 Geneva Summit, Dulles agreed with Soviet prime minister Nikolai Bulganin's suggestion that the United States "get in touch with the People's Republic." Eisenhower asked Soviet defense minister Georgy Zhukov to use his government's "influence with the Chinese in order to persuade them that problems should not be settled by fighting." When Zhukov suggested that "direct talks" between the United States and China should occur," the president said he was "not averse" to such talks.[1]

The British government, which had recognized the PRC in 1950, successfully brokered an agreement whereby the United States and China would resume talks at the Ambassadorial level. On July 25, 1955, the two governments issued a joint statement explaining that the talks would resume on August 1 in Geneva and would cover issues such as the repatriation of civilians of both countries and the release of all American POWs held in China since the Korean War. In a July 30 speech to the Chinese National People's Congress, Zhou hoped the talks would result in "a reasonable settlement of the question of the return of civilians to their respective countries" and negotiations between China and the United States for "relaxing and eliminating the tension in the Taiwan area." He also claimed that, as he had said at Bandung, "the Chinese people want no war with the United States." The Chinese, in a gesture of goodwill, released eleven American "agents" a day before the talks began.[2]

Over the next two years, the Ambassadorial talks failed to achieve any results, and in December 1957 they were suspended. Yafeng Xia has shown that after the Korean War ended in a stalemate, Mao concluded that the PRC "had truly stood up" to the United States. A meaningful rapprochement with the United States, Mao concluded, was not worth the effort and might actually harm Chinese security.[3]

Meanwhile, the Eisenhower administration stepped up its support for Taiwan. In November 1957 the Seventh Fleet performed military maneuvers off Taiwan's coast, while Taiwan engaged in a pattern of what Gong Li has called "harassment and sabotage" against the Mainland from their bases on Jinmen and Mazu. In August, Mao began to shell Jinmen again, launching the second and arguably more dangerous Taiwan Crisis. The United States contemplated, but ultimately rejected, the use of nuclear weapons in a form of "brinksmanship" against Chinese threats to Taiwan.[4] While the Crisis petered out just like the first Taiwan Crisis, the already fractious Sino-US relationship further deteriorated.

It is worth noting that recent scholarship has demonstrated that as he started the second Taiwan Crisis, Mao also had his own domestic agenda, which both depended upon and ultimately further radicalized his foreign policy. China, he believed, had to work on its own "self-reliant socialist development" while the US embargo remained in place. He therefore launched the "Great Leap Forward," a radical attempt to "surpass economically Great Britain in fifteen years through a technological revolution." Mao also intended to undertake the Great Leap Forward in order to implement his theory of "continuous revolution" throughout all sectors of the economy, and by extension the polity. The confluence between the Second Taiwan Crisis and the Great Leap Forward created what Lorenz Luthi has called "a warlike atmosphere that allowed him to mobilize the Chinese people." These two events not only further undermined Sino-American relations, but the famines resulting from forced collectivization and industrialization failed miserably and killed tens of millions of Chinese.[5]

Khrushchev was appalled by the human costs of the Great Leap Forward, given that Stalin had implemented similar programs in the 1930s that had also failed and killed millions. He remarked, "there was no excuse for the Chinese to be repeating our own stupid mistakes." By 1959, Khrushchev began to have serious misgivings about Mao's reliability. He therefore "reconsidered his decision to supply China with a prototype nuclear weapon." As Sergey Radchenko has shown, however, this decision could not stop China's nuclear program, but it did make "Mao think that Khrushchev was trying to 'tie China by hands and feet.' Nuclear capability symbolized for Mao socialist China's power, and he resented Soviet efforts to sabotage the Chinese nuclear program."

Still, Khrushchev tried to foster closer Soviet-Chinese military cooperation, and proposed the creation of a joint submarine fleet and the construction of a long-wave radio station in China for use by the Soviet Navy. Mao, however, "interpreted the Soviet proposal as an attempt to control China or even turn it into a Mongolia-type satellite." Meanwhile,

Khrushchev visited the United States in September for the Camp David summit. Mao and Zhou made their displeasure known during Khrushchev's visit to Beijing in October and criticized peaceful coexistence. The so-called "Spirit of Camp David" combined with Khrushchev's decision to remain neutral in the dispute over Taiwan convinced Mao that Moscow could not be relied upon to pursue anti-imperialism.[6]

In 1960, the Sino-Soviet split burst into public view. Mao, angry that Khrushchev would be meeting with Eisenhower, DeGaulle, and MacMillan in Paris in May, sent the "ultraleftist" Kang Sheng to represent him at a Warsaw Pact meeting in Moscow on February 4. After calling the United States "an untrustworthy and warmongering power that was trying to destabilize China," Kang Sheng attacked peaceful coexistence by criticizing "the modern revisionists" who "continuously dream of changes in their favor." At a banquet, Khrushchev, not to be outdone, said China did not want to help "the interests of the socialist camp." Mao subsequently ordered the publication of an attack on peaceful coexistence, the so-called "Lenin Polemics," in *Honqqi* (Red Flag, the CCP magazine) on April 19. Khrushchev was infuriated that Mao seemed to consider himself "the master theoretician in the socialist camp." When an American U-2 plane was shot down over Soviet territory on May 1, Khrushchev walked out of the Paris summit, and Mao pounced on the debacle as proof that neither Eisenhower nor Khrushchev could be trusted.

Khrushchev, meanwhile, went after China. During a Romanian Party congress session on June 22, he slammed the Great Leap Forward and the border mess with India. Charges and countercharges between Beijing and Moscow flew throughout the summer. On July 18, Khrushchev informed Mao that he would withdraw all civilian specialist and advisors from China. Zhou, meanwhile, began to complain about the Sino-Soviet border, and the Chinese army initiated a series of border incidents over the next decade.[7]

While the split between the two communist giants became obvious, the new US president, John F. Kennedy, inherited his predecessors' antipathy toward China. Neither he nor his Secretary of State, Dean Rusk, believed that the Warsaw Talks could produce a fundamental shift in Beijing's attitude toward the United States. Kennedy said he had taken office with "an open mind" on China and "had been prepared to take such steps as might be possible to bring about a less tense atmosphere and to make it possible to seek some sort of a developing relationship." But it had become quickly apparent that "the Chinese Communists were just as hostile" toward him as they had been toward Eisenhower.[8] When a Taiwanese U-2 plane was shot down over Chinese territory on September 9, 1962, the Chinese protested that the United States supported Taiwanese "aggression" against the PRC. After this incident, Mao called the United States "China's main enemy."[9]

Despite his rift with Mao, Khrushchev continued to criticize US policy toward Taiwan. During his contentious summit with Kennedy in Vienna in June 1961, the Soviet Premier declared that Sino-US relations "could not be improved until the United States ended the occupation of Taiwan." Furthermore, the United States should pursue a "realist policy," recognize the PRC, and allow it to replace Taiwan at the UN. "What kind of United Nations is it," he asked, "when it does not have among its members a nation numbering 600 million people?" He actually praised Chinese restraint, declaring that if his country "were in China's place, it would probably have attacked Taiwan long ago." The president replied that if the United States withdrew from Taiwan, US "security" would be threatened. He also pointed out that Mao continued to demonstrate "hostility," proving he had no interest in improving relations with the United States.[10]

Kennedy also dreaded that the PRC would successfully test a nuclear weapon. In a meeting with CIA Director John McCone and National Security Advisor McGeorge Bundy, Kennedy called a nuclear weapon in Chinese hands "the most serious problem facing the world today" and "unacceptable to us." He later told the NSC that he considered the Chinese Communists "our major antagonists of the late 60's and beyond." Khrushchev agreed about the nature of the Chinese threat, and joined Kennedy in hoping that a global test ban would prevent China from acquiring a nuclear weapon. China, on the other hand, condemned the subsequent LTBT as a "U.S. nuclear fraud" that would "manacle the socialist countries."[11] Eventually China successfully tested an atomic weapon in October 1964.

The escalating war in Vietnam also prevented any improvement in Sino-US relations. At first, as Kennedy increased the number of American advisors in South Vietnam from a few thousand in 1961 to 15,000 in 1963, China sent economic and military aid to North Vietnam. But after Kennedy's assassination on November 22, 1963, the new US president, Lyndon B. Johnson, significantly increased the US military presence in South Vietnam. When a North Vietnamese patrol boat attacked the US destroyer *Maddox* in the Gulf of Tonkin on August 2, 1964—to this day historians still debate whether or not the *Maddox* was in North Vietnamese territorial waters or international waters—Johnson received authorization from the House and the Senate to use military force to protect any SEATO signatories threatened by communist aggression without an official declaration of war. Shortly thereafter, Johnson retaliated with airstrikes against North Vietnam.

The PRC responded to the airstrikes by stepping up its military support for Hanoi and preparing its own military forces for a potential war with the United States. It transferred older fighter jets to Hanoi, provided Chinese pilots to train their North Vietnamese counterparts, and began building supply depots near its border with North Vietnam. When Johnson initiated Rolling Thunder and sent combat troops to South Vietnam in March 1965, Mao began negotiating a military assistance treaty with Hanoi, and PLA infantry and anti-aircraft crews started arriving in June. Zhou, meanwhile, warned the United States that while "China would not take the initiative to provoke a war with the United States," it would "honor whatever international obligations it has undertaken" vis-à-vis Hanoi. Both the Johnson administration and the PRC subsequently signaled that they did not want a repeat of the direct military confrontation that had occurred in Korea. Johnson in particular ruled out an American invasion of North Vietnam, which surely would have prompted a Chinese attack similar to that of 1950. The fact that China had nuclear weapons also prompted Johnson to eschew an invasion.[12]

Still, the PRC viewed American intervention in Vietnam as an attempt to defeat China after its failure to do so during the Korean War. It therefore became necessary for Beijing to support Hanoi's "war of national liberation" in order to "break 'the ring of encirclement' by US imperialism and thus increase the security of China." Mao also considered Hanoi's war "a vital part of a world proletarian revolution revolutionary movement" that would enable him to wrest control over the world communist movement from the Soviet Union. As Sergey Radchenko has written, when Brezhnev and Kosygin removed Khrushchev in 1964, "Mao appeared unwilling to mend fences" with Moscow. Indeed, he continued to condemn Soviet "revisionism" in foreign policy under the new leadership as he had done when Khrushchev ran the Soviet Union.[13] Recently released Chinese and Soviet documents reveal that the Vietnam War became yet another battleground in the now-public Sino-Soviet split, as the two communist giants competed for influence over Hanoi through the supply of arms, matériel, and military and technical advisors. Meanwhile, Mao considered a Soviet "peace plot" to be "the most disturbing aspect of Soviet involvement in the Indochina War." Accordingly, "Chinese leaders did their utmost to oppose DRV-American peace talks" in 1965.[14]

Mao made any Sino-US accommodation virtually impossible when he plunged China into the Great Proletarian Cultural Revolution during a March 18, 1966 CCP Politburo meeting. He began to purge his domestic critics—many of whom had criticized the Great Leap Forward—and labeled them "revisionists," thereby linking them with the Soviet Union's heretical approach to world revolution. Radical Red Guards, Mao's youthful paramilitary organization, began to harass and detain politicians, professors, teachers, engineers, and other "bourgeois" members of Chinese society who allegedly wanted to restore capitalism to the nation and who dared to disagree with Mao. Sultan M. Khan, then Pakistan's Ambassador to China, described scenes of "drum beats, flag-waving processions, shop fronts, walls and doors plastered with revolutionary writings, frightened men and women with hands bound and ropes round their necks being dragged in the streets for a 'trial' by angry-looking male and female Red Guards who thought they were following in the footsteps of Mao and creating a new order in China."[15]

The foreign minister, Chen Yi, who had advocated reconciliation with the Soviet Union, was criticized by Red Guards and exiled by Mao to the countryside. Although he was not officially replaced, Zhou Enlai assumed Chen Yi's duties. Mao recalled all of his ambassadors except for Huang Hua, who remained in Egypt. Only Zhou's personal intervention on behalf of the moderates prevented an actual bloodbath in the Foreign Ministry. Mao essentially "adopted a revolutionary line of intense militancy and turned inward toward inescapable isolation," and cut ties with virtually every other government except for Albania and Romania. But even Albania's radical Marxist leader, Enver Hoxha, called "the actions of the Red Guards 'dangerous'" and argued that "the Cultural Revolution had led the PRC into 'total self-destruction'." In January 1967, after Soviet militia prevented a group of Chinese students from reading quotes from Mao at Lenin's tomb in Red Square, millions of Chinese protested in front of the Soviet Embassy in Beijing. In August, Red Guards burned the British Chargé d'Affaires office in Beijing.[16]

The CCP leadership also lashed out at the nuclear powers. The French embassy in Beijing reported that Mao had charged that the United States, Britain, and the Soviet Union had colluded against China by signing the LTBT and the NPT. Far from being beneficial to mankind, he called the Treaties an attempt "to establish a US-Soviet nuclear military alliance against China and the people of all countries." The American and British "imperialists" and the Soviet "revisionists," Beijing argued, actually wanted to "encircle" China. Moreover, China said the "revisionist clique [the Soviets] is practicing the restoration of capitalism" internally while externally, they were "accomplices with American imperialism" who had committed "treason" at the Glassboro Summit.[17]

The Johnson administration signaled that it wanted to improve relations. At the 129th meeting of the Ambassadorial talks in March 1966, Ambassador John Gronouski said the United States was willing to establish "bilateral relations with 'the People's Republic of China.' Until that moment, the United States government had never addressed China by its official name." But because China was engulfed in the Cultural Revolution, Ambassador Wang Guoquan's report to Beijing "did not receive sufficient attention" and he was recalled a year later.[18]

Still, Johnson kept trying. On June 26, 1967, he told Romanian prime minister Ion Gheorge Maurer, who was close with the Chinese government, that "just as we do not wish to destroy North Viet-Nam, we do not want war with China or to change the system of government in China. We hope that China will join the society of nations. We have no designs on her territory or her philosophy. All we want to do is to trade with China and get along with her to the extent that she will permit." He also wanted to "talk with the Chinese about a non-proliferation treaty and work out ground rules so that we can avoid nuclear war." Maurer said he was "very pleased" to hear this, and said he would be visiting China in a week. Johnson also told Maurer "it would be the height of folly, it would be prehistoric and like a cave man's approach, for the United States to want to go to war with China. Nothing was farther from his mind."[19]

In his 1968 State of the Union Address, while he criticized the "radical extremism" of the Chinese government, Johnson nonetheless said he remained willing "to permit the travel of journalists to both our countries; to undertake cultural and educational exchanges; and to talk about the exchange of basic food crop materials." Like his comments to Maurer, this message fell on deaf ears in Beijing.[20]

After the Chinese repeatedly postponed the Warsaw Talks in 1968, a mood of pessimism subsequently blanketed the Johnson administration. The NSC's China expert, Alfred Les Jenkins, said the Cultural Revolution's social and political unrest, self-imposed isolation, and strong xenophobia had produced a situation that precluded a "direct approach" to a hostile enemy. "So long as the Maoists are in control," he wrote, "we are confronted by secular religionists, who have insistently cast us in the devil's role for their own purposes. No compromise is possible," and China's rigid ideological enmity had only been intensified during the "last two years of lunacy."[21]

Actually, the period 1968–1969 proved to be the time when Mao began to reconsider the efficacy of the Cultural Revolution and his hostility toward the United States. A series of events occurred that convinced him that the Soviet Union, not the United States, had become China's main enemy. First, the August 1968 Warsaw Pact invasion of Czechoslovakia, and Moscow's evocation of the "Brezhnev Doctrine," which declared that it had the right to intervene in any socialist country that deviated from Moscow's line, infuriated Mao. He interpreted the Doctrine not only as an attack on his own legitimacy, but worried whether the invasion "should be interpreted as the prelude to a more general war, which he believed might trigger 'revolution' and could only be prevented by 'revolution'. In any case, China had to be prepared" for any contingency.[22]

A series of violent skirmishes between Chinese and Soviet soldiers in the disputed border areas on the Zhenbao Island (Damansky Island in Russian), located in the Ussuri River, in March 1969, and one in Xinjiang in August 1969, also convinced Mao that the Soviet Union wished to encircle China with military force. The Sino-Soviet split had gone beyond rhetoric to existential danger, and Mao believed that he had to put an end to China's self-imposed isolation. He therefore began to explore rapprochement with the United States.[23]

Coincidentally, the new American president, Richard M. Nixon, had taken office determined to pursue rapprochement with the PRC. In 1967, before he announced his candidacy, he wrote in the influential journal *Foreign Affairs* that the United States must "urgently come to grips with the reality of China." China, he said, could become a partner for stability if the United States brought it into the international order.[24] In his acceptance speech at the 1968 Republican Party convention, Nixon argued that "after an era of confrontation, the time has come for an era of negotiation." If elected, he would work to establish "an era of peaceful competition, not only in the productivity our factories but in the quality of our ideas. We extend the hand of friendship to all people, to the Russian people, to the Chinese people, to all people in the world."[25] In his Inaugural Address, Nixon said he wanted "an open world" where "no people, great or small, will live in angry isolation." Mao, who had read Nixon's *Foreign Affairs* article and recommended it to Zhou, ordered the CCP's official news organ, *Renmin Ribao* (*People's Daily*), to publish the Address.[26]

Nixon's choice for National Security Advisor, Harvard Professor Henry Kissinger, agreed with Nixon's reconceptualization of American foreign policy. He believed that the American power had declined relative to the Soviet Union, and like Johnson, he worried about Moscow's massive strategic arms buildup. The United States would have to adopt a hard-headed, "realistic" approach to foreign policy that meant negotiating with the communists despite the way they treated their own citizens. Kissinger, in classic realist fashion, essentially said that the United States should accept the world the way it was, not the way it would like it to be, and must de-emphasize ideology.

As for relations with China, Kissinger wrote an important speech for his mentor, Governor Nelson Rockefeller (R-NY), one of Nixon's opponents during the 1968 Republican presidential primaries. The speech called for "a new policy toward communist China." Like Nixon, Kissinger said that "aiding or encouraging the self-isolation of so great a people" would hurt American interests, and more important, he argued that "in a subtle triangle with communist China and the Soviet Union, we can ultimately improve our relations with each—as we test the will for peace of both." Rockefeller promised to "begin a dialogue with communist China" if elected.[27]

The PRC initiated the first Sino-Soviet fight in the remote border area on the Amur and River on March 2, 1969, which left 50 Soviet soldiers dead. Beijing, however, immediately accused Moscow of starting the battle. A second confrontation on March 15, apparently directed by military commanders in Beijing, killed another 60 Soviet soldiers.[28] The United States, meanwhile, reacted cautiously to the incidents and refused to take sides. Kissinger told Soviet Ambassador Dobrynin that the United States did not want to "capitalize" on the Sino-Soviet dispute but instead wanted to improve relations with both nations, "while simultaneously avoiding entanglement in their quarrels and disagreements, since that could rebound against the U.S. itself in one way or another." At this early stage, therefore, the Nixon administration did not adopt "triangular diplomacy," that is, it did not try to exploit the Sino-Soviet split to its advantage, until later in the Sino-US rapprochement process, as I will demonstrate below.[29]

Shortly before the March border clashes, Mao had asked Chen Yi, now being rehabilitated, to conduct a study of the international situation. Zhou asked him to work with fellow Marshals Ye Jianying, Nie Rongzhen, and Xu Xiangqian, who had been exiled to factories during the Cultural Revolution. In their first report, submitted on July 11, they argued that "the U.S. imperialists and the Soviet revisionists are two 'brands' of representatives of the international bourgeoisie class. On the one hand, they both take China as the enemy; on the other, they take each other as the enemy. U.S. imperialists and Soviet revisionists are hostile toward China, spreading slanderous rumors about China's 'expansionist ambition'." However, unlike previous US administrations, "Nixon takes China as a 'potential threat,' rather than a real threat" and would not wage a "large scale war" against China because he wanted to withdraw from Vietnam.

While they dismissed the likelihood of a Soviet attack on China, the Marshals stated that the "Soviet revisionists have made China their main enemy, imposing a more serious threat to our security than the U.S. imperialists" and "creating tensions along the long Sino-Soviet border." Equating the Soviet and American threats was an important conceptual change, but it is important to note that they did not dismiss the US threat. They argued instead that the United States was "pushing the Soviet revisionists to stand on the first front of a major war against China" so it could enjoy the benefits of a Sino-Soviet clash.[30]

Nixon, meanwhile, sent direct and indirect signals that he wanted to change the Sino-US relationship. In March, knowing that France enjoyed somewhat cordial relations with China, he told French president Charles de Gaulle that he wanted to develop a "long-range" policy based upon developing "parallel relationships" with both China and the Soviet Union. He conceded, however, that relations with the former would be "largely theoretical" because "it was difficult to have relations with the Chinese." In July, the administration announced that it would ease travel restrictions between the United States and the PRC for US citizens and journalists. On August 1, Nixon visited Pakistan and asked President Yahya Khan to act as an intermediary between the United States and the PRC. Nixon said, "Asia could not 'move forward' if a nation as large as China remained isolated," and "asked Yahya to convey his feeling to the Chinese at the highest level." Yahya agreed to do so.[31] A day later the president told Romanian prime minister Nicolae Ceausescu, "when China changes its approach to other nations, we want to open communications channels with them to establish relations. One billion Chinese fenced in is a bomb about to explode." He asked Ceausescu to play "a mediating role between us and China." Ceausescu agreed and promised to "tell our opinion to the Chinese, and of your opinion of this problem. We shall act to establish relations on the basis of mutual understanding."[32]

The new administration also publicly sent signals to Beijing. In a speech in Australia, Secretary of State William Rogers said that the United States wanted to "open up channels of communication" with China in order to "remove irritants in our relations and to help remind people on

FIGURE 4.1 *Nixon and Ceausescu (smiling at camera) participate in a traditional folk dance during the former's visit to Romania. White House.*

mainland China of our historic friendship for them." Referring to Beijing's cancellation of the Warsaw Talks in 1968, the Secretary said, "We would welcome a renewal of talks with Communist China. We shall soon be making another approach to see if a dialogue with Beijing can be resumed." He also promised that the United States would "stand unaligned in the Sino-Soviet conflict while persisting in efforts to engage in a constructive dialogue with both."[33]

The Xinjiang border incident of August 13 (which the Soviets initiated and in which 30 Chinese soldiers died) seems to have catalyzed both the United States and China to make more serious moves toward rapprochement. Nixon told the NSC that he had initially "assumed that the Chinese are hard liners and the Soviets are more reasonable. But I think this is open to question." Now, he said, based on this new incident and his recent conversation with Ceausescu, he believed "the Soviets are tougher and more aggressive than the Chinese. We must look at China on a long term basis." China, the president argued, used "the dispute with Russia for internal use. But to me the Soviets are more aggressive." The Assistant Secretary of State for the Bureau of East Asian and Pacific Affairs, Marshall Green, warned that the crisis could spin out of control, and worried that the "Soviets are certainly probably tempted to surgically remove the Chinese nuclear threat." Indeed, a member of the

Soviet embassy staff—likely a KGB officer—asked a State Department staffer "point blank what the US would do if the Soviet Union attacked and destroyed China's nuclear installations." The latest border incident was the "last straw as far as the Soviets were concerned" and they would not allow the Chinese to "get away with these acts."[34]

Nixon nevertheless again ordered his national security team not to take sides in the Sino-Soviet dispute. For example, on September 5, Under Secretary of State Eliot Richardson told the American Political Science Association that "[i]n the case of Communist China, long run improvement in our relations is in our own national interest." But the administration would not side with either belligerent because US national security "would in the long run be prejudiced by associating ourselves with either side against the other." Once again, the strategy of "triangular diplomacy" did not factor into the administration's calculations.[35]

While the United States took Moscow's threat as a feeler, Mao took it seriously. He quickly "laid out the strategy of 'digging the cave deeply, accumulating grain extensively, and preparing for war and famine'...Mao was preparing for nuclear war." On August 28 he ordered the mobilization of Chinese armed forces as well as the citizenry.[36]

The most important result of the third border incident was the second and most important Marshals Report, which they submitted on September 17. The incident proved that the "Soviet revisionists indeed intend to wage a war of aggression against China." Moreover, they contended that the Soviets "are scared by the prospect that we might ally ourselves with the U.S. imperialists to confront them." The PRC, the Marshals concluded, "should respond positively when the timing is proper" to the US suggestion to resume the Warsaw talks.

In a separate piece, Chen Yi argued that the Warsaw Talks had failed, so the PRC should take the radical step of suggesting direct, high-level negotiations with the United States given the signals Nixon had already sent. "Because of the strategic need for dealing with the Soviet revisionists," he explained, "Nixon hopes to win over China. It is necessary for us to utilize the contradiction between the United States and the Soviet Union in a strategic sense, and pursue a breakthrough in Sino-American relations." If Washington suggested higher-level talks first, Beijing should accept. Second, and even more important, he argued that the PRC should not make Taiwan or any other issue a "prerequisite." Instead, he said that Taiwan should be "gradually solved by talks at higher levels." Mao accepted these arguments and, as Yang Kuisong and Yafeng Xia have written, conducted his own version of triangular diplomacy when he "approved Zhou's proposal of promoting high-level Sino-American contact in order to 'increase the suspicion of the Soviet revisionists, and to enlarge American-Soviet contradiction'."[37]

Nixon, meanwhile, continued to push for rapprochement. Not content with working solely through Pakistan and Romania, on September 9 he ordered the US Ambassador to Poland, Walter Stoessel, to "pass a message to the Chinese privately," either by a letter or by direct talks with a Chinese diplomat, and say that he "had seen the President in Washington and that he was seriously interested in concrete discussions with China." Two weeks later, Nixon took an even more significant step. The State Department informed the Taiwanese government that the administration had "reluctantly" decided to modify the Seventh Fleet's patrols in the Taiwan Straits to an "intermittent basis." Foggy Bottom wanted the Embassy to assure Taipei that Southeast Asian and NATO patrols would also be reduced, emphasize that the move implied no "change in US defense commitment" based on the 1954 Mutual Defense Treaty between the United States and Taiwan, and promise that the Fleet would still make "visible" calls at Taiwan ports. Later that day, Kissinger asked Pakistani General Sher Ali to inform China that the administration had decided to remove the destroyers from the Straits. Sher Ali passed along Kissinger's message to Yahya in a coded cipher.[38]

Stoessel did not achieve a breakthrough until December 3 when he saw a man who he believed to be the Chinese Chargé in Warsaw, Lei Yang, and his interpreter at a reception at a Yugoslav fashion show in Warsaw. The ambassador followed them out of the building and told the interpreter that the president "wished to have serious concrete talks with the Chinese." Although it was likely Stoessel had seen second secretary Li Juqin, Lei Yang was informed about Stoessel's approach, and immediately contacted Zhou. The Premier in turn told Mao, who "said excitedly 'We have found the door; it is time to knock on it, and here is the knock'."[39] A few days later, the interpreter informed Thomas Simons, an officer at the US embassy, that China had released two American citizens whose yacht had strayed into Chinese territorial waters, a gesture almost as symbolic as Nixon's removal of the Seventh Fleet. Simons thanked him for the news and reiterated that the United States wanted to talk formally with China. This exchange restarted the Warsaw Talks, and Stoessel met with Lei Yang four times over the next two months.[40]

On April 30, US and South Vietnamese forces invaded Cambodia. The Chinese responded by canceling the Stoessel–Lei Yang meeting scheduled for May 20. Over the summer, Nixon tasked Major General Vernon Walters, the Senior US Military Attaché at the US Embassy in Paris, with reigniting the talks. Walters repeatedly tried to contact his counterpart at the Chinese Embassy but was rebuffed. In October, Nixon told *Time* magazine "If there is anything I want to do before I die, it is to go to China." Shortly thereafter he told Yahya that he wanted to establish "direct talks" between himself and Chinese leaders. Kissinger suggested that either Pakistan or France could host such a meeting. Yahya said he would tell the Chinese during his upcoming state visit.[41]

Despite having to deal with a terrible humanitarian crisis caused by a cyclone hitting East Pakistan (Bangladesh), on November 23 Yahya wrote his Ambassador in the United States, Agha Hilaly, that Zhou, Mao, and Lin Biao had a message for Nixon that read

> Taiwan and the Straits of Taiwan are an integral unalienable part of China which have now been occupied by foreign troops of [the] United States for the last fifteen years. Negotiations and talks have been going on with no results whatsoever. In order to discuss the subject of vacation of China's territory, called Taiwan, a special envoy from Pres. Nixon will be most welcome in Peking.

In order to preserve the secrecy of the offer, he instructed the ambassador to "convey the foregoing to Dr. Kissinger orally." Hilaly received the letter on December 9 and immediately delivered it to Kissinger at the White House. The Ambassador subsequently became the direct channel between the United States and China, bypassing the State Department in favor of the White House. This preserved the secrecy of the channel and kept control over the process in Nixon's and Kissinger's hands.[42]

Nixon replied that at this proposed meeting, the two nations should discuss Taiwan and "other steps designed to improve relations and reduce tensions." Significantly, for the first time, at Nixon's insistence, the message officially referred to China as "the People's Republic of China." Kissinger handed the message to Hilaly on December 16 and said "it would not be difficult" to comply with Beijing's request to withdraw US forces from Taiwan. In February 1971, the administration released its second Foreign Policy Report and referred to the "People's Republic of China" twice, publicly using that moniker in an official document for the first time.[43]

In an interview with the expatriate American journalist Edgar Snow, Mao also praised Nixon, and said "if he wishes to visit Beijing, tell him to come secretly and not make it open." He also conceded that China bore some of the blame for the deep freeze that had defined Sino-US relations for an entire generation: "we also have to criticize ourselves, that is to say, reflect on our mistakes and faults and weaknesses, as well." However, the interview remained secret, apparently under Mao's orders, until it appeared in print in the spring of 1971 in *Life* magazine.[44]

Mao publicly embraced rapprochement in April at an international table-tennis (Ping-Pong) tournament in Japan. The US team met the Chinese team, and Graham Steenhoven, the manager of the American team, jokingly suggested that because the United States had just eased restrictions on travel to China, the US team should play the Chinese team in China. The Chinese team liked the idea and contacted Beijing. Mao said that the team should be invited because it "offered a very good opportunity to open the relations between China and the United States." A simple game of table tennis, he contended, had become "much larger" in politics than it had in sport. The offer was made public on April 8 and the US team, after checking with the State Department, accepted the invitation, and arrived in Beijing on April 12. Zhou personally oversaw the arrangements for their reception in the Forbidden City. "Ping-Pong diplomacy" caused a sensation in both Beijing and Washington.[45]

Ping-Pong diplomacy thrilled the White House. Kissinger credited it and Nixon's China policy for creating a surge in "goodwill" between the two countries. Nixon's patience and his decision to pursue better relations with China secretly had clearly convinced Mao to make the gesture. They also agreed that "the whole China thing had given us maneuvering room with the Russians because now we're not backed against the wall." Nixon's Chief of Staff, H. R. "Bob" Haldeman, wrote that "Henry feels that our whole policy and the current moves on China will help to shake the Soviets up, as will Brezhnev's need to make a big peace move of some kind, which should play in our favor for a SALT agreement and a Summit conference." For the first time, Nixon and Kissinger considered the idea of triangular diplomacy. The administration could extract concessions from both communist giants by playing them off one another.[46]

Beijing quickly moved to make concrete plans for the high-level meetings with Washington that had been discussed since early 1970. On April 27, Hilaly gave Kissinger a handwritten message from Zhou, which requested "direct discussions between high-level responsible persons of the two countries." Zhou reaffirmed Beijing's desire to "publicly receive an emissary in Beijing," perhaps "even the President of the U.S. himself for direct meetings and discussions." On May 10 Kissinger handed Hilaly a Note stating that President Nixon "is prepared to accept the suggestion of Premier Zhou that he visit Beijing for direct conversations with the leaders of the People's Republic of China." Should the PRC desire that a public visit to Beijing occur between this proposed trip and a presidential visit, "Dr. Kissinger will be authorized to arrange it" through Hilaly and Yahya. Once Nixon decided to send Kissinger for the first meeting, Hilaly and Kissinger agreed that in order to keep the visit secret, the White House would announce that he would make an "inspection" visit to South Vietnam, then travel to India and Pakistan to discuss issues on the subcontinent. Kissinger would secretly travel to China to meet Zhou during the second week of July.[47]

As the Americans made preparations for the visit to China, the Chinese leadership began to prepare party members about its decision to host a high-level US official. In a May 26 Politburo meeting, Zhou argued that the United States needed to simultaneously withdraw from Vietnam and "establish contact with China." This was a perfect "opportunity to improve Sino-American relations," which would "be beneficial to the struggle against the imperialist expansion and hegemonism, beneficial to maintaining peace in Asia as well as in the world, and beneficial to maintaining our country's security and pursuing the unification of the motherland in a peaceful way."[48]

The Pakistani government fabricated a story so that Kissinger's visit to China would remain secret. Initially, Yahya Khan suggested that they explain his unavailability by saying that Kissinger had decided to go hunting, but after he told Hilaly he had never even picked up a gun, let alone hunted, in his life, they decided to say that Kissinger had suffered a stomachache (so-called "Delhi belly") that required rest and recuperation. Interestingly, the visit nearly became public because at the airport, a reporter for a British newspaper recognized Kissinger. He immediately cabled his editor that Kissinger must be secretly leaving for China. The editor, however, called the reporter "crazy," and "spiked" the story.[49]

As China's top diplomat, Zhou "displayed an extraordinary personal graciousness" in dealing with the secret visit. He sent a group of four English-speaking Chinese foreign ministry officials, including his close confidante, former Ambassador to Pakistan, Zhang Wangzhen, and Mao's personal interpreter, the American-born [Nancy] Tang Wensheng, to Pakistan to escort Kissinger and his team. Marshal Ye Jianying (one of the Marshals who had recommended rapprochement) and Huang Hua, one of Zhou's close allies, met the plane in Beijing on July 9.

Huang Hua and NSC Staffer John Holdridge rode in the same limousine, and "no sooner had the motorcade begun to move" than the ambassador "broached with me a matter that evidently weighed heavily in the minds of many of the Chinese": the handshake incident at Geneva. The Chinese feared that Kissinger would do the same thing. Holdridge assured Huang Hua "that we hadn't come all of this distance by such a circuitous route in such a high degree of secrecy just to repeat the errors of previous administrations." The administration looked "to the future, not the past."[50]

Zhou, as China's premier, despite of the gap in protocol rank, called on Kissinger, as National Security Advisor (equivalent of that of deputy Cabinet secretary, three levels down) at the state guesthouse. Kissinger remembered this "gesture of considerable courtesy" that indicated Chinese eagerness for rapprochement. Kissinger shook Zhou's hand, and the photograph of which was later published in Chinese newspapers.[51]

Kissinger later called his seventeen hours of conversations with Zhou "the most intense, important, and far reaching of my White House experience." The two debated Taiwan, Vietnam, Korea, how best to keep Japan from re-militarizing, and the Soviet threat. Seven of those hours occurred on that first day. Zhou asked Kissinger to begin, and the American began a long statement about why the United States wanted rapprochement, and how the administration looked forward to the talks and the responsibilities that went along with it. He closed by remarking that "Many visitors have come to this beautiful, and to us, mysterious land." Zhou, Ji Chaozhu recalled, "raised his hands. Startled, Kissinger stopped in midsentence." But Zhou, "[s]miling slightly," merely "said 'when you have become familiar with China, it will not be as mysterious as before.' This broke the ice."[52]

Kissinger said that their meeting signified an exchange "where each country recognizes each other as equals," a very important point, for, as Yafeng Xia has noted, Zhou demanded that the United States demonstrate "full respect for China's sovereignty and national independence, the question which had bothered the Chinese nation for more than a century." Furthermore, Kissinger remarked that a "strong and developing People's Republic of China poses no threat to any essential U.S. interests." Zhou agreed that different ideologies should not preclude "coexistence, equality, and friendship," and reiterated that the PRC expected "equality, or in other words, the principle of equality" in order to make rapprochement a reality. He also praised the administration's desire to reach agreement on "fundamental" rather than "small" questions.

Moving to substantive issues, Zhou argued that the United States must recognize the Mainland's historical claim to Taiwan "unreservedly" and recognize the PRC as the "sole legitimate government of China" in the same way as the PRC recognized US sovereignty over Hawaii and Long Island. He demanded that the United States withdraw all its forces from Taiwan, and called the 1954 US–Taiwan Mutual Defense Treaty "illegal." Kissinger acknowledged the mistakes made by previous administrations on Taiwan, yet stressed that Nixon would uphold any agreements the United States had made with Jiang Jieshi. Still, since "the general direction" of US foreign policy had shifted toward Beijing's position—he noted Nixon's force and patrol reductions in the Straits—US troops would leave Taiwan once the war in Vietnam ended.

Turning to Vietnam, Kissinger began by saying the United States wanted to withdraw with its honor intact and would therefore not betray its South Vietnamese ally. Rather than sharing Dulles's "mission to fight communism all around the world," President Nixon instead believed the United States should conduct relations with individual communist nations based on their actions, not "as an abstract crusade." The United States, therefore, wanted to withdraw from Vietnam based "on the realities of the present and not on the dreams of the past." Zhou replied by reminding Kissinger that the United States had not honored the 1954 Geneva accords. The United States must immediately withdraw all its forces without conditions and let the three Indochinese countries choose their own futures.

After a dinner break, the two argued about Japan. Zhou accused the United States of supporting a "militaristic" Japan that if allowed to rearm would threaten China. Kissinger replied that Washington's defense relationship tied it to Tokyo in order to prevent it from pursuing "aggressive policies." If the United States abandoned Asia, Japan would rearm and then they could threaten the PRC.[53]

The talks continued over the next two days, although Zhao's tone was more confrontational in their second discussion. In some ways his comments seemed to be more befitting China's position vis-à-vis the United States in 1968 rather than in 1971. He accused the United States of colluding with the Soviet Union and Japan to "carve up" China. This was at Mao's instruction; he wanted to see how Kissinger reacted. Kissinger didn't take the bait, but instead declared that the United States wanted rapprochement and, eventually, friendship with the PRC.[54] The two sides also began to work on what NSC Staff member Winston Lord called "the real negotiating," the wording of the communiqué that would announce Kissinger's visit to the world. Lord recalled "We wanted to make it look essentially that the Chinese wanted President Nixon to come to China. The Chinese essentially wanted to make it look as if Nixon wanted to come to China and that the Chinese were gracious enough to invite him." They settled on some compromise language: the Chinese agreed to say that "Zhou, 'knowing of' the President's desire, had extended the invitation," which the United States accepted. Zhou then issued an invitation for a formal summit. They also agreed that they would sever the Pakistani channel and replace it with one between Huang Zhen, the Chinese Ambassador to France, and Nixon's hand-picked representative, General Walters.[55]

On July 11, Kissinger cabled "Eureka" to the White House, and informed Nixon about the invitation for Nixon to come to Beijing. Nixon replied that "if we play the game up to the hilt from now on out, history will regard your effort as the most significant foreign policy achievement of this century."[56]

Nixon revealed Kissinger's visit to the world in a July 15 announcement on national television and said he had accepted "with pleasure" the PRC's invitation to visit China sometime before May 1972. His new policy, he promised, would not occur "at the expense of our old friends," nor was "it directed at any other nation. We seek friendly relations with all nations. Any nation," he continued, "can be our friend without being any other nation's enemy." The so-called "Nixon Shock" reverberated around the world and caused the administration to scramble to assuage its Asian allies and the Soviet Union that "all nations" would benefit from Sino-US rapprochement.[57]

The Nixon administration spent the rest of the summer and much of the fall trying to prevent Taiwan from being expelled from the UN. Nixon and Rogers knew they would have to bow to the political realities—each successive vote to expel Taiwan had received more votes in UNGA over the past five years—and find some way to allow the PRC to be admitted to the UN. In a July 22 conversation, the president understood that "in terms of this new initiative with China, it looks like we're being tricky as hell. If we, on the one hand, say we're going to communist China, and on the other hand we're voting against communist China coming into the UN, I wonder if that doesn't just make us look like hypocrites." Nixon asked if they would have to resort to subjecting a vote on Chinese Representation as an "Important Question" (requiring a two-thirds majority) in UNGA. Rogers replied "in order to save Taiwan, we'll have to do it that way," and warned "if we don't succeed on that, we don't have a chance." Rogers concluded that the United

States would have to vote for the PRC's admission but figure out a way to preserve Taiwan's membership in the organization.[58]

Accordingly, on August 2 Rogers issued a carefully worded statement announcing that the United States would support the seating of both Taiwan and the PRC in the UN. The US Ambassador to the UN, George H. W. Bush, introduced the so-called "Dual Representation" Resolution, which was co-sponsored by Japan, to the UN on September 22.

An unexpected political crisis in the CCP leadership in September 1971 could have impacted Kissinger's second visit, scheduled for October. Lin Biao, Mao's anointed successor, who had been known as Mao's "closest comrade-in-arms" and "best and most loyal student," allegedly plotted a coup to assassinate Mao. Lin, together with his wife, his son and a handful of supporters, fled from Beijing but died in a mysterious plane crash in the People's Republic of Mongolia on September 13.[59]

The Nixon administration was in the dark about the Lin Biao incident. It knew that since September 12 almost all military flights had been suspended, members of the top brass had not been seen in public, and rumors that the annual National Day observances had been canceled throughout the country ran rampant. Kissinger speculated whether the PRC leadership had become embroiled in one of its periodic factional struggles, noted that similar military stand-downs had occurred during the Cultural Revolution, and wondered whether Mao or Lin Biao had fallen seriously ill or died. He also warned that if China became embroiled in another Cultural Revolution, the Beijing summit could be jeopardized.

The State Department, meanwhile, learned that all army leaves had been canceled and heard rumors that foreign businessmen had been told to leave Beijing. Not until November 16 did the administration receive confirmation from the consulate in Hong Kong about the Lin Biao episode, which reported that "the regime has gone to such lengths to blacken Lin's reputation indicates that he fell in a power struggle of major proportions." Hong Kong noted—correctly, as it turned out—that "Lin's fall has not produced any discernable alteration in Beijing's foreign policies and may have strengthened Zhou Enlai's hand." This meant that rapprochement would continue, and accordingly, Beijing notified Nixon through the Huang Zhen–Walters channel in Paris that the Lin Biao Incident would not change its preparations for Nixon's visit.[60]

Kissinger's second, public visit occurred during the UNGA debate over Chinese representation, and initially it seemed to lack the drama of his secret trip. However, his entourage's reception on October 20 indicated that something serious was afoot in China. Someone, perhaps Mao's wife or other radicals, had ordered that posters bearing slogans in English calling for "the people of the world to 'overthrow the American imperialists and their running dogs'" be hung up on the walls of the guesthouse and on the route of the motorcade. Holdridge recalled that the situation was "eerie" and "It struck me then that it was a city like Warsaw, having been bombed out, because it was so still. People looked dazed." The Lin Biao incident and his presumed opposition to US–China rapprochement had clearly not been resolved.[61]

Despite the atmosphere on the streets, the trip, as Lord put it, also served as a "dress rehearsal" for the Beijing summit, as Kissinger and Zhou discussed technical aspects of the summit. The United States wanted permission to construct a temporary installation at the airport, connected to a satellite, that would handle not only television, radio, and other communications but also the "secure" links the president required to stay in touch with the White House. Kissinger noted that over a thousand members of the media had initially applied to accompany Nixon, though they had reduced that number down to between 250 and 300 people.

Turning to political issues, Kissinger argued that Taiwan was "the crucial issue" regarding Sino-US rapprochement. Resolution of the war in Vietnam, the division of Korea, the status of Japan, the growing tensions in South Asia, and the Soviet Union rounded out his list of political issues. Zhou wryly noted that these represented the "uniting together of various forces to commit aggression against China from four sides." This was a telling—and for the Chinese—central point. Kissinger also wanted to ensure that neither side used rapprochement "as a means to drive a wedge" between old friends and allies. Doing so, he warned, might tempt "everyone" to "withdraw back into the rigidity we are all attempting to escape." Zhou answered that "we should recognize an old proverb: the helmsman who knows how to guide the boat will guide it well through the waves. Otherwise he will be submerged by the waves." China, he promised, wanted a "relaxation of tensions" with every nation.[62]

On October 21, the two leaders officially set February 21, 1972 as Nixon's arrival date in Beijing. They also tentatively discussed who would and would not be included in negotiating sessions from each nation, and pledged that all such arrangements would remain secret. Despite Kissinger's repeated requests, Zhou rejected Nixon's suggestion that he meet with Mao individually during the Summit. Instead, Zhou argued that his and Kissinger's presence would allow the issues to be discussed "more directly and in a more deep-going way." Only after Kissinger rather patronizingly commented that even a half-hour Nixon–Mao conversation would aid "the psychology of the President" did Zhou finally agree to raise the issue with Mao.

Regarding political issues, Kissinger reiterated the administration's desire to withdraw troops from Taiwan once the war in Vietnam ended and its repudiation of the "two Chinas" doctrine. Zhou interjected that this position clashed with Rogers's dual representation proposal. Kissinger reassured the Premier that Nixon would not stand in the way of "historical evolution" when it came to Taiwan's expulsion from the UN and stated that the administration believed that "there's only one China and that Taiwan is part of that China." Nixon would "abrogate" the 1954 Taiwan–US defense treaty once it reverted to Mainland control.

When it came to the Vietnam war, the White House, he assured Zhou, "would like nothing better than to have ended the war when we come to Beijing," but it would not be stampeded into a dishonorable withdrawal. Zhou, however, called a withdrawal a "glorious thing" from which Nixon would receive "the respect of the world." Beijing, because of its own history of colonialism, sympathized with Hanoi and therefore would neither "put the Vietnamese people aside" nor dictate a settlement that would help the United States withdraw with "honor." Zhou was also concerned about the issue of Japanese expansion to Taiwan after the US withdrawal and wanted a promise from Kissinger that the United States would prevent this from happening. For the moment, however, Kissinger could not provide an absolute guarantee, but made it clear that the United States wanted to withdraw its troops from Taiwan as soon as possible.[63]

The negotiations over the communiqué draft turned out to be tortuous. When Kissinger handed a draft to Zhou on October 22, the Chinese premier did not respond right away. While listening to Zhou's briefing on his meetings with Kissinger, Mao told the premier that if the American side wanted to talk about "peace, security, and no pursuit of hegemony," the Chinese side should emphasize "revolution, the liberation of the oppressed peoples and nations in the world, and no rights for big powers to bully and humiliate small countries." Zhou carefully explained to Mao that the Nixon administration faced a dilemma: as Kissinger had noted, the United States could not withdraw from Taiwan before it had left Vietnam, nor would it end the war without preserving its honor. Kissinger was therefore initially surprised to receive the Chinese draft communiqué on October 24. But after reading the document full of "empty cannons," he "began to see that the very novelty of the [Chinese] approach might resolve our perplexities." He wrote that "the unorthodox format appeared to solve both sides' problem. Each could reaffirm its fundamental convictions, which would reassure domestic audiences and uneasy allies."[64]

The second visit ended on the eve of the UN vote. Rogers and Bush warned Nixon that Kissinger's return to Washington on the same day could impact the vote. Nixon agreed and ordered Kissinger's assistant, General Alexander Haig, to tell Kissinger to delay his return until the vote occurred. Haig replied that this would appear "contrived" and could "give credence to rumors that the trip was connected in some way to the U.S. attitude in the UN vote." Rogers disagreed and said that "many fence-sitting nations" would see Kissinger's arrival before the vote as an indication that the dual representation resolution had been a sham all along.[65] Kissinger reluctantly agreed to delay his arrival in Washington, even though he insisted that his visit would have no impact on the Chinese representation vote. The Dual Representation Resolution failed, Taiwan was ultimately expelled from the

UN, and the PRC assumed China's seat in both the GA and the Security Council. It seems clear that Kissinger correctly predicted that his visit would not impact the vote.

Despite a brief war between India and Pakistan, the planning for the Beijing summit proceeded in the winter of 1971–1972. In early January, Haig traveled to Beijing for a final pre-summit meeting with Zhou. The Chinese, Haig recalled, "chose to treat our presence as a dress rehearsal for Nixon's visit, with me as stand-in," and the Chinese gave him an "exceptionally cordial" reception at the airport. As his motorcade passed Tiananmen Square on the drive from the airport, he saw a group of pedestrian and bicyclists on the other side of a deserted street. "As the days passed," he recalled, "my host continued to open the curtain wider, apparently as a subtle signal of increasing trust and openness. By the last day, the curtains were wide open, and as the car made its way through a sea of bicycles we were gazing through the windows into the curious and friendly faces of the crowd." Although he and Zhou repeatedly argued about Vietnam, he was impressed by his hosts' dedication to putting on the best summit possible, in particular the role the press and television would play in disseminating each nation's message. Both the White House and the PRC leadership understood that the Summit would not just include discussions and negotiations but reflect the crucial role that public diplomacy played in Sino-US rapprochement.[66]

Kissinger, having met with Zhou twice, explained what Nixon could expect in China. "It's hard to understand these Chinese leaders because they *are* different from the others," he explained on February 15, 1972. Unlike the Soviets, who were "capable of great brutality," the Chinese had caused "a revolution in which millions got killed" and called it a 'Cultural Revolution'." Nixon interjected, "Their brutality is Chinese, not communist." Kissinger replied "yes" and said "they lay enormous stress, you'll have to read the verbatim record, on principle. It is important to be tough with them, that is, when Zhou attacks, one has to hold firm because otherwise he'll follow. But when Brezhnev attacks one has to slap him brutally." Still, Kissinger urged Nixon to realize that "They don't expect us to agree with them. It's important, however, that we show we understand their point of view, not that we share it." For the Chinese, "cooperation in the abstract is of no interest to them. Peace in the abstract is of no interest to them."[67]

In the final days before his departure for Beijing, Nixon privately debated the pros and cons of rapprochement and reflected on the summit's significance. He particularly wanted to end the feeling of "mystery" that surrounded mainland China because Americans feared "what we do not know." The summit would "shake the world," and Ping-Pong diplomacy had shown how symbolism could break down even the most intractable barriers. He particularly acknowledged that the Summit could not eradicate the differences between the United States and the PRC, but if they could meet in a spirit of "honesty and candor," neither would have to give up their fundamental interests. As long as each acted with the international framework in mind, the world would become a safer and more prosperous place in spite of their disagreements on policy and ideology.[68]

On February 17, 1972, the president's plane, which he had renamed *Spirit of 76* specifically for the summit, left Washington. Kissinger recalled that Nixon had been reminded at least a dozen times about shaking Zhou's hand, so he told Rogers and Kissinger to stay on the plane because he "was determined to have no other American distract the viewer's attention while he rectified the slight." The plane arrived at 11:30 a.m. Beijing time on February 18, 10:30 p.m. on Sunday night in the United States (for maximum television exposure). Nixon walked down the steps alone, shook Zhou's hand, reviewed an honor guard, and hopped into a waiting limousine. During the ride, Zhou said that "your handshake came over the vastest ocean in the world—twenty-five years of no communication."[69]

Mao, meanwhile, awaited his meeting with Nixon with anticipation. Despite his poor health—he had been suffering from heart problems and a lung infection—Mao believed that Nixon's visit would confirm China's "equal" position in the world of nations. As a result, he agreed to undergo physical therapy so he could walk and be in a condition to receive visitors.[70] On February 21 Nixon and Kissinger arrived at Mao's residence in the Imperial City, and were struck by his strength despite his obvious sickness. Kissinger mistakenly believed that Mao had suffered a series of strokes, and noted how words "seemed to leave his bulk as if with great reluctance; they were ejected from vocal cords in gusts, each of which seemed to require a new rallying of physical force until enough strength had been assembled to tear forth another round of pungent declarations." Still, Kissinger recalled, "I have met no one, with the possible exception of Charles de Gaulle, who so distilled raw, concentrated willpower." Nixon recalled that after his "girl secretary helped him to his feet," the two shook hands in front of the cameras. Nixon called this "the most moving moment," because Mao held his hand for about a minute. Mao admitted, "I can't talk very well," but Nixon remarked that Mao's writings "moved a nation and have changed the world."[71]

After a few moments of banter, Nixon asked if they could discuss substantive issues. Mao, however, said he would prefer to talk about the "philosophic questions" and that Zhou would handle the "troublesome problems." The president agreed and said that the "hard questions" of the moment were whether the PRC feared the United States or the Soviets. Mao replied that "the question of aggression from the United States or aggression from China is relatively small; that is, it could be said that this is not a major issue." He acknowledged that Nixon had withdrawn some troops from Vietnam and claimed that PRC soldiers "do not go abroad." Zhou, however, interjected that "the main thing was John Foster Dulles' policy." Nixon conceded that he had once been opposed to relations with

FIGURE 4.2 *Mao and Nixon shake hands in Beijing. White House.*

China, but said "a new situation in the world" now existed. The two nations could find common ground, he continued, because neither wanted world domination.[72]

After a two-hour break, Nixon, Rogers, Kissinger, and Zhou met at the Great Hall of the People. Zhou lamented his country's long isolation and thanked Nixon for traveling so far to meet with him and Mao. Zhou again raised Dulles's refusal to shake his hand in 1954, and Nixon promptly stood up and shook his hand again. Zhou then highlighted recent positive events, noting that Mao had "personally" decided to invite the US table tennis team to China, and suggested that in their subsequent meetings that they discuss "basic matters" and the larger relationship, including Taiwan. That evening the Chinese gave a banquet in Nixon's honor during which the Red Army band played a number of songs, including "America the Beautiful" and "Home on the Range."[73]

In a four-hour meeting on February 22, Nixon and Zhou spent most of their time on Vietnam and Taiwan. After asking Zhou if he could make a "general statement" about the world scene, Nixon said the United States accepted the fact that "there is one China, and Taiwan is a part of China." He promised not to support Taiwanese independence, and would "discourage" Japan from doing so. He also promised that Japanese troops would not replace American troops once he withdrew them from Taiwan after the Vietnam War and said he wanted a "peaceful solution" to the Taiwan issue. Finally, he said the United States wanted normalization of relations with China "within the framework I have previously described."

Zhou thanked Nixon for his comments and urged him to make "a bold move" and withdraw completely from Indochina. Beijing, meanwhile, would continue to support Hanoi. The discussion shifted to the relationship between China and the Soviet Union. The Premier said that he wanted to reduce tensions with Moscow, but he remained pessimistic, however, because the Soviets rejected the Five Principles of Coexistence. China wanted relations with the Soviet Union, but he assumed that Nixon's visit and Sino-US rapprochement worried them. Nixon told Zhou that the United States would reject any attempt by Moscow to set up an anti-Chinese "cabal," but he did not believe the Soviets wanted war with the United States. He would therefore deal with them through a policy of "firmness but not belligerency." Zhou concurred with both sentiments.[74]

February 23 turned out to be a snowy day, but indoors Nixon and Zhou engaged in a wide-ranging conversation. Zhou began by defending his nation's support for "revolutions waged by the peoples of the world," but argued "we don't send a single soldier abroad. The revolution of any country must depend on the people of their country." He compared the PRC's actions to those of George Washington during the American Revolution and Abraham Lincoln during the Civil War. Both American leaders, he explained, were successful because they "relied on the people." Regarding Sino-US relations, he argued that "although our philosophies differ, we think in managing our state relations we should act in accordance with the five principles of peaceful coexistence."

After a discussion about the recent war in South Asia, Nixon noted, "I believe it is very useful to think in philosophic[al] terms. Too often we look at problems of the world from the point of view of tactics. We take the short view." The United States and China should instead "look at the world not just in terms of immediate diplomatic battles and decisions but the great forces that move the world. Maybe we have some disagreements, but we know there will be changes, and we know that there can be a better, and I trust safer, world for our two peoples regardless of differences if we can find common ground."

Zhou turned to Korea, and asked Nixon if he would withdraw US forces from the peninsula as well as prevent Japanese forces from replacing American forces. Nixon essentially dodged the question and countered that both nations should "restrain" their allies. "The Koreans," he continued, "both the North and the South, are emotionally impulsive people. It is important that both of us exert influence to see that these impulses, and their belligerency, don't create incidents which would embarrass our two countries." Another conflict between the United States and the PRC over Korea, he argued, would be "silly."

Japan continued to concern the Chinese. Zhou warned that Tokyo's economic growth would inevitably lead to its military expansion. Nixon, however, said that allowing Japan to remain "an economic giant and a military pygmy" would lead to renewed militarism. The US-Japanese "partnership" would instead restrain Japan. Zhou, however, worried more about Japan's "tradition of militaristic thinking," which he believed would undermine East Asian stability. Nothing but a "new, independent, peaceful and democratic" Japan "friendly" to both nations, he argued, could ease his concerns about a renewed Japanese threat to China.

Regarding the Soviet Union, Nixon asked why they had been so critical of his visit. Zhou replied that "the policy of the Soviet Union, although they don't admit it themselves, is actually a policy of expansion." The Soviet invasion of Czechoslovakia proved that they were "people who were socialist in words but imperialist in deeds." He complained that Moscow had used the border incursions "as a pretext to shift the main body of their forces from the Western border to the Far East." Border talks, he said, had "stagnated" since his September 1969 meeting with Kosygin. Nevertheless, Zhou asserted that Moscow remained "very frightened" of a Sino-US rapprochement and this, along with their increased nuclear strength, fueled their imperialist and expansionist ambitions. Nixon concurred, but said that "the best policy towards the Soviets" was "one of firmness but not belligerency," and a willingness to negotiate.

Zhou also launched into a long history of the Chinese-Soviet border dispute. While he hoped that the Soviets would want to "relax tensions" with his country, he held out little hope since they did not believe in the Five Principles of Coexistence. "Therefore," he concluded, "these two ideologies are diametrically opposed." He then excoriated Khrushchev for exaggerating his combat record during the Second World War, condemned both Khrushchev and Brezhnev for "rewriting Party history," and blamed the Soviets for creating the split with China. Nixon said that in spite of his differences with Brezhnev, he had no choice but to conclude arms control treaties with him and hoped that these would convince Moscow to curb their strategic arms buildup.[75]

The following morning the presidential party visited the Great Wall and the Ming tombs. Nixon and Zhou met again that evening, this time for a relatively short three hours, to discuss the general tone of the joint communiqué that would be issued at the end of the Summit. Zhou said he wanted it to reflect each nation's belief that neither had "territorial designs" nor wanted to "dominate" and "impose its will" on the other. This required four principles. First, the two nations must "normalize" relations because, he argued, it "is not only in the interest of the two peoples but also in the interest of the peoples of the world." They should also take care to emphasize that normalization did not signify an "anti-Soviet alliance." Second, both nations should agree to "reduce the danger of international military conflict." Third, no nation should be allowed to "seek hegemony in the Asia-Pacific region." Fourth, the two nations should agree that neither would "negotiate on behalf of third countries" nor "enter into agreements or understandings directed at other states."

Turning to Taiwan, Zhou noted that the United States had still not set a date for the "liberation" of the island. The president replied that he wanted normalization with China and realized "that solving the problem of Taiwan is indispensable to achieving that goal." But he did not want to be accused of flying "16,000 miles in order to repudiate a commitment" to Taipei. He needed to reassure the American people that "no secret deals" had been cut on Taiwan. Once the war in Vietnam ended, he could leave Taiwan, but he refused to provide a firm timetable for withdrawal from both.

Speaking of Vietnam, Zhou again called for an immediate American withdrawal. Nixon said that he now realized that China "cannot help us in Vietnam." But he argued that his critics would say that Zhou got what he wanted from the United States on Taiwan, but he had gotten nothing in return on Vietnam. The United States, he declared, would not withdraw until Hanoi returned all American prisoners. A settlement on Vietnam was "inevitable," but could only be "done in the right way" and consistent with America's honor. He added that if China refused to help end the war, the least it could do was to "not encourage" the North Vietnamese to refuse to negotiate. Zhou simply replied that China "could not meddle" in Hanoi's affairs.[76]

While Nixon and Zhou talked, Rogers, Green, and PRC foreign minister Ji Pengfei, much like Byrnes, Molotov, and Eden during the Potsdam Conference, debated specific, bilateral issues under negotiation between the two nations in the so-called "Counterpart Meetings." With the exception of their first meeting, these were very contentious talks, and reflected the fact that Rogers, despite his status as Secretary of State, had been frozen out of the process of Sino-US rapprochement by Nixon and Kissinger. As such, he was at a disadvantage against the more combative Ji, who likely acted so belligerently at Mao's instruction.

They first met on February 22, and after an exchange of pleasantries, Rogers said he wanted to build on Nixon and Mao's dialogue. "The history of the last twenty years," he proclaimed, had "been an aberration and not the norm. It was time that we returned to the norm," find common ground, and "develop a spirit of trust." For the moment, however, he said that "We are looking for an improvement in relations which will move us in the direction of normalization." The United States believed trade and cultural exchanges could best improve and eventually normalize relations. Ji Pengfei, however, countered that China defined normalization as the restoration of diplomatic relations with the United States. "Since we have none," he explained, "our relations are not normal." Nonetheless, China had decided to pursue "people-to-people" exchanges, including trade, in the absence of full diplomatic relations.

Before turning to how they could specifically create those exchanges, Ji asked Rogers whether or not the United States still required the fingerprinting of some visitors to the United States, calling it "a sensitive subject in China because in the old days landlords required the fingerprint of their tenants on feudal agreements." After checking and assuring Ji that it no longer applied to tourists and other visitors, the Secretary said they must build "direct communications" in order to create lasting contacts, especially in trade.

Ji agreed with Rogers but called Taiwan the major roadblock to lasting contacts between the two nations. While he didn't mind whether the United States set up a trade organization in China, his government would not establish one in the United States because of the "Chiang Kai-shek embassy in Washington." As for exchanges, Ji believed that because Ping-Pong diplomacy had been so successful they could extend it to basketball, tennis, badminton, and gymnastics. He also hoped that the PRC could receive Most-Favored Nation status—the idea that China would receive the same trade advantage that any of America's trading partners received—in the near future.[77]

Ji became more aggressive the next day during their second meeting. He dismissed the Secretary's August 2, 1971 dual representation speech as evidence that the Nixon administration "still clings to the errors of the past." He called the proposal "incompatible with the desire for better relations" and demanded that the United States withdraw its troops from Taiwan. To be fair, he did conclude his opening statement on an optimistic note, claiming that "the Chinese and American people are friends," and he expected that the visit would be a "turning point" in Sino-US relations. Rogers took the high road and simply repeated that Nixon accepted the fact that Taiwan was part of China and that only one China existed. His dual representation proposal, meanwhile, had become "academic" since it had been defeated by the UN, and the United States accepted the vote.[78]

Kissinger, meanwhile, spent much of his time negotiating the specific language of the communiqué with Vice-Foreign Minister Qiao Guanhua. The tone of these discussions was much more positive than the Counterpart meetings. Nevertheless, the issue of Taiwan continued to be difficult as each man tried to include language that would satisfy their nation's political needs. Kissinger explained that China had to respect Nixon's problems with pro-Taiwan conservatives. The White House did not want to be accused of being "taken in" by the Chinese in Beijing, so it wanted a document that "indicate[d] a general direction" on Taiwan rather than one that bound the United States to specific timetables or promises.

Qiao disputed Kissinger's last point, asking "if we don't have that objective in mind where will be the direction?" China believed that the United States must declare unequivocally that it would leave Taiwan, for it had domestic concerns of its own (likely a reference to those who opposed US–China rapprochement). China also wanted to know why the United States had decided to drop any mention of the US–Taiwan Defense Treaty from a draft communiqué that Haig had delivered in January. China could not agree to this formulation.[79]

Their third meeting, held on February 24, was even testier. Qiao Guanhua said the United States had originally agreed to call Taiwan a "province of China," but in the current draft communiqué it now called Taiwan a "Chinese territory." He called this "a step backward" because "Taiwan is our territory." Kissinger again referred to the domestic dilemma Nixon faced. If the president agreed to withdraw from Taiwan, it would look as if he had "sold out a friend in the capital of another country. The resulting storm," Kissinger argued, would "undo much of the good that has been accomplished and will reduce our ability to do what we have said we will do." This continued to be a sticking point throughout the Summit, and ultimately the English version of the Final Communiqué differed from the Chinese version and omitted any reference to the 1954 US–Taiwan Defense Treaty.[80]

In their final full session in Beijing on February 25, Zhou suggested that they hold one last, short plenary to be held the following morning at the airport. Nixon agreed and hoped that they could include "some of our people who have not had a chance to sit in on the private sessions feel that they have had a part to play, too" in the Summit. Zhou said Rogers in particular should be included. After Nixon agreed to that suggestion, Zhou turned to the "great tension" between China and the Soviet Union. China, he promised, wanted to solve the border problem without resort to force, but he again claimed that Moscow had little interest in solving the problem. This had forced China to begin building underground shelters and to warn the Soviets that if they attacked China, they would themselves be attacked. On the bright side, Zhou remarked that "changes" in tensions between the United States and China had occurred so that "the question of aggression by the United States against China or the question of aggression by China against the United States was not a major problem." Nixon replied by promising that when he visited Moscow in June, "under no circumstances will I negotiate about or discuss our relations with the People's Republic of China" without Zhou's "approval or knowledge." He repeated that the United States had no interest in trying to stir up tensions between the Soviet Union and China.[81]

The final half-hour meeting at the airport on February 26, before the *Spirit of '76* flew to Hangzhou and Shanghai, featured the two foreign ministers. Ji Chaozhu has written that Zhou had asked that Rogers be present so he could receive "the face his own government had taken away" when it had confined him to bilateral discussions with Ji Pengfei. In fact, Zhou had earlier hosted Rogers at a private lunch and treated him "as a respected official and friend, thanking Rogers for his contribution to Sino-US understanding and the success of the Nixon visit." The president and Premier, meanwhile, agreed on the importance of airing their differences as well as clarifying their areas of agreement. Rogers added that he and Ji Pengfei had conducted their sessions "in the same spirit" as those of Zhou and Nixon. "They were frank," he added, "but never at any time unfriendly," and he looked forward to continuing to develop relations between the two nations.[82]

During the Huangzhou stopover, Green read the communiqué and immediately detected "a major flaw which I immediately drew to Rogers' attention." The United States had reaffirmed its support for ANZUS and SEATO but not the Taiwan Defense Treaty. Rogers, Green recalled, "could see my point right away. He, too, remembered how Secretary of State Dean Acheson had come under heavy fire for excluding South Korea from a map showing those areas in East Asia of primary defense concern to the United States." Kissinger, however, was furious at what he called Green's "poor-mouthing of the Communiqué." Green replied "Since when was the Secretary of State offering constructive criticisms defined as poor-mouthing?" That was Rogers's job. Ultimately, Kissinger and Green handled the issue at a February 27 press conference in Shanghai. Kissinger, with Green at his side, said that "'we stated our basic position with respect to this issue in the President's World Report, in which we said that this Treaty will be maintained. Nothing has changed on that position'."[83]

At a reception at the Shanghai Municipal Revolutionary Committee on February 27, Nixon closed what he called "the week that changed the world" by saying that his meetings with Mao Zedong and Zhou Enlai had built "a bridge across 16,000 miles and twenty-two years of hostility which have divided us in the past." Together, the two nations, despite their very real differences, could "build a new world, a world of peace, a world of justice, a world of independence for all nations." Future generations, he said, would "thank us for the meeting we have held in this past week."[84] The CCP Central Committee, meanwhile, distributed the communiqué throughout the country and said the summit had "shaken the international community." Mao's willingness to use his own brand of revolutionary diplomacy through his "brilliant decision to invite Nixon to China" had not only created "a new beginning in Sino-American relations," but had "played a very important role" in using "contradictions, dividing up enemies, and enhancing ourselves." The communiqué had "broken up the slanders of the Soviet revisionists, and has inspired the people of the world."[85]

The success of the Beijing Conference ushered in a brief respite in the Cold War. Flush from the praise he received from all quarters for meeting with Mao and Zhou, Nixon, who in the fall of 1971 had accepted an invitation from Brezhnev to visit the Soviet Union, traveled to Moscow in May 1972. There, he and Brezhnev signed the SALT I Interim Agreement, fulfilling the Johnson administration's quest to reach an agreement on the limitation of ICBMs. As for missile defenses, they also signed the Anti-Ballistic Missile (ABM) treaty, which limited strategic missile defenses to 200 interceptors each and allowed each side to construct two missile defense sites, one to protect the national capital, the other to protect one ICBM field. Lastly, they signed the Biological Weapons Convention, which prohibited the development, production, and stockpiling of biological weapons. In November, Nixon was overwhelmingly reelected.

Although Nixon's personal political fortunes soon soured thanks to the growing Watergate scandal, US foreign policy for the most part remained successful during his presidency. On January 27, 1973, Kissinger and the North Vietnamese diplomat Le Duc Tho, a long-time friend and ally of Ho

Chi Minh, who had been secretly negotiating since 1970, signed the Paris Peace Accords. The agreement imposed a ceasefire between North and South Vietnam, US troops would begin to withdraw from South Vietnam within sixty days, American POWs would be released, and reunification of Vietnam would be carried out by peaceful means.

US-Soviet relations stayed cordial. In June 1973, Brezhnev visited Washington, and the two leaders signed the Agreement on the Prevention of Nuclear War. Some historians have noted that the two adversaries nearly went to war during the October 1973 Yom Kippur War. After the Israeli army surrounded the Egyptian Third Army, Kissinger interpreted a Brezhnev letter to Nixon that called for a joint US-Soviet intervention to compel an Israeli retreat as a threat of *unilateral* Soviet intervention. Indeed, Nixon called the letter "the most serious threat to US-Soviet relations since the Cuban Missile Crisis." But this incident soon passed, and Nixon and Brezhnev continued to pursue SALT II in hopes of signing a permanent arms limitation agreement.[86] After Nixon was forced to resign in August 1974, the new US president, Gerald R. Ford, pledged to continue the talks.

The US-Chinese relationship also became closer. In 1973, the United States established a Liaison Office in Beijing, the first official US diplomatic presence in the PRC since 1949. Kissinger visited China numerous times over the years, and President Ford met with Mao and Zhou in Beijing in December 1975. The tone of those conversations was similar to with Nixon: both sides continued to work toward normalization of relations and remained vigilant about the Soviet threat. In 1976, however, both Zhou and Mao died, and China entered a period of turmoil as the radicals and the moderates battled to see who would succeed Mao. Ultimately, Deng Xiaoping, who like Chen Yi and the Marshals had been purged during the Cultural Revolution because of the economic reforms he advocated, gradually assumed power over the next two years.

CHAPTER FIVE

The Vienna Summit: The Beginning of the End of Détente

Despite their other disagreements, the issue of strategic arms control symbolized détente between the United States and the Soviet Union. Nixon had built upon Johnson's concern about the never-ending costs of arms race, while Brezhnev also wanted an agreement so that he could address his own security and economic concerns. In July 1974, shortly before he was forced to resign from office, Nixon and Brezhnev signed the Threshold Test Ban Treaty (TTBT), which prohibited nuclear tests with a yield exceeding 150 kilotons. Nixon's successor, Gerald R. Ford, continued to pursue both détente in general and a SALT II agreement in particular. In November 1974, Ford met with Brezhnev for a two-day summit. The two leaders agreed to limit both nations to an "equal aggregate number" of various weapons, including Intercontinental Ballistic Missiles (ICBMs) and Submarine-Launched Ballistic Missiles (SLBMs) fitted with MIRVs. The Vladivostok Agreement became the guiding principle behind the SALT II Talks.

In 1975, Ford and Brezhnev traveled to Helsinki, Finland, to sign the Final Act of the Conference on Security and Cooperation in Europe (CSCE). While not a treaty and therefore not technically binding under international law, the Act signified that the West acknowledged the Soviet Union's and Eastern Europe's post–Second World War borders, including Soviet control over the Baltic states. In return, the Soviet bloc agreed to respect human rights and Western-style civil liberties. The Act created numerous nongovernmental organizations such as the Moscow Helsinki Group to monitor Soviet compliance with the Act.

However, détente had many detractors in the United States, and as Nixon's standing began to be impacted by Watergate, his critics began to publicize their concerns. His critics included conservative Republicans such as California Governor Ronald Reagan, Nixon's second Secretary of Defense James Schlesinger, and intellectuals such as William F. Buckley.

Détente, they charged, ceded both America's moral and technological superiority to the Soviet Union. They also worried that the Soviet Union could not be trusted to uphold the arms treaties it had signed. Indeed, one of their major criticisms of SALT I was the lack of verification procedures, and in particular the absence of On-Site Inspections (OSI) in favor of National Technical Means (NTM). They pointed out that new weapons systems could easily be hidden from electronic intelligence.

Meanwhile, a growing number of conservative Democrats, led by Senator Henry "Scoop" Jackson of Washington, also worried about détente. In early 1973, the so-called "Senator from Boeing" successfully pressured Nixon to replace most of the senior members of the Arms Control and Disarmament Agency (ACDA), accusing them of being "too eager" to make agreements with the Soviet Union.[1] Jackson opposed SALT I because he did not believe the United States could accurately estimate the number of missile launchers and warheads in the Soviet stockpile.

Moreover, Jackson argued that the United States should protect human rights around the world. In particular, Jackson believed that the Soviet Union must allow more emigration of Soviet Jews. In October 1972, he and Congressman Charles Vanik (D-Ohio) introduced an amendment to the Trade Act that made the granting of Most-Favored Nation status to communist countries contingent upon their willingness to allow their citizens to emigrate without penalty. Although the amendment did not single out the Soviet Union, it was clearly aimed at Moscow. The Amendment passed the House 319–80 on December 11, 1973 and the Senate in late 1974.[2]

Ford, meanwhile, began to face problems from members of his administration who resented détente, not to mention Kissinger's dominant role in policymaking. White House Chief of Staff Richard B. "Dick" Cheney and Ford's second Secretary of Defense, Donald Rumsfeld, argued that détente had actually strengthened the Soviet Union and weakened the United States. An imbroglio over whether Ford should publicly host the Soviet dissident and Nobel Prize winner Alexander Solzhenitsyn at the White House exposed the rift to the public. After Kissinger successfully convinced Ford not to extend the invitation, Cheney remarked "I think the decision not to see [Solzhenitsyn] is based up on a misreading of détente. Détente means nothing more and nothing less than a lessening of tension. Over the last several years it has been sold as a much broader concept to the American people. At most, détente should consist of agreements wherever possible to reduce the possibility of conflict, but it does not mean that all of a sudden our relationship with the Soviets is all sweetness and light."[3] The incident seemed to be the final straw for the conservative wing, and Reagan challenged Ford for the 1976 Republican presidential nomination. Although Ford won the nomination, the conservatives forced the Republicans to include a plank in the party platform on "Morality and Foreign Policy," which praised Solzhenitsyn.[4]

Jimmy Carter, the Democratic nominee for president in 1976, sided with Jackson and Reagan on the issue of human rights, and pledged that he would reverse his predecessors' emphasis on foreign policy realism. The former Governor of Georgia promised to make human rights, respect for international law, and arms control an integral part of his presidency. After defeating Ford, he called for respect for human rights in his Inaugural Address, and pledged "perseverance and wisdom in our efforts to limit the world's armaments to those necessary for each nation's own domestic safety. And we will move this year a step toward ultimate goal—the elimination of all nuclear weapons from this Earth."[5] His National Security Advisor, Zbigniew Brzezinski, has argued that Carter wanted to make US foreign policy "more humane and moral" and believed that as president "he could shape a more decent world."[6]

A more decent world depended upon arms control. In his memoirs, Carter wrote "It was always obvious that both nations had far more weapons than would ever be needed to destroy every significant military installation and civilian popular center in the lands of its potential enemies, and in the process kill tens of millions—perhaps a hundred million—people on each side ... That horror was constantly on my mind." He also recognized that for SALT II to have any teeth, the agreement would have to be verifiable. Carter, however, acknowledged two important points. First, "There is another imbalance which American negotiators do not like to discuss." Moscow had legitimate fears about the "much more formidable" number of nuclear weapons arrayed against them, "not only from the United States and our allies, France and Great Britain, but also from a seemingly implacable Chinese adversary." Second, he conceded, "we were leapfrogging each other" in technological breakthroughs "in this frightening competition, and this in itself was a destabilizing factor in United States-Soviet relations."[7]

In his first six months in office, Carter and Brezhnev exchanged a number of personal letters. The two leaders pledged to continue negotiations on SALT II as well as on other arms control issues such as a chemical weapons ban; an agreement on a comprehensive nuclear test ban (CTB), including "Peaceful" Nuclear Explosions (PNEs); the non-proliferation of nuclear technology, even if it was for ostensibly peaceful purposes; and Mutual and Balanced Force Reductions (MBFR) by NATO and the Warsaw Pact in Central Europe.

The Soviet Union, on the other hand, worried about Carter's emphasis on human rights. They were used to Nixon, Kissinger, and Ford, who had paid only lip service to the idea of pressing for internal Soviet reforms. Carter's public decision to make human rights the key component of his overall diplomacy, which might be called conditional détente, shocked the Soviets.[8]

Carter's first encounter with Dobrynin on February 1, 1977 highlighted many of the issues that ultimately complicated US-Soviet arms control discussions. The two immediately tangled over the issue of the Soviet

Backfire bomber—a long-range strategic bomber that could be refueled during flight, which would give the Soviet Union first-strike nuclear capability—and argued about whether cruise missiles should be included in the SALT II discussions. Under Ford, the Joint Chiefs of Staff had refused to allow cruise missiles to be included in the SALT aggregate unless the Backfire was counted in the Soviet aggregate. Dobrynin denied that the Backfire had strategic capability and hence should not be counted in the Soviet aggregate. Carter complained about the Soviet advantage in throw-weight, which Dobrynin said was necessary since the United States enjoyed an advantage in accuracy.

The president then proposed a "radical" idea: strategic arms *reductions*, rather than limitations. Only a "minimal level" of nuclear weapons were necessary, he contended, so "each country had a sufficient number to deter an attack but not big enough to inspire fear that its arsenal could annihilate the other side in a first strike." In his memoirs, Dobrynin admitted that Carter was "far ahead of his time" with his proposal, but said that "they could not then have been realistically accomplished. Carter had taken a shallow approach to SALT negotiations and relations with the Soviet Union in general." Moscow instead wanted a "gradual, stage-by-stage process" of arms limitations, not arms reductions, which would preserve MAD.[9]

FIGURE 5.1 *Carter, Brzezinski, and Vance meet with Dobrynin at the White House, March 1977. White House Photo.*

The issue of human rights came up at the end of their discussion. While Carter said he did not want to interfere in Soviet internal affairs nor "embarrass" Moscow, "he felt it was necessary for him to express human rights concerns from time to time." Dobrynin replied that his country had "an abundance of human rights in their country, such as in health and housing. He mentioned that at some time the Soviets might feel it appropriate to comment on the Equal Rights Amendment. More seriously," he worried that "the public debate on this issue would be disadvantageous to both sides." Carter said he would "try to be reticent" and Dobrynin urged "quiet diplomacy" on the issue.[10]

The new president's apparent distancing from the Vladivostok framework infuriated Moscow. Carter told Brezhnev on March 4 that "no final agreement" on the Backfire and cruise missiles had been reached at Vladivostok. Brezhnev replied that the Backfire was not subject to SALT negotiations, and warned that if cruise missiles did not make into the discussion, then further talks would be "counterproductive."[11] Meanwhile, the Soviets viewed Carter's repeated calls for human rights as a "convenient propaganda weapon to keep on wielding in public at the expense of agreements on other major issues in Soviet-American relations," in particular Vladivostok, "whether by design or not."[12]

A late March visit by Secretary of State Cyrus Vance to Moscow to meet with Gromyko was dominated by discussions about what the Soviets called "Forward Based Systems" (FBS), or the US deployment of medium-range nuclear missiles and bombers in the NATO countries. Moscow had wanted these included in the SALT negotiations since at least 1970, but the United States had refused to allow these numbers into the aggregates, instead concentrating on limiting ICBMs. Vance said these "European" missiles therefore should not be subject to SALT II negotiations. He also refused to make cruise missiles subject to the negotiations.. Dobrynin called the visit "a predictable failure" due to Carter's "wrenching departure" from the Vladivostok framework, upon which the Soviet government "had staked its prestige."[13]

On the other hand, the Soviets also saw that Carter had signaled his desire to move beyond détente. In a commencement address at Notre Dame University in May 1977, Carter contended that while the US-Soviet competition continued, and he remained determined to gain control of the arms race and push for human rights, "we are now free of that inordinate fear of communism which once led us to embrace any dictator who joined us in that fear. I'm glad that that's being changed. For too many years, we've been willing to adopt the flawed and erroneous principles and tactics of our adversaries, sometimes abandoning our own values for theirs."[14] Carter's contradictory public policy would continue to undermine his secret negotiations with the Soviets on almost every issue.

The Arab-Israeli dispute remained another area of superpower contention. Given the two wars that had occurred in the past decade, a major change occurred in the region during the late 1970s that few expected. On May 17, 1977, the candidate of the Israeli conservative Likud party, Menachem Begin, won a plurality of seats in the Knesset, the Israeli parliament. For years, Begin had criticized the Eshkol government's 1967 "Land for Peace" proposal and UN Resolution 242. He also urged that Israel build settlements in what he called, from the Bible, "Judea and Samaria" (the West Bank), and the Gaza Strip. Begin's ascension to Prime Minister on June 20 initially made a peace between Israel and the Arabs seem impossible. But his appointment of Moshe Dayan, a hero of the 1948 war, Labor Party Defense Minister during the 1967 war, and proponent of land for peace, as his foreign minister indicated that he was not as hawkish as his public profile suggested.

Meanwhile, Egyptian president Anwar Sadat, Nasser's vice-president during the Six Day War, and the initiator of the Yom Kippur War, began hinting to Carter that he wanted peace with Israel. On November 9, 1977, he stunned the Egyptian Parliament by saying he would be willing to address the Knesset in person if it would lead to peace. Ten days later he arrived in Tel Aviv, and on November 20 he told the Knesset that "any life that is lost in war is a human life, be it that of an Arab or Israeli." Extensive negotiations by Vance and Carter convinced Begin and Sadat to meet at Camp David in September 1978. After thirteen days of arduous discussions, Begin and Sadat signed the Camp David Accords on September 17, which contained two frameworks for peace. The first accepted UN Resolution 242 and full autonomy and self-governance for the Palestinian people in the West Bank and Gaza following discussions among Israel, Egypt, Jordan, and the Palestinians. The second contained an outline of a peace treaty between Israel and Egypt in which Israel agreed to return the Sinai in exchange for Egypt's diplomatic recognition of Israel as well as freedom of Israeli passage through the Suez and the Straits of Tiran. On March 26, 1979, Begin and Sadat signed the Egypt–Israel Peace Treaty.[15] The Soviets, however, opposed the Treaty.

To be sure, to blame the new frost in the Cold War solely on the United States would not only be unfair but historically inaccurate, for the Soviets were hardly acting as if they accepted détente. The Soviets, Cubans, and East Germans had intervened in the Angolan civil war in 1975, and followed this by sending troops to Ethiopia in its war with Somalia in 1977–8. Combined with Soviet support for the Marxist regimes in North Yemen and Afghanistan, it appeared as if the vital Persian Gulf region would soon be encircled by the Soviet Union or its proxies. Moscow had also begun deploying a new IRBM, the SS-20, in Eastern Europe. These new missiles were mobile and contained three MIRVed nuclear warheads with a range of 5,000 kilometers (3,000 miles), which put them under the category of Intermediate-Range missiles. Every city in Western Europe was now vulnerable to a nuclear attack. The SS-20s were not subject to the SALT II negotiations, which strictly covered ICBMs.

Indeed, the Soviet Union under Leonid Brezhnev interpreted détente differently than the United States. The conservatives had a point when they argued that détente did not mean that the Soviet Union had given up its desire for communist revolution and, in particular, its desire to achieve parity with the West when it came to the strategic nuclear balance.[16]

A November 22, 1978 Brezhnev speech to a Political Consultative Committee of the Warsaw Pact in Moscow is instructive on this point. He told his allies,

> *The strengthening of the positions of socialism* in the world in recent years is an incontrovertible fact. Our countries' defenses have become even stronger. Today we are not weaker than the imperialist powers and their main military alliance, which is aimed at the socialist world…However, even the tentative parity in armaments and armed forces is perceived quite nervously in the ruling imperialist circles. In those circles—especially in the USA and in the ruling leadership of NATO—they obviously do not want to let go of the hope of achieving some kind of breakthrough, of overturning the existing correlation of forces, and of gaining an opportunity to impose their will [and] their ways on the rest of the world.

As galling as these developments were, the West's deepening ties with the PRC endangered the socialist bloc. Brezhnev charged that "imperialism has now acquired an ally—today's China. Beijing's policy, directed against the Soviet Union and other countries of the socialist commonwealth, makes it a very attractive partner for world imperialism."[17] When Carter announced on December 15, 1978 that he would establish diplomatic relations with the PRC on January 1, 1979, and that Chinese Premier Deng Xiaoping would visit the United States at the end of January, Brezhnev warned that the new US-Chinese relationship not be directed against the Soviet Union.[18]

The February 14, 1979 kidnapping and assassination of the US Ambassador to Afghanistan, Adolph Dubs, by Afghan terrorists also impacted US-Soviet relations. Deputy Secretary of State Warren Christopher laid into Dobrynin, expressing "our shock over the role played by Soviet advisers to the Kabul police" in the bungled raid that resulted in Dubs's death. Christopher warned that this incident "may well cause serious damage to our relations," especially when Capitol Hill found out about the role of the Soviet advisors in the rescue attempt.[19] Tempers further flared when China invaded Vietnam on February 17. Carter immediately condemned the attack, but Brezhnev replied that it exemplified Beijing's "expansionist, hegemonic aspirations," and asked Carter whether it was merely a coincidence that the invasion occurred shortly after Deng's visit. The Soviet Union, he warned, could not remain "indifferent" to China's actions.[20]

Ten days later, Carter told Dobrynin that he wanted "to talk to you briefly and seriously. There is no more important relationship than maintaining peace between our two countries. I am concerned about the state of that relationship," and noted that plans for a superpower summit had still not been finalized. Carter pointed to three areas of disagreement. First, while he stressed that the United States "had negotiated in good faith on SALT, two issues remain: definition of new missiles, and encryption." Although Vance interjected that the encryption issue "had been resolved," it will become clear below that this important verification issue had *not* been resolved. Carter continued, "I am anxious to resolve SALT, and we should try to wrap it up before and pursue other issues at the summit."

Second, he made it clear that the United States had "no secret agreements with China," and not only had not encouraged the Chinese attack on Vietnam, but had urged Beijing to act with restraint. Third, he said he was especially "concerned about the South Yemeni attack on North Yemen. South Yemen is a friend of the Soviet Union, and we believe the Soviet Union has encouraged this altercation." Vance noted that the Yemeni situation could provide "an opportunity for the Soviet Union and the U.S. to cooperate in ending a conflict." Continuing on Vance's more positive point, Carter also said he "would like Soviet help in Namibia and Rhodesia," where the United States and Britain were trying to convince the white minority governments to allow blacks to vote and create democratic institutions based on the majority vote. "We would like to have a constructive relationship on these issues," the president continued," and "we would like to enhance our trade with you... Rapid conclusion of SALT would help to resolve these concerns." Carter concluded that he wanted a summit with Brezhnev "so that we can prove that we are as friendly with the Soviet Union as with China. I want you to extend to President Brezhnev my deep friendship and my commitment to better relations."[21]

As noted above, the issue of telemetry (electronic signals that are used during tests to transmit information about weapons systems) encryption had not been solved, and it nearly torpedoed the SALT II negotiations. Carter wrote a blistering letter to Brezhnev on March 7 warning that telemetry encryption was "critical" to the SALT II treaty. He called the continued use of electronic encryption to mask information about weapons systems, which would have prevented each side from verifying whether they were complying with the treaty, "unnecessary and ill-advised." Furthermore, the president wrote, "I must tell you in all candor that the terms and future observance of our agreement concerning telemetry encryption is an issue that goes to the heart of the prospects for SALT II ratification, the verification and viability of the SALT II treaty, and the future stability of the strategic relationship between us."

In a March 11 response, the General Secretary said he was "frankly... surprised that you return to this issue once again since it is considered already closed by mutual agreement of the sides." His government, Brezhnev insisted, had nevertheless shown "good will" by having Gromyko reiterate to Vance that each side reserved "the right to use various methods of transmitting telemetric information during testing, including its encryption, except for those cases when it would impede verification of compliance with the provisions of the agreement. We confirm that we intend to strictly adhere to the reached agreement having in mind *that in practice* there should be no encryption of such telemetric information which could become necessary for verification of the provisions of the concluded Treaty."[22]

I have emphasized the words "that in practice" because this rhetorical shading is crucial to understanding what each side meant by telemetry encryption, and why the verification issue made reaching critical arms control agreements so difficult during the Cold War. Carter, worried that he could not convince the Senate to ratify a treaty that contained such a loophole, insisted that no encryption be allowed. Brezhnev, however, said that the Soviet Union retained the theoretical right to maintain encryption, though it would never do so.

Three weeks of further negotiations finally produced an acceptable agreement on the issue. Carter wrote Brezhnev that both sides would allow telemetry encryption only when it concerned non-verification of arms control agreements. He added, "It is my hope and expectation that the negotiating record on this issue may be considered complete and that with the agreed common understanding and this letter we can consider the telemetry issue as resolved."[23] Still, the Soviets continued to complain that the US SALT negotiators kept "raising new questions primarily of a technical nature." Indeed, Brezhnev charged that "an impression is created that these American proposals aimed at regulating certain technical decisions proceed from the unilateral interests of the United States, ignoring the fact that each side has formed over a period of years its own practice in the resolution of technical questions of one sort or another." In this context, then, Brezhnev questioned why Carter wanted to set a signing date so quickly. Soviet signature of such a treaty, he charged, would "be politically unsuitable" to his country.[24]

One important issue in this period of Soviet-American relations has recently received more attention: Brezhnev's increasingly poor health. By the end of the 1960s, Vladislav Zubok has shown that he had developed "a gradual brain atherosclerosis [hardening of the arteries that often leads to strokes] that produced periods of asthenia [loss of strength] after moments of strain." The head of the KGB, Yuri Andropov, apparently knew that Brezhnev had become addicted to prescription drugs and secretly supplied him with pills. Brezhnev's doctor believed that his patient's "progressive malaise," which exhibited itself in the form of a shortened attention span and a lack of attention to detail, caused him to become "more suspicious and peevish and less open to understanding and compromise."

Brezhnev had a seizure after his first discussion with Ford in Vladivostok in 1974, and after the summit ended, he collapsed and spent two weeks in recovery. At the Helsinki Conference, he was apparently in a "semi-coma and barely managed to affix his signature to the Final Act." These reports gradually increased over the next five years. As I will show below, however, while Brezhnev might have been doddering, he and his advisors, especially Gromyko, were certainly not fools, and their performances during the Vienna summit were eerily reminiscent of Khrushchev's in that city in 1961.[25]

While the arguments over encryption occurred secretly, public opposition to a SALT II treaty became more pronounced. Senator Jackson claimed that the loss of intelligence sites in Iran (Washington's longtime ally, the Shah, had abdicated and left the country in February) that had been used to verify Soviet compliance with the SALT I treaty would make the monitoring of a SALT II treaty impossible. Meanwhile, some of the more liberal members of the Democratic caucus in the Senate said their support for SALT II had become contingent upon the treaty "actually curbing the arms race." Despite these objections, on May 9, 1979, Vance declared that he and Dobrynin had reached an agreement on SALT II, and two days later he announced that Carter and Brezhnev would meet in Vienna from June 15 to June 18 and sign the treaty.[26]

Carter and Brezhnev met for the first time on June 15 in the office of Austrian president Rudolf Kirchschlaeger, who co-hosted the opening of the Summit with Austrian prime minister Bruno Kreisky. Carter had been briefed by intelligence reports to expect a "frail and not always alert" Brezhnev and "hoped that he would be vigorous and able to conduct the long discussions that lay ahead. There was no need for me to worry." The Soviet leader "seemed a little hesitant about approaching me, but I moved forward immediately and greeted him warmly." Brezhnev "seemed to have a little trouble hearing the interpreter, but was otherwise forceful and alert. After the first few moments of small talk, we were adequately at ease with one another. We walked together into President Kirschschlaeger's office and sat for a long time, until the silence became very uncomfortable. I gently reminded the Soviet leader that he was to speak first."[27]

According to the official US record of the meeting, Brezhnev "haltingly and laboriously" began to read his prepared comments, which included thanking the Austrians for hosting the summit. He stated that the "central purpose" of the summit was to "try and find means to slow the arms race and to try and debate and possibly resolve other matters." Most importantly, they would sign the SALT II treaty, which he believed the entire world would welcome.

In his remarks, Carter called their meeting "long overdue," and said that while he recognized that Brezhnev "had a strenuous schedule each day" (including a date at the opera that night), Carter believed that both sides wanted a successful outcome. Kirchschlaeger said that he was struck by how Carter's and Brezhnev's opening remarks mirrored those of Eisenhower and Khrushchev during the 1955 Geneva Conference, and that this augured well for the remainder of the summit. The Austrian then asked whether Brezhnev would attend the opera that night. Brezhnev said that he was feeling tired, and Carter interjected that while he and his wife would attend, Brezhnev should skip it. Brezhnev "haltingly and after some deliberation" replied that he would attend, at least for the first act. As they were leaving the room, Brezhnev, Carter recalled, "startled me by placing his hand on my shoulder and saying 'If we do not succeed, God will not forgive us'."[28]

The opera apparently gave Brezhnev a shot in the arm, because in their first plenary the following morning at the US Embassy in Vienna, he broke protocol and spoke first, again reading from a prepared statement. After expressing his happiness at meeting Carter, he said nothing could replace personal contact between leaders of states. In what was clearly a shot at the Chinese, he noted that while the world "was riveted" on the summit, "not everybody would wish them success. There were some people in the world who thought of nothing but what they could do to worsen Soviet-American relations, to frustrate détente and intensify international tensions." Brezhnev wanted to engage in "frank and constructive" discussions aimed at getting "to the bottom of the problems" between the two rivals and attempt to solve them. The two superpowers, he contended, "bore a special responsibility for the destiny of peace." Nuclear war, Brezhnev emphasized, could not erupt between the United States and the Soviet Union, and this fact made the conclusion of the SALT II Treaty so crucial.

Détente, he contended, demonstrated that the two nations had "agreed to structure the relations between them on the principle of complete equality, equal security, respect for each other's legitimate interests, and non-interference in each other's affairs—in brief, the principle of peaceful coexistence." The Soviet Union, Brezhnev claimed, foreswore the "export" of both revolution and counter-revolution, and he promised that his country had no "hostile designs against" the United States. As long as the United States reciprocated, he believed that peaceful coexistence could flourish.

After praising Carter for publicly trying to rid "mankind of the threat of war," Brezhnev reversed course and criticized the president for increasing military spending. Did the United States want to "achieve military superiority over the Soviet Union?" The Soviet Union could not allow this to happen. "Experience clearly showed," Brezhnev argued, that "an arms race did not result in greater security or peace, but rather the opposite. The true path toward strengthening security was to lower levels of military confrontation, reduce existing stocks of arms, nuclear as well as conventional."

Carter replied that "it was his firm hope and highest goal" to ensure that Soviet-American relations stayed on "a stable basis in order to preserve peace through our common interests and in the interests of people throughout the world." Calling the signing of the SALT II treaty "the most important single item" for the summit, he emphasized that the two nations had "different interests and different goals in some respects," but sought "greater security" as well as "peace between our nations and peace in the world." Moreover, each clearly wanted "the development of a stable and productive relationship." Oftentimes, however, "unnecessary differences" had occurred, the result "of a lack of understanding and lack of adequate consultations on a regular basis." Despite the fact that Vance and Gromyko had met on numerous occasions, he "had the impression that the two Foreign Ministers did not share the same objectives."

Gromyko protested, "That is a very bold statement." Carter, however, continued that he "wanted to salute President Brezhnev for initiating the concept of détente, which provided for increased stability between us." Interestingly, he did not mention either Johnson's or Nixon's role in establishing détente, but noted that Glassboro had laid the groundwork for SALT I. In any event, Carter chose not to reply to Brezhnev's accusations, and instead emphasized the issues that had been under negotiations in the SALT II talks. He noted that the two countries had moved from limiting Anti-Ballistic Missiles (ABMs) to the conclusion of the SALT II talks, "which for the first time set ceilings on missiles and in some instances provided for reductions, but still permitted both sides large increases in the number of warheads." SALT III negotiations, he predicted, would be "different," given that because of "increasing accuracy our missiles would become increasingly vulnerable, and that was a destabilizing factor." This made verification "much more important and concealment of information by both sides much more serious." He urged Brezhnev to consider joining him in exploring "deep cuts in nuclear arms, non-use of force, and limitation or termination of the production of nuclear weapons."

Carter continued that "peaceful competition was inevitable, but some elements of that competition are of deep concern to us and are potentially destabilizing." Both sides should instead discuss those issues "fully so as to understand them, alleviate concerns and resolve difficulties." Neither nation, he stressed, "can hope to dominate the other," and he called their nuclear and conventional arms competition an "enormous waste of natural and human resources."

At this point, Brezhnev interrupted and, after saying he wanted to say something off the record (which was preserved in the official record), again asked a fair question: why had Carter approved a budget that increased military spending by billions of dollars? He didn't know whether he could believe Carter's words when his actions belied a commitment to peace. SALT II, Brezhnev said, was "a major step," but they had still not eliminated "mankind of the risk of perishing in an all-out war." They must move toward SALT III. Carter replied ("off the record," which was also recorded) that he understood that the Soviet Union had spent billions on arms of all kinds, and at "a much greater rate than the United States." Both sides, he said, must "exercise greater restraint."

Carter then praised the Soviet Union as "a great and powerful nation, not afraid, and very confident in its own abilities and strength," and that the world looked upon both nations as "being of approximately equal strength." He closed by calling arms control and strategic parity between the two superpowers "the centerpiece" of the current state of the US-Soviet relationship and repeated his belief in the importance of verification.[29]

The talks resumed shortly after 5:30 that evening, again at the US Embassy. As host, Carter asked Brezhnev to speak first, and the Soviet Premier, again reading from prepared notes, said that the completion of the SALT II Treaty had "proven to be no easy task." Nevertheless, the two sides must realize that the treaty "would not, of course, be enough to end an arms race. The Treaty contained what it had proven possible to achieve at this stage." He then read a statement about the new types of cruise missile carrier aircraft that both sides had agreed to make. Both nations pledged not to deploy during the time of the treaty "new types of aircraft equipped with more than 20 cruise missiles capable of a range of over 600 kilometers." In addition, he reminded Carter that the United States had pledged that "modernized U.S. Minuteman II ICBM launchers did not contain Minuteman III missiles and did not have the capability of launching such missiles."

More important, Brezhnev seemed to make a major concession by stating that the Backfire would not gain "the capability of operating at intercontinental distances. In this connection, the Soviet side states that it will not increase the radius of this airplane in such a way as to enable it to strike targets on the territory of the USA." He also pledged that the Soviet Union would not increase production of the plane. After handing over a written copy of his statement, he stressed that this was "being made strictly as an act of good will" since he had always said that the Backfire was not subject to the Treaty.

Once the president had himself made the two statements about cruise and Minuteman missiles, Brezhnev said he considered all the issues pertaining to the SALT II treaty "resolved." He then called for the quick ratification of the treaty by both sides, which would be granted in the Politburo given Brezhnev's control of the votes. He recognized, however, that the treaty would face significant opposition in the US Senate, but urged Carter to recognize that these opponents were nothing more than "proponents of war." Brezhnev also declared that the Soviet Union would not be the first to use arms against the United States or its NATO allies, and he hoped that Carter would make a similar promise to him.

Before turning to SALT III, Brezhnev noted that he had read a June 8 statement that the administration intended to develop and deploy the considerably more accurate, land-based, and mobile MX (Missile Experimental) ICBM. "He wanted to say quite candidly that adoption of that decision, especially on the eve of the signing of the SALT II Treaty, could hardly be viewed as promoting the objectives of that Treaty, that is, to limit strategic offensive arms and to curb the arms race in general." He could not understand why Carter was doing this, since development of the MX "meant building a foundation for the further intensification of the arms race." The silo and tunnel modes, which would enable the missiles to escape detection by NTM, were "contrary to the present Treaty," which was supposed to allow for verification of missiles. Any new system that prevented verification "would be tantamount to undermining follow-on negotiations and the prospects for concluding a SALT III Treaty."

Brezhnev also wished to discuss the issues that had been left out of SALT II but that he believed must be addressed by SALT III talks. These included the number of sea-based and land-based long-range cruise missiles, as well as the arsenals of the NATO allies and the PRC. While he conceded that involving these countries in the SALT III talks was "certainly a difficult question," it must be resolved, because the Soviet Union could hardly be expected to reduce its nuclear arsenals while others were increasing theirs. Brezhnev closed with yet another broadside against FBS. Pointing at a match book on the table, Brezhnev said that if it were a US missile with a range of 10 kilometers, it would not be included with ICBMs, yet if deployed in Europe it could "strike very important centers in the Soviet Union." Brezhnev argued that this imbalance should be addressed in the SALT II treaty.

Carter replied that he agreed that SALT II was part of a continuing process and that, while the talks had indeed been difficult, he praised Brezhnev for being such a good negotiator that the Soviet Union had seemed to have "prevailed." After reading the statement on cruise and Minuteman missiles that Brezhnev had mentioned above, he turned to the Backfire. Despite his "serious concerns" about its capabilities, "in the interests of completing SALT II, the U.S. had agreed to exclude the Backfire from the SALT II aggregate limits, conditioned on the Soviet Union's making a statement on this issue." Carter asked for confirmation that the Soviets would not increase production of the Backfire. Gromyko replied that "no answer was required" since Brezhnev had already replied in the affirmative.

Turning to verification, the president said that "the success of our future negotiations" on SALT III required strong verification methods. The two sides had, after a long, hard slog, agreed to use telemetry to verify that each side was conforming to the limits of the SALT II treaty. Nonetheless, encryption of the elements of telemetry that were "not relevant to verification" of the treaty was not prohibited, and he wanted Brezhnev to confirm that both sides accepted this understanding of the uses and, when necessary, the encryption of, telemetry. Brezhnev concurred and stressed that neither side should be allowed to "impede verification" by NTM.

Carter promised that the United States would uphold the terms of the treaty no matter how long Senate ratification took, just as it had done with the LTBT and the Vladivostok understanding. He asked Brezhnev to make the same pledge. Gromyko replied that "there was no international tradition, no universally accepted tradition, under which treaties or agreements entered into force immediately after signing, if they required ratification." None of the previous 11,000 treaties or agreements the Soviet Union had concluded, Gromyko claimed, contained such a provision. Brezhnev asked, "what was troubling the President?" to which Carter replied that he wanted "to pursue this matter one more time." While he conceded that the Soviets would make the final decision, he noted that the two sides had extended the SALT I Interim Agreement. The President "thought that a departure from the practice would set a bad precedent and it was of concern to us," but he would not pursue the question further.

The president noted Brezhnev's earlier pledge that the Soviet Union would not be the first to use nuclear weapons and hoped that they could craft a joint statement saying such a promise would also cover conventional arms. Brezhnev agreed that such a statement was possible. Meanwhile, Carter said Brezhnev need not worry about the MX so much because it "was not nearly as formidable a system as the Soviet SS-18 missile and that in throw-weight and other characteristics it was equivalent to the SS-19. This was not a new or drastic escalation of weapons in a qualitative sense beyond what the Soviet Union was familiar with over years of experience." More importantly, the MX would be subjected to NTM.[30]

Shortly thereafter, the two delegations got together for drinks and dinner. Carter, however, lamented the fact that while much of "the formality and restraint dissipated," he couldn't pull any of the Soviets aside for "anything but nonsubstantive subjects." Although Brezhnev seemed tired, they offered numerous toasts, and Brezhnev "bottomed up his glass of vodka each time, teasing me when I failed to do the same." Despite this bonhomie, Carter wrote "All in all, it was not a very successful evening."[31]

The two leaders met again the following morning at 11:00, this time at the Soviet Embassy. Carter began by expressing his happiness that the SALT II treaty would be signed the following day, but regretted that the treaty didn't go far enough, since it allowed both nations to retain more than 10,000 nuclear warheads. Both nations would also be allowed to pursue technological advances, which he called "destabilizing." The United States, he said, wanted to end the arms race, and he repeated his call for the elimination of telemetry encryption in favor of OSIs and other forms of verification that would develop "mutual trust" between the two nations. Looking toward SALT III, he explained that he was ready to reduce the number of launchers, warheads, and throw-weight, as well as conclude "an immediate moratorium on the construction of any new nuclear launchers and missile warheads" with the Soviet Union.

The Soviet Defense Minister, Marshal Dimitri Ustinov, asked whether such reductions could make each side vulnerable to an attack, and would this not require "new weapons"? Carter answered that "only in a defensive way was he talking about missiles less vulnerable to a pre-emptive attack," and he used the example of allowing a "safe haven" for strategic submarines in certain areas of the ocean.

Ustinov's comment, of course, exposed the heart of the problem. The whole premise of SALT, the idea of *limiting* both sides' arsenals, still left massive stockpiles since both sides accepted Mutually Assured Destruction. In the curious chicken-and-egg dilemma of nuclear strategy, each side needed to reserve the right to annihilate the other in order to prevent a first strike from occurring. Thus any *reduction* in arsenals, under this thinking, could truly destabilize the US-Soviet strategic balance.

Carter seemed to recognize that the idea of reducing weapons systems could open up a difficult can of worms, so he suggested that ideas such as this could be explored privately. He then moved to safer ground and said he wanted to proceed with a CTB, and hoped that he could persuade the British, the French, and even China to join, although he conceded it would "be difficult to persuade" Beijing.

For his part, Brezhnev agreed with Carter's assessment of the SALT treaty, and called the arms race "disquieting." Carter, however, should recognize that he had proposed a halt in the production of nuclear weapons as well as reduction in stockpiles, and envisioned "their complete elimination." But he cautioned that his government would not reduce its stockpiles in such a way as to harm "the balance" between the two sides, nor do so while other nations increased their own stockpiles. While he agreed with Carter's call for non-proliferation, he noted that the West was "engaged in helping China to build up their military might, including their nuclear potential." Given these developments, he wondered why the United States spent so much time decrying India's refusal to sign the Non-Proliferation Treaty while giving China a pass.

He too agreed on the need for a CTB, but complained that the failure to sign such a treaty had been "slowed and delayed, and by no means through any fault of the Soviet Union." He hoped that the United States and Britain would "change their inflexible approach, in particular, to questions of verification." Regarding MBFR, the Soviets, he said, were eager to move on, but all Moscow and its allies had heard were "the very same unacceptable demands on which the West had insisted all along." Gromyko seconded Brezhnev's complaint about the MBFR negotiations, and in particular claimed that the West had overestimated the true number of Soviet and Warsaw Pact forces in Central Europe by some 150,000 soldiers. He protested that Western negotiators had said an agreement was impossible unless and until Moscow accepted this number. When Carter asked how the issue could be reconciled, Gromyko first replied "when the East asked where that 150,000 figure came from, it received no answer. He could only conclude the West had unreliable sources." Gromyko then claimed that the best way to solve the problem was that only the United States and Soviet Union declare the respective number of their own soldiers and armaments.

He urged Carter to "take a fresh look at this business, because he felt the present delay was entirely artificial." Carter agreed that this issue could be solved "today."

Brezhnev asked Gromyko to "review the general state" of the various non-nuclear arms talks. The chemical weapons talks, Gromyko contended, were "proceeding badly and in an unsatisfactory way." The two sides were far apart on the verification issue, and a chemical weapons agreement could not be reached until every major power, in particular China, joined the talks. The same could be said about the antisatellite negotiations.

As Gromyko attempted to steer the conversation toward the conventional arms talks (CAT), Carter interrupted to say that the United States had not complained about the Soviet-manned space flights and did not consider them antisatellite systems. Why, he wondered, did the Soviet Union consider the US space shuttle an antisatellite system? The shuttle was not designed for an antisatellite capability, but instead "was the very center of our space effort in the future." Carter said he hoped such a mischaracterization did not jeopardize the antisatellite discussions. Gromyko replied that while the Soviet Union wanted such talks to continue, "it would be impossible to reach agreement on the basis of the U.S. position."

Regarding CAT, Gromyko again complained that the Soviet Union wanted an agreement but had been stymied by Washington's demands that they discuss transfers on a regional basis, and in particular those regions in which the United States was interested. "When Soviet representatives mentioned other areas and countries of concern to both sides," he claimed, the US side had not only refused to talk about them, but then walked out of the talks. Carter replied that the United States believed that "we should not begin with areas where each country was deeply involved," specifically mentioning South Korea and Japan on the US side and Vietnam and Ethiopia on the Soviet side. Talks should instead focus on "areas where there was not that much controversy."

Gromyko turned to talks on limiting military activities in the Indian Ocean. Yet again, he contended that the United States had "unilaterally suspended" the talks, continued to strengthen its facilities on Diego Garcia, and had "intensified naval activities in that area." The Soviets, he warned, would not resume these discussions until the United States changed its position. Carter in turn said that the United States would "never" renounced using the island as a base, and blamed his buildup on the "massive Soviet arms supply to Ethiopia and before that Somalia." Now the Soviet Union was building up its position in Afghanistan. Stability in the region, the president warned, would not be achieved until both sides renounced intervention and demonstrated "respect for international borders," and the Soviets and Cubans stopped "inject[ing] themselves into regional military altercations. Such involvement caused us deep concern." Gromyko ignored these comments and instead said both should renounce deploying nuclear-equipped ships in the Mediterranean. He also suggested they revisit the idea of giving each other advance notice of military exercises and missile tests.

After saying that this concluded his remarks about "the entire complex of issues involved in curbing the arms race," Brezhnev read a prepared statement that confirmed that his comments about limiting the production of the Backfire bomber from the previous day remained in effect. He then suggested that the joint communiqué include phrasing to mean that each agreed not to be the first to use nuclear weapons against the other side or other side's allies. Carter said he would consider the no-first-use statement and asked if Brezhnev's statement meant that production of the Backfire would not exceed 30 per year. Gromyko interjected that "the Soviet Union would not rebut" Carter's understanding.

Vance said that he understood that the Soviets would not produce more than 30 Backfires per year and that Carter "had received no confirmation from the Soviet side." Brezhnev replied that the two sides had "an identical understanding on this score. He said that the Soviet Union will not produce more than thirty per year." Carter replied "perfect," to which Gromyko "jokingly" replied, "President Carter loves concessions." Carter said he now considered the Backfire issue resolved.[32]

When the meeting broke for lunch, Carter gave Brezhnev a handwritten note offering some "new ideas for disarmament," such as "deep" reductions in stockpiles and the inclusion of medium-range nuclear missiles in the SALT III negotiations. That night, Brezhnev convened a meeting of his advisors to talk about the proposals. Ustinov, Dobrynin recalled, was "dead against the proposals as too far-reaching." Gromyko said they couldn't make a decision quickly and should present the proposals to the rest of the Politburo. Brezhnev agreed that he didn't want to "tackle new difficult questions" that called MAD into question.[33]

Their fourth meeting, also held at the Soviet Embassy, began that evening at 5:30. Carter stated that he was "very gratified" that the "spirit of détente which had originated in Europe under President Brezhnev's leadership" could spread "elsewhere in the world." However, today's discussions might be "unpleasant" because they were going to speak "in a full and frank fashion" about some of the world's hot spots. In particular, he wanted to focus on two areas "where the U.S. and its allies had absolutely vital interests": the Arabian Peninsula and the Persian Gulf. Only through "maximum restraint" could the two superpowers "avoid a serious confrontation" in these regions. Other "troubled areas," Carter continued, included the Middle East, the Horn of Africa, Southern Africa, and Southeast Asia. He hoped that both sides would "discourage armed combat and bloodshed, and to encourage peaceful solution of differences," in these areas. He also criticized Cuba's "extensive military of activities" and said the United States viewed Havana as a "proxy" or "a surrogate or at least an ally" of the Soviet Union in Africa, the Caribbean, and Central America.

Vietnam, meanwhile, had violated China's border, invaded and occupied Cambodia, and Moscow's use of naval and air facilities in Vietnam "causes us grave concern."

The president hoped that the two rivals could "cooperate where possible," even as he conceded that they had "different perspectives." The progress that had been made in the peace talks in Namibia and in the Arab-Israeli dispute, including the recent Camp David accords, would benefit from Moscow's support. While he recognized that Washington's relationship with Iran had changed, he promised that the United States would not interfere in its—or Afghanistan's—internal affairs.

While he recognized Moscow's "concerns" about the relationship between the United States and China, he believed that "after 30 years, normalization of relations…was long overdue." The new relationship, Carter argued, "would contribute to peace and stability" in the world. Furthermore, "It was not directed against other countries of the world," and would not be done at Moscow's expense.

Brezhnev began his comments by returning to SALT. He repeated his insistence that any further arms control negotiations include the arsenals of other powers, asked for "full clarity" about the issue of FBS, and urged that any negotiations be based on what he called the "holy of holies from which the Soviet Union could not depart," that is, "the principle of equality and equal security." Otherwise, it would be "abnormal" to negotiate any reductions in strategic arms.

Turning to international issues, the Soviet leader said that his country wanted to reach "a common understanding" with the United States in world affairs. In order to achieve this goal, however, it was important to "make note of the factors which were preventing this." Such understanding was "hampered when one of the sides attributed changes in the world, movements for national liberation and independence, as well as social progress, to the malevolent will of one of the sides." He also expressed disbelief that "a rather strange theory has gained currency in the United States," a Brzezinski theory called "the arc of crisis," which contended that the Soviet Union wanted to expand from Western Africa to Southern Asia, "seeking to surround the Middle East, to the detriment of the United States and western countries in general." This "was an absolute fairy tale." He also expressed amazement at "how lightheartedly some corners of the world were being declared spheres of vital interests of the U.S. This was not only contrary to elementary norms of international law, but also complicated the international situation even more when there were sufficient complications as it was."

The Soviet Union, Brezhnev continued, "attached particular importance to European affairs," and did not want a repeat of the Second World War. That being said, he "had to take into account reality," and he recognized that there were some areas in Europe that had "different social systems." The Soviet Union, he promised, "did not pursue an anti-American course or try to prejudice legitimate interests of the United States." He expected, needless to say, the same "approach" from the United States and its allies. He wanted to finalize the Helsinki Accords, but worried that the NATO countries had begun "accelerating their military preparations to such an extent that questions arise." The Soviet Union, he insisted, wanted a balance of forces in Europe and to reduce them "without changing the existing correlation of forces."

Turning to the Middle East, he accused the United States of following an "anti-Arab policy" and said that the Egyptian-Israeli treaty "had failed to tranquilize the Middle Eastern situation, but has aggravated it." Israel, he claimed, was waging war on Lebanon under Egypt's protection. Thus the positions of the United States and the Soviet Union in this region were "fundamentally different... and not through any fault of the Soviet Union." His government, he promised, would "resolutely oppose any efforts to use the UN to bolster the separate deal between Egypt and Israel," and said "no firm peace" could be achieved in the region until Israel returned all the occupied territories and a Palestinian state created.

Moving on to Southeast Asia, Brezhnev blamed China's "dangerous expansionist and jingoist policy" for turning the area into a "dangerous flashpoint of tension." Vietnam had simply stopped China's "aggression" during the recent war. His government, at the same time, had exercised "restraint and had acted very responsibly." But he warned that such restraint had its limits, and Moscow had certain "obligations" under its friendship treaty with Vietnam. The United States must warn China that its "methods of dictation, blackmail and threats were inadmissible in international relations and that the world would not tolerate aggression." As for Cambodia, he said "one could only be happy" that it had freed itself "from a regime of rapists and killers imposed by Peking," a regime that the United States had also condemned as "abhorrent and inhumane."

It was time for the situation in Africa, Brezhnev declared, to be "clarif[ied]." Africans had merely declared their independence and rebelled against "the economic and political legacy of colonialism." The Soviet Union, for its part, wanted the "full liquidation" of this legacy, but "did not pursue any other goal" on the continent. "The President," he said, "should not believe absurd tales to the contrary." Moscow believed that "wherever colonialists imposed bloodshed on the African peoples, the victims are free to take the path of armed struggle and in this they deserve the support of the Soviet Union." Still, he wanted a "peaceful solution" to the unrest in Southern Africa.

After praising the "social revolution" that had occurred in Afghanistan and saying the "traditional friendship" between Moscow and Kabul "was not aimed against any third country," Brezhnev turned to Cuba. The Soviet Union, he claimed, had "complied strictly with the 1962 understanding. It had done nothing nor was doing anything that would be contrary to that understanding." To say that his country "was using Cubans to interfere in other areas" was untrue. "Cuba was an independent country and ... rendered assistance at the request of legitimate governments which were threatened by aggression," as it was allowed to do under international law and the UN. Hadn't George Washington's army contained foreign soldiers? If necessary, he could point out "genuine instances" of US interventions overseas. But he "had no desire to do so."

Returning to Asia, he told Carter that the Soviet Union didn't have any military bases in Vietnam. "Soviet ships," he explained, "entered Vietnamese ports for business and for friendly visits." Soviet aircraft did the same. The true "threat to peace," on the other hand, came from China. The Soviet-Vietnamese friendship treaty, Brezhnev warned, "was designed to compel China to come to its senses and to refrain from its expansionist policy." The other "destabilizing factor" in Asia were the American military bases in Japan, South Korea, and the Philippines. He noted that these bases were close to Soviet borders, and that American aircraft carriers and submarines equipped with nuclear weapons could easily reach the Soviet Union.

Carter thanked Brezhnev, said he had listened closely to Brezhnev's comments, and noted that they differed on a number of issues. But these differences just made further talks more necessary. The signing of the SALT II treaty, he emphasized, could serve as the foundation for more talks.[34]

Later that day the two leaders issued a joint statement, which, in addition to reaffirming the statement Brezhnev and Nixon had signed at the 1972 Moscow Summit, included a promise to meet annually for summit meetings.[35] Carter invited Brezhnev to come to the United States in 1980 and Brezhnev accepted "in principle." Their foreign ministers would meet at least twice a year, each nation's defense minister and senior military officials would meet periodically, while lower-level diplomats would meet more frequently. These contacts would "enhance mutual understanding and strengthen the traditional respect of the two countries' armed forces toward each other," while noting that the sides had never fought a war against each other.[36]

The Soviets put on a spread for dinner that evening that Carter admitted far outshone the one the Americans had offered the previous evening. "Our banquet had been adequate," he recalled, but the Russian one was "exquisite." Never one to resist a dig at the United States, Brezhnev "was particularly proud of the menu, which was printed in both Russian and English; he pointed out to everyone that he had not been able to read the one at our meal, which had only been in English." This time, Carter said, "It was really a very pleasant evening, during which we addressed some of the serious issues in more relaxed language." He ended his evening with a two-mile run by flashlight around the embassy residence with his daughter.[37]

On the morning of June 18, Carter and Brezhnev met privately for 90 minutes at the US Embassy with only their interpreters present.

Brezhnev, again reading from prepared notes, began by saying they could consider the summit "necessary, useful and productive." While that afternoon's signing of the SALT II treaty would be the summit's highlight, he considered it "significan[t]" that they had talked about a number of issues. True, differences remained between the two nations. But "they now had a better understanding of the positions and the thought processes of each other, and that was also very important." He urged Carter to join him in establishing "the kind of level of mutual understanding and confidence that would completely rule out the possibility of war breaking out" between the two countries. Should "a third country" attack either or both countries, they would "join forces in repelling the aggressor." With such an understanding, no third country "would embark on such madness."

Not surprisingly, he segued into another attack on China, and called the new relationship between Washington and Beijing "a dangerous thing." He warned Carter that "if some people ventured to use Peking's anti-Sovietism to their own advantage, he would have to say outright that such schemes would not bring any benefit to the United States, but could inflict a great deal of harm." China's invasion of Vietnam demonstrated that Washington's policy of "smiles and bows in the direction of the Chinese was totally unproductive." He reminded Carter that China was not bound by any international agreement limiting nuclear weapons. The "future encouragement" of China's "hostile policy toward the Soviet Union, Brezhnev warned, "would seriously aggravate Soviet-American relations," and any progress of limiting and reducing arms "would become quite impossible." If Washington moved any further toward Beijing, "it could only produce a drastic deterioration of the entire international situation." He hoped Carter would not go down that road.

Turning to the issue of human rights, which he had considered inappropriate for their previous "official" meetings, he explained that Carter could have "his own views on human rights and freedom of the individual" and that it was all right that this and other issues became "the subject of ideological argument." Given the way that the two nations had developed, such differences were indeed "inevitable." However, he objected to the elevation of such issues "to the level of official state policy and when attempts were made to exploit them in the relations between states." Carter, he assumed, would bristle if Brezhnev linked the US-Soviet trade relationship to "the issues of U.S. unemployment, racial issues, or equal rights for women." Such issues were outside the realm of state-to-state relations, and he reminded Carter that in a recent speech, the president had called the "right to life" the "most fundamental human right." Therefore, he asked Carter to do "all in his power" to prevent another war that would take millions of lives.

After Brezhnev invited Carter to visit the Soviet Union, Carter had a chance to respond to the Secretary General's comments. He called normalization of relations with China "good for us, good for China, good for the Soviet Union and for world stability and peace." Brezhnev disagreed, but Carter insisted that "whatever influence we have at this time or will have in the future on the leaders of China will be used to urge peaceful relations" between Moscow and Beijing. He promised that the United States would "never let relations between us and China be at the expense of the Soviet Union, nor will we ever permit an alignment develop between us against the Soviet Union."

Brezhnev again interrupted Carter, this time to ask, "Why don't you prod them to sign an agreement with us?" Carter answered that he would be "pleased to do so," since that would be good for the United States. But now he wanted to again speak "frankly" on issues that held both "symbolic and substantive significance" for both countries. One such issue was telemetry encryption. He noted that the United States did not use this particular method to hide its missile tests, but he was worried that the Soviets did use this technology to mask its SS-20 missile tests. While he conceded that these missiles were not covered by the SALT agreement, the loss of US "observation" stations in Iran meant that the United States could not verify that the Soviet Union was in compliance with SALT. In order to do so, he wished to "fly airplanes over Turkey on peaceful missions." While he was not asking for the Soviets to approve these flights, he wished Brezhnev to inform the Turks that he did not object to these flights.

Brezhnev's interpreter handed him a typed briefing paper, which he began to read. He noted that "from the very beginning" of the SALT talks, both sides had agreed to use NTM to verify compliance. "There were no grounds whatsoever," he contended, "to alter that principle in any way." While the Soviet Union opposed such "cooperative" measures, he wanted them to "fit into the framework of verification by national technical means." Regarding the specific instance of proposed US flights over Turkey, he said that his government's position regarding reconnaissance flights over that country was "well known and hardly needs to be set out again." Given Turkey's border with the Soviet Union (and in an obvious reference to the fact that Khrushchev had vehemently criticized the deployment of Jupiter missiles in Turkey back in the 1950s), "nothing in that position would change even if the U.S. side were to propose that this matter be resolved on the basis of reciprocal change, providing for flights of Soviet airplanes from Cuban territory." The United States and the Soviet Union, he contended, could not address questions "affecting the sovereign rights of other states."

Carter replied that this was "an important matter to us," and that it would help build "mutual trust between our countries, and it is important for ratification of the SALT II Treaty." He asked Brezhnev to "consider carefully" what a "more forthcoming response" from the Soviet side could do for détente. Brezhnev agreed to do so but said he could not promise anything more.

Carter in turn said he needed to raise "another difficult issue": he asked that the Soviet Union not veto the continued ability of a UN peacekeeping force to monitor the Israeli withdrawal from the Sinai. Using a brief provided by his interpreter, Brezhnev said he had repeatedly told Carter that his country remained "resolutely opposed to any attempt to sanctify a separate Egyptian-Israeli deal through the authority and prestige of the United Nations," in particular through the use of UN peacekeeping forces in the Sinai. The maintenance of the force, Brezhnev charged, "cannot lead to lasting peace in the Middle East, but only the opposite. To expect the Soviet Union to support such a force in this matter would be hopeless." Carter said he understood, but in the written copy of the memoranda, he wrote "but disagreed with" Brezhnev's comment. He hoped instead to work with the Soviet Union on Lebanon and "other troubled areas" in the region.

After repeating his call for the two nations to consult and cooperate in the world's trouble spots, Carter raised the issue of human rights. Noting that the American people had been "warmly gratified" by Brezhnev's decision to release the Baptist Pastor Georgi Vins from five years of internal exile, he asked that Anatoly Scharansky, a prominent Soviet Jew who had been convicted of spying for the United States and was imprisoned in a gulag in Siberia, also be released. Reading again from a typed brief, Brezhnev replied that "he could do nothing that would violate Soviet laws" given that Scharansky had been convicted of espionage by a Soviet court. The two leaders closed by affirming their willingness to continue talking since many of the issues facing them could be easily solved, and Brezhnev gave some autographed copies of his books to Carter.[38]

In their final, half-hour meeting before the SALT II treaty signing ceremony, Carter and Brezhnev traded kudos over how the summit had helped further the cooperative relationship between the two superpowers. Brezhnev, again reading from a prepared statement, also said he wanted to pursue "regularization of trade between our two countries" and decried the fact that trade had been "turned into a constant object of various linkages." The issue of emigration from the Soviet Union, he declared, was a "purely internal affair," and his government was angry about all the "discriminatory legislation" that had caused Soviet-American trade to be brought to a "state of stagnation." He understood that Carter was studying the "normalization of trade" between the two superpowers and called this a "positive thing." The Soviet market, he said, "could offer much" to American businesses.

Unfortunately, Brezhnev lamented, "artificial obstacles had been created" that prevented the improvement of relations in the areas of maritime shipping and air travel. However, after complaining about "[r]idiculous accusations" that the Soviet Merchant Marine fleet intended to seize American shipping markets, he praised the level of cooperation that occurred in science and technology. Brezhnev concluded by hoping that he hadn't "offended" Carter, but he wanted to develop a "stable and long-term" relationship with the

United States. Happy at having met Carter, he expected their new personal relationship would help improve overall Soviet-American relations.

Carter noted that since time was almost up, he would not respond to each of Brezhnev's remarks. But he promised to "investigate" Brezhnev's complaints and respond through Vance. Any misunderstandings that occurred, he assured his counterpart, will be cleared up so that "each side can understand the attitudes of the other." At the treaty signing ceremony, the two leaders not only shook hands but also "embraced warmly in the Soviet fashion."[39]

Brzezinski offered a brutal description of Brezhnev at this meeting in his memoirs. He wrote that "he seemed to be on the verge of senility. The other Soviets treated him with affection and patience, guiding him gently…Brezhnev struck me as a genuinely pitiful figure, struggling valiantly to represent the Soviet Union as best he could in spite of grave physical infirmity. At times, he was quite energetic, and one could sense that in his prime he must have been a man of great ebullience and dynamism." Dobrynin called Brezhnev's reliance on prepared papers "a source of amusement."[40] But when one reads the transcripts of the Vienna summit, one is struck by how tough Brezhnev sounded, and when Gromyko stepped in, how tough he was, and how implacable their government remained on all the issues. The Kremlin could have driven a truck through the Backfire statement, which Brzezinski and Carter touted as a concession. Nor did they accept OSIs, which hampered the verification of any arms control agreement for the next decade. Neither Brezhnev nor Gromyko gave any ground on their increased activities in Africa, Afghanistan, Cuba, the Persian Gulf, and Southeast Asia.

Carter, on the other hand, came across as either weak or too interested in accommodating the Soviets. With the exception of the SALT discussions, he offered only tepid counterarguments when Brezhnev made his various demands. The transcripts show Carter bending over backwards to sign the SALT II treaty, and while he maintained that cruise missiles and FBS were not subject to the treaty and pressed for an official promise that the Soviets limit their production of the Backfire, he didn't convince the Soviets to agree to stringent verification procedures.

Both sides seemed cautiously pleased by the summit. Dobrynin called the SALT II Treaty "a major achievement" and conceded that it was "a marked improvement over the Vladivostok agreements." But he complained that the administration's delays had allowed its critics to launch numerous broadsides not only against arms control talks but against the overall US-Soviet relationship. At the same time, he argued that "Brezhnev had grown physically and mentally more decrepit," while the rest of the leadership "began to write off Carter because of the unstable condition of Soviet-American relations, which they blamed on him." Brzezinski told Dobrynin that the meetings had allowed Carter to experience "a psychological relaxation of tension which led him to believe in the possibility of a

FIGURE 5.2 *Carter and Brezhnev signing the SALT II Treaty at Vienna. Behind Carter are Brzezinski, Secretary of Defense Harold Brown, and Vance. Gromyko, Dobrynin, and Ustinov are behind Brezhnev. United States Information Agency.*

reasonable dialogue and further agreements with the Soviet Union." Brzezinski said that he left Vienna "feeling fairly satisfied" about SALT II, especially because the Soviets had made concessions on telemetry encryption and Backfire. But he claimed that "At the same time, there was at best only a limited dialogue on the issues that I considered most important," such as Africa, Southwest Asia, and Cuba. Carter claimed that while he was "somewhat disappointed" that they hadn't made even more progress on issues other than SALT, he believed they had a "clearer understanding of the many differences between us, and the sure knowledge that both of us wanted to avoid war with the other had made the Soviet-American summit conference worthwhile."[41]

On June 22, Carter submitted the SALT II treaty to the Senate for ratification and hearings began on July 9. The treaty became, as Vance said, "the catalyst of a broadening conservative challenge to détente," as the treaty's opponents successfully created "political linkage between the treaty and the problem of restraining Moscow's attempts to expand its influence." Kissinger brought considerable weight to bear on this question, because even though he had spent so much time negotiating the treaty, he only "guardedly" supported the treaty while criticizing the Carter administration for not linking it to Soviet behavior elsewhere. This allowed centrist Senators who might have otherwise supported the treaty to question whether the

United States could trust the Soviet Union. The conservative Republicans and Jackson argued that the treaty favored the Soviet Union because it retained its 308 land-based launchers with their enormous throw-weight, nor did it count the Backfire under the aggregate ceiling. They also expressed serious concern that the United States could not verify Soviet compliance. Liberal Senators, on the other hand, wanted actual arms reductions and didn't believe the treaty went far enough. They pointed to Carter's approval of the MX and, like the Soviets, noted that medium-range nuclear missiles were not subject to the treaty. Their criticisms, Vance lamented, allowed the Right to use such arguments to block ratification.[42]

Other events hurt détente and the prospects for ratification of SALT II. In July, the US press reported that the Soviets had stationed a combat brigade in Cuba, in apparent violation of the 1962 US-Soviet understanding on Cuba. Dobrynin believed that this "discovery" (the brigade had been training Cuban soldiers since 1962, but this fact had not been publicized) had been leaked by opponents of SALT II and détente as proof that the Soviets could not be trusted.[43] On November 4, Iranian students overran the American Embassy in Tehran and took 52 Americans hostage, beginning a diplomatic crisis that crippled Carter for the rest of his term. Shortly thereafter, Pakistani students nearly succeeded in taking over the American Embassy in Islamabad, and radicals seized the Grand Mosque in Mecca, Saudi Arabia. The resulting instability plunged the US and the Western economies into a second energy crisis.

Although the Senate Foreign Relations Committee recommended ratification of the SALT treaty by a vote of 9–6 on November 9, the Armed Services Committee—of which Jackson was a member—took a decidedly different stance. On December 4, it reported to the Senate that the treaty favored the Soviet Union, lacked adequate verification protocols, and therefore was "not in the national security interest" of the United States. On December 12, NATO adopted the so-called "dual track" policy: the United States would install Pershing II ground-launched cruise missiles while NATO would negotiate with the Soviet Union for the removal of all IRBMs in Europe. The timing was not propitious given the SALT II Treaty's troubles in the Senate. Five days later, a bipartisan group of 19 Senators, including Carter's friend and fellow Georgia Democrat Sam Nunn, wrote Carter that they remained "uncommitted" on voting for the treaty because of many of the concerns raised by the Armed Service Committee, including "the ongoing slippage in America's comparative military position, and recent international events."[44]

SALT II, and détente, officially died on December 25 when the Soviet Union invaded Afghanistan. On January 3, 1980, Carter asked the Senate to delay ratification of the treaty. Carter responded to the invasion by boycotting the 1980 summer Olympics in Moscow, embargoing grain sales to the Soviet Union, creating a "Rapid Deployment Force" to protect the oil fields in the Persian Gulf, and increasing covert funding of Afghani

Islamic rebels, the *mujahideen*, who fought the Soviet military.[45] In March, the United States learned that the Soviets had violated the 1972 Biological Weapons Convention when word leaked that an accident had occurred at a biological weapons factory in Sverdlovsk that spread anthrax throughout the surrounding area.[46] The administration raised the issue throughout the summer, and also complained that the Soviets had resumed high-yield nuclear tests in violation of the 1974 TTBT.

In August 1980, striking shipyard workers in Gdansk founded *Solidarity*, a free trade union that worked closely with Roman Catholic Church officials to challenge the communist regime. In December the Carter administration learned that Soviet troops had been moved to the Polish-Soviet and Polish-East German borders. With the expectation of another Czechoslovakia on the horizon, Carter warned Brezhnev not to intervene. Brezhnev, recently released documents have revealed, had no intention of invading Poland, but he did warn the Polish First Secretary, Stanislaw Kania, "If we see that you are being overthrown" by *Solidarity*, "then we will go in." To further intimidate Kania, the Warsaw Pact held military exercises in Poland and near its borders.[47] The crisis further soured the already tense US-Soviet relationship as Carter left office.

Carter's political fortunes also took a beating. Reagan ran again for president and this time he won the Republican presidential nomination. He strongly criticized SALT and détente in general along the same lines as he had Ford and Kissinger in 1976, promised to sharply increase defense spending, and ridiculed Carter's handling of the Iranian hostage crisis. Senator Edward Kennedy, on the other hand, opposed Carter from the left in the Democratic primaries and also assailed Carter's handling of the hostages. Although Carter won the nomination, Kennedy's challenge lasted all the way to the Democratic Convention in August (just like the Reagan–Ford nomination fight of 1976). The combination of the split within the Democratic Party, the awful American economy, Carter's failure to secure the release of the hostages, and the seeming collapse of American foreign policy resulted in Reagan's victory over Carter in November.

CHAPTER SIX

The Malta Summit:
The End of the Cold War

The Cold War entered a new and more dangerous phase in 1981. The new US president, Ronald Reagan, argued that Nixon, Ford, and Carter had "seemed to accept as inevitable the advance of Soviet expansion." Détente, he claimed, had allowed the Soviets to "interpret our hesitation and reluctance to act and our reduced sense of national self-confidence as a weakness" and had been exploiting it "to achieve a Communist-dominated world."

Reagan, however, also believed that the "nuclear standoff was futile and dangerous for all of us," and ultimately he wanted to reduce and eventually eliminate nuclear stockpiles. Like Johnson, he believed that the superpowers could spend their money on other, more important priorities. For the time being, however, he agreed to abide by the SALT II Treaty, but reserved the right to renounce it whenever he deemed it appropriate.[1]

In his first press conference, when asked if he believed détente with the Soviet Union was still possible, Reagan declared "so far detente's been a one-way street that the Soviet Union has used to pursue its own aims." Moscow, he charged, had "openly and publicly declared that the only morality they recognize is what will further their cause, meaning they reserve unto themselves the right to commit any crime, to lie, to cheat, in order to attain" its goals. The United States, on the other hand, operated "on a different set of standards," and he argued "I think when you do business with them, even at a détente, you keep that in mind."[2]

The new administration also sent a private, but more substantial, message to the Soviets. Only a few hours after Reagan's press conference, Dobrynin arrived at the State Department for his first meeting with the new Secretary of State, Alexander Haig. The Ambassador, who had been accustomed to entering the State Department's garage and taking a private elevator to the seventh floor, was forced to back his car out and enter via the same entrance as the other diplomats. In his memoirs, Haig conceded that the incident "conveyed so aptly the change in American attitudes toward Moscow."[3]

After the incident, Dobrynin wrote, "it soon became clear that in ideology and propaganda Reagan turned out to be far worse and far more threatening." During his long career as ambassador, "the collective mood of the Soviet leadership had never been so suddenly and deeply set against an American president."[4]

In a November 18, 1981 speech to the National Press Club, Reagan offered to cancel Washington's planned deployment of Pershing IRBMs in Western Europe if the Soviets withdrew its SS-20s and other IRBMs from Eastern Europe. The so-called "zero option," he argued, would "be an historic step. With Soviet agreement, we could together substantially reduce the dread threat of nuclear war which hangs over the people of Europe." Reagan genuinely believed that reducing rather than limiting nuclear weapons was more "rational" than the so-called "rational" Mutually Assured Destruction.[5]

In the meantime, Poland was becoming more of a problem. In March 1981, Brezhnev had told Kania and the head of the Polish military, General Wojtech Jaruzelski, "our patience is lost!…We give you two weeks ultimatum to restore order in Poland!" He followed up this threat with a military exercise similar to the one in December 1980. But in reality, Brezhnev and the rest of the Politburo had no stomach for another invasion. In October, Jaruzelski became the leader of the party, and on December 13 he imposed martial law, which for the moment "removed the immediate challenge to the Warsaw Pact."[6]

Reagan was incensed. On December 21 he told the NSC that "this may be the last chance in our lifetime to see a change in the Soviet Empire's colonial policy re Eastern Europe. We should take a stand & tell them unless & until martial is lifted," the United States would "quarantine the Soviets & Poland with no trade or communications across their borders." During his Christmas address to the nation, Reagan blamed the crackdown on Moscow. Brezhnev in turn warned Reagan not to intervene in Poland.[7]

Reagan instead began a propaganda push designed to back Moscow into a corner. In a May 9, 1982 commencement address at his alma mater, Eureka College, he charged that the Soviets had used arms control talks to "enhance Soviet power and prestige." Now, he proposed something different. "I'm asking my START—and START really means—we've given up on SALT—START means 'Strategic Arms Reduction Talks,' and that negotiating team," he declared, "to propose to their Soviet counterparts a practical, phased reduction plan. The focus of our efforts will be to reduce significantly the most destabilizing systems, the ballistic missiles, the number of warheads they carry, and their overall destructive potential."[8] Reagan later told a joint session of the British Parliament that the West must adopt "a plan and a hope for the long term—the march of freedom and

democracy which will leave Marxism-Leninism on the ashheap of history."
He also praised the "freedom-fighters" who fought Marxist or Soviet- and
Cuban-supported regimes in El Salvador, Poland, and Afghanistan.[9]

On June 24, Reagan replaced Haig—who had clashed with Weinberger
and others—with George Shultz, an economist and former Secretary of
Labor and Treasury under Nixon. Shultz, along with the new Soviet expert
on the NSC staff, the longtime diplomat Jack Matlock, had different ideas
about the Soviet Union. Shultz, as James Wilson has written, "believed that
the Soviets had the capacity to change," and he tried to convince Reagan to
develop a better relationship with his Soviet counterparts.[10]

But getting there proved to be far more difficult for two reasons. First,
Brezhnev died on November 10. His successor, the longtime head of the
KGB Yuri Andropov, was ill with kidney problems.[11] Second, Andropov,
like Brezhnev, simply did not accept the idea of nuclear arms reductions.
He and a majority of the Politburo believed in MAD, and interpreted the
abandonment of SALT as an attempt by the United States to achieve
nuclear superiority. Moreover, as Dobrynin later wrote, they regarded
Reagan's policies, like Carter's, "as a kind of betrayal of the agreements
they had laboriously reached with previous administrations." Reagan's
attempt to achieve both American superiority and the reduction, and
the eventual abolition, of nuclear weapons, confused a Kremlin already
uninterested in making the conceptual leap from arms limitations to arms
reductions.[12]

Despite this entrenched opposition, Reagan initially made some
conciliatory gestures. First, he unexpectedly, but Dobrynin conceded
"characteristically," visited the Soviet Embassy in Washington to personally
offer his condolences for Brezhnev's death. Second, he sent Vice-President
George H. W. Bush and Shultz to Moscow to attend the funeral.

Andropov, Bush cabled Reagan, "conveyed strength, but not in a
bellicose way." Bush admitted, "It is of course too early to predict how things
will evolve in Moscow, but for some reason I feel up-beat, opportunity
may well lie ahead, though much of the rhetoric was predictable and
accusatory."[13] Shultz wrote that Andropov "looked more like a cadaver
than did the just-interred Brezhnev, but his mental powers filled the room.
He reminded me of Sherlock Holmes' deadly enemy, Professor Moriarty,
all brain in a disregarded body … I put him down as a formidable ally."[14]

Shultz's attempts to moderate Reagan's tone did not initially succeed. On
January 17, 1983, Reagan approved National Security Decision Directive
(NSDD)-75. The United States would now "contain and over time reverse
Soviet expansion by competing effectively on a sustained basis with
the Soviet Union in all international arenas." The United States would also
promote, "within the narrow limits available to us, the process of change in
the Soviet Union toward a more pluralistic political and economic system."
NSDD-75 argued that "Soviet aggressiveness has deep roots in the internal
system," and "relations with the USSR should therefore take into account

whether or not they help to strengthen this system and its capacity to engage in aggression." Thomas Reed, one of Reagan's advisors, called NSDD-75 "a declaration of economic and political war."[15]

In a March 8, 1983 speech in Florida, the president ratcheted up his rhetoric and asked his audience to resist the temptation to label "both sides equally at fault, to ignore the facts of history and the aggressive impulses of an evil empire, to simply call the arms race a giant misunderstanding and thereby remove yourself from the struggle between right and wrong and good and evil." The Soviets believed he was now "challenging the legitimacy of the Soviet regime."[16]

Two weeks later, he announced he would begin research and development on the Strategic Defense Initiative (SDI), a space-based antimissile system designed to protect the United States from a nuclear attack. Reagan believed it was necessary to achieve what he called his "ultimate goal of eliminating the threat posed by strategic nuclear missiles. This could pave the way for arms control measures to eliminate the weapons themselves. We seek neither military superiority nor political advantage," he contended, but rather peace in the nuclear age.[17]

Dobrynin wrote, however, that his government regarded SDI "as a move designed to destabilize the strategic situation and create a large-scale antimissile defense system for American territory, in order to deprive the Soviet Union of the chance to retaliate in case of nuclear war." In other words, SDI could provide a first-strike capability that would prevent Moscow from responding in kind and eradicate MAD as a strategic doctrine.[18]

Superpower relations further deteriorated in the fall. On September 1, Soviet fighters shot down an unarmed passenger plane, Korean Air Lines Flight 007, killing all 269 passengers, including a US congressman and sixty other Americans. The plane had accidentally strayed over the Soviet-occupied Kurile Islands, and the Soviet air defense command mistook it for a US spy plane. Despite an international uproar, Andropov angrily accused the United States of concealing a spy flight behind the passenger plane and called the flight a deliberate US provocation.

Two months later, US and NATO forces conducted a ten-day war games exercise code-named "Able Archer 83." During the exercise, NATO forces used a new communications system to simulate a higher level of nuclear alert. Soviet intelligence officials incorrectly feared that NATO was about to launch a preemptive nuclear attack on Soviet forces, and in turn put Soviet nuclear facilities in East Germany and Poland on high alert.[19] On November 23, the United States began to deploy the Pershings in Western Europe. The Soviets responded by walking out of the START talks in Geneva.

There is evidence that these events sobered Reagan. On November 18, he and Shultz talked about "setting up a little in house group of experts on the Soviet U. to help us in setting up some channels. I feel the Soviets are so defense minded, so paranoid about being attacked that without in any way being soft on them we ought to tell them no one here has any intention of doing anything like that."[20]

Accordingly, Shultz began a series of breakfast meetings with Bush, Weinberger, CIA Director William Casey, and National Security Advisor Robert McFarlane. Matlock recalled that "nobody argued that the United States should try to bring the Soviet Union down. All recognized that the Soviet leaders faced mounting problems, but understood that US attempts to exploit them would strengthen Soviet resistance to change rather than diminish it." Essentially they had agreed to jettison NSDD-75. On January 16, 1984, Reagan publicly stated that "we have common interests and the foremost among them is to avoid war and reduce the level of arms."[21]

Any opportunity to capitalize on this new approach was dashed when Andropov died on February 9. Once again, Reagan sent Bush to attend the funeral. After meeting with the new General Secretary, Konstantin Chernenko, Bush reported "He said that it is by no means certain we will have a fatal confrontation; that we are not inherently enemies. I told him that we, too, were ready for dialogue and progress."[22]

Vladislav Zubok has argued, however, that Chernenko was actually "a walking mummy, who suffered from severe asthma and lived on tranquilizers."[23] The arch-conservative Gromyko quickly seized control of foreign affairs. On May 8 the leadership announced that it would boycott the summer Olympics in Los Angeles. Two days later, Dobrynin accused the United States of wanting "the 'militarization' of space."[24]

As Chernenko's health declined, a young Politburo member, Mikhail Gorbachev, slowly increased his power. During the summer of 1984, Dobrynin recalled that Gorbachev "often chaired" Politburo meetings because of Chernenko's illness. "Without much publicity," he wrote, the Politburo "took two important decisions, first to renew the disarmament dialogue with the American administration ... and second to move toward a summit with Reagan."[25] In December Gorbachev traveled to London to meet with British prime minister Margaret Thatcher. He told her he wanted to reduce the dangers of armed confrontation between the East and the West, argued that it made little sense to continue an arms race that could destroy both sides, and shared his plans to reform the Soviet system. Afterwards, Thatcher famously remarked on television, "I like Mr. Gorbachev. We can do business together."

Gorbachev's public reception was reminiscent of Zhou Enlai's at Bandung. His youth, his Western mannerisms, his sense of humor, and his vivacious and stylish wife, Raisa, contrasted sharply with his predecessors. Thatcher quickly flew to Washington and told Reagan that Gorbachev "was an unusual Russian in that he was much less constrained, more charming, more open to discussion and debate." More important, he "was an advocate of economic reform and was willing to slacken Soviet control over its economy."[26]

On March 10, 1985, Chernenko died, and Shultz and Bush attended the funeral in Moscow. At Shultz's recommendation, Reagan wrote Gorbachev suggesting a meeting and inviting him to visit the United States. After the funeral, Gorbachev told the two Americans that the Soviet Union had "no expansionist ambitions" and did not want to fight the United States. Most significant, he promised to renew the START negotiations in Geneva. Impressed, Bush cabled Reagan and warned that "Gorbachev will package the Soviet line for Western consumption much more effectively than any (I repeat any) of his predecessors." Moreover, he noted "This Gucci Comrade brings the General Secretariat a quantum leap forward in overall appearance."[27]

The reforms that Gorbachev mentioned to Thatcher fell under the rubric of perestroika, or "restructuring." It is crucial to understand, however, that Gorbachev, like Khrushchev, wanted to strengthen and revive the Soviet system, not turn it into a democratic, capitalistic society. Perestroika represented the political and economic components of what Gorbachev called "New Thinking." It required that the Soviet Union eliminate corruption; fight rampant alcoholism; increase industrial and agricultural production; and introduce technological, administrative, and bureaucratic innovations.

Perestroika could not succeed, however, if the Soviet Union continued to spend approximately 30 percent of its gross domestic product on the military. The decades-long quest for nuclear parity with, or even superiority over, the United States had bankrupted the economy. The invasion of Afghanistan had not only cost billions of rubles and tens of thousands of killed, wounded, and disabled soldiers but had taken on the appearance of a colonial occupation, which true communism rejected.[28]

Reagan and Gorbachev exchanged a total of seven letters between March and October in anticipation of their first Summit. Meanwhile, Gorbachev acted boldly. On April 7 he announced a moratorium on further deployment of SS-20 missiles in Europe until November. If the United States agreed to stop deploying Pershings and cruise missiles in Western Europe, he would extend the halt indefinitely. The United States and NATO, however, rejected the offer, since Soviet IRBMs still outnumbered NATO's 10–1. Gorbachev, however, kept trying. In July he announced a moratorium on nuclear tests effective from August 6, 1985 to January 1986. He would extend that moratorium if the United States agreed to stop its testing. Reagan also rejected this offer because he suspected that, like the SS-20 proposal, it was a propaganda ploy.[29]

In September, Reagan told the new Soviet foreign minister, Eduard Shevardnadze, "I really meant 'arms reductions' & I wasn't interested in any détente nonsense." Shevardnadze gave Reagan a letter from Gorbachev that contained arms control proposals that Matlock dismissed as containing "only minor changes in previous positions." Shultz, however, called the proposals "a breakthrough of principle, even though the specifics were not remotely acceptable; it was a victory for the president's policy of seeking significant reductions in offensive nuclear arms." Reagan also saw something positive in this meeting: "for the first time they talked of real verification procedures."[30]

The Geneva Summit began on November 19, 1985. In their first meeting, Reagan remarked, "Countries don't mistrust each other because of arms, but rather countries build up their arms because of the mistrust between them." All nations, he stressed, needed to live together. Each "could follow its own way, but with peaceful competition." Gorbachev agreed, and emphasized that "this meeting is important in itself." He was "convinced that he and the President could not ignore each other." He also stressed that despite "squalls in the bilateral relationship" between the two superpowers, "I can definitely state that in the USSR there is no enmity toward the United States or its people."[31]

Throughout the Summit, both stuck to their guns on arms control. Gorbachev repeatedly told Reagan that SDI would not only touch off an arms race in space but even worse, give the United States a first strike capability. Reagan countered that it was not an "offensive" weapon but rather "an effort to find a more civilized means of deterring war than reliance on thousands of nuclear missiles which, if used, would kill millions on both sides." He offered to share the technology with Gorbachev "in order to end the nuclear nightmare for the US people, the Soviet people, for all people." Gorbachev, however, accused Reagan of proposing a 50 percent reduction in nuclear arms while "advocating a new class of weapons. Describing these weapons as a shield was only packaging."[32]

Despite their deep disagreements on SDI, it became obvious when they appeared together at the International Press Center on November 21 that, as Shultz wrote, their "personal chemistry was apparent. The easy and relaxed attitude toward each other, the smiles, the sense of purpose, all showed through." The Geneva Summit allowed the two sides to begin seeking a more permanent and constructive relationship.[33]

Gorbachev's advisor Anatoly Chernyaev wrote in his diary that in spite of the logjam over arms control, "a turning point in international relations is taking shape. We are coming closer to acknowledging that no one will start a war; to understanding that we cannot keep provoking it either in the name of communism, or in the name of capitalism." At the conclusion of the Summit, the two leaders issued a joint statement declaring that "nuclear war cannot be won and must never be fought." Gorbachev's interpreter Pavel Palazchenko called this point "revolutionary" considering Reagan's first-term rhetoric about challenging the Soviet Union with nuclear diplomacy.[34]

Unwilling to lose any momentum, Gorbachev announced on January 15, 1986, that the Soviets would unilaterally give up all their nuclear weapons by 2000 and proposed that the two nations remove all their IRBMs from Europe. He also extended his nuclear test ban moratorium by three months and offered the United States the chance to conduct on-site inspection of stockpile eliminations, a concession that his predecessors had rejected.

Of course, Reagan would have to scrap SDI in return. In his diary, Reagan called the proposal "a h–l of a propaganda move. We'd be hard put to explain how we'd turn it down." Still, he refused to give up SDI, but pressed forward with arms reductions negotiations.[35]

However, before anything constructive could be worked out, disaster struck: on April 26, 1986, an explosion at the Chernobyl nuclear power plant in Ukraine released an enormous cloud of radiation that drifted throughout Europe. Not until alarms went off at a Swedish nuclear power plant did the Soviets admit to the world what had happened. The Chernobyl disaster likely convinced Gorbachev to move even further into arms reduction talks and push perestroika. Gorbachev told the Soviet foreign ministry he would "loosen the vice of defense expenditures," and urged his diplomats to ditch the old Brezhnev style of "senseless stubbornness." In a July 3 Politburo meeting, he called Chernobyl "an extraordinary event bordering on the use of a nuclear weapon."[36]

Another Gorbachev advisor, Andrei Grachev, has written that Gorbachev now "realized that to obtain the desired result he would have to pay a substantial price." The Politburo decided to propose a cut in the Soviet ICBM stockpile, accept the "zero option," and abandon the demand that Forward-Based Systems be included in any arms agreement. Knowing that he could not convince Reagan to drop SDI, Gorbachev decided to accept a "promise to honour the Anti-Ballistic Missile Treaty for the next ten years while confining SDI to laboratory testing." Keeping up with SDI, he had concluded, would mean "exhausting our economy." Gorbachev was therefore preparing to inform Reagan that he, unlike his predecessors, was ready to move beyond MAD.[37]

The negotiations for another summit hit a snag on August 30, when Soviet authorities arrested Nicholas Daniloff, a reporter for *U.S. News and World Report*, in retaliation for the arrest of a Soviet spy in New York. Reagan told Shevardnadze "no progress could come in the US-Soviet relationship without Daniloff's release." A letter from Gorbachev proposing a summit in either London or Reykjavik, Iceland, arrived at the height of the affair. Reagan said he "would not even consider such a meeting" while Daniloff remained in custody. Shultz and Shevardnadze finally worked out a deal on September 28. The Soviets released Daniloff and the Soviet spy pled no contest to the charges and was expelled. The Soviets also agreed to release and let emigrate a prominent dissident and his wife. On September 30 the two governments announced that Reagan and Gorbachev would meet in Reykjavik for two days starting on October 11.[38]

In their first meeting in Reykjavik, they agreed that they must reduce arms stockpiles and verify arms reductions agreements. Reagan uttered his famous phrase, quoting the Russian proverb "Doveryai, no proveryai," or "trust but verify." If they signed an arms reduction agreement with real verification procedures, the president said "the world will applaud." Gorbachev agreed with this idea.

Gorbachev informed the president about his proposals: the 50 percent cut in strategic weapons, the elimination of IRBMs from Europe, and his "major concession," that he had dropped the long-standing Soviet demand that British and French nuclear forces be included in the US aggregate. He also urged that they eliminate all nuclear weapons by 1996, a more ambitious goal than his original year 2000 target. Reagan was thrilled to hear these proposals, but his good mood soured when Gorbachev said that SDI research and testing should be confined to laboratories, which would accord with the 1972 Anti-Ballistic Missile Treaty, and again accused Reagan of planning to use the technology to achieve a first strike capability. Reagan replied that SDI was not an offensive weapon and that it would eliminate all nuclear weapons. Gorbachev, however, remained unmoved.[39]

Despite this fundamental disagreement, Reagan recalled that he had gotten some "amazing agreements" such as "the most massive weapons reductions in history." But on October 12, "Gorbachev threw us a curve. With a smile on his face," Gorbachev said that the arms reductions depended on "you giving up SDI." Not just confining the research and testing to a lab, but a complete renunciation of the system. Reagan said he "couldn't believe it and blew my top." He said that if SDI was "practical and feasible, we'll make that information know to you and everyone else, so that nuclear weapons can be made obsolete. Now with all we have accomplished here, you do this and throw in this roadblock and everything is out the window. There is no way we're going to give up research to find a defense weapon against nuclear missiles." Shultz recalled that as the two men gathered up their papers and made to leave, Reagan said "I still feel we can find a deal." Gorbachev, however, replied "I don't think you want a deal...I don't know what more I could have done." After Reagan said "you could have said yes," Gorbachev answered "We won't be seeing each other again."[40]

Although the international press reported that the summit had ended in disaster, and both leaders initially were upset that it had ended on such a discordant note, upon reflection, they considered Reykjavik a significant step in arms reductions talks. Both men explained that each understood and respected the other's position and decided to concentrate on where they agreed rather than harp on SDI.

Reagan's private reassessment of the Reykjavik summit was shattered on November 3 when a Lebanese magazine reported that McFarlane had secretly visited Tehran in September on a plane carrying US military equipment purchased from international arms dealers in violation of the US embargo against Iran. In return for the weapons, "moderates" within the Iranian government would secure the release of seven Americans who had been kidnapped in Lebanon. The United States had violated its most sacred tenet of counter-terrorism: that it would never negotiate with terrorists. Shocked by the revelation, Shultz remarked "This has all the feel of Watergate."[41] On November 13, however, Reagan appeared on national television and said that while he had authorized the sale of a small shipment of weapons to Iran, he had not traded arms for hostages.

The administration was later rocked when Attorney General Ed Meese reported that some of the proceeds from the arms sales were diverted to the contras, the anticommunist army in Nicaragua. This action apparently violated the Boland Amendment to the Defense Appropriation Act of 1983, which the House of Representatives passed 411–0 and which Reagan signed. The Amendment prohibited US assistance to the contras for the purposes of overthrowing the Sandinista government. The Reagan administration was plunged into a year-long constitutional crisis due to the Iran–Contra scandal.

While the press and the Congress investigated the scandal, US-Soviet relations continued to improve. In January 1987, Victor Karpov, the chief Soviet negotiator at the Geneva space and arms talks, said his government might resume the talks separately from SDI or the ABM treaty. On February 28, Gorbachev announced that he would agree to reduce Intermediate Nuclear Forces (INF) in Europe regardless of whether or not Reagan continued to develop SDI.[42]

Gorbachev had to make this concession because perestroika had failed to make even a small dent in reforming the Soviet economy. Industrial production had decreased by 6 percent, while Moscow's foreign debt had increased. The occupation of Afghanistan was also bleeding the Soviet treasury dry. Meanwhile, an unexpected plunge in the price of oil and the fall in sales from Gorbachev's antialcohol campaign led to a massive revenue shortage. Despite all his talk, Gorbachev had not implemented any of the even modest temporary capitalist reforms he had called for when he began perestroika.

As the Geneva Talks heated up again, plans for another Reagan–Gorbachev summit in the United States moved forward. Reagan nevertheless kept up the pressure. In West Berlin in front of the Berlin Wall on June 12, Reagan demanded that Gorbachev "tear down this wall." The speech electrified the world.[43]

On December 8, 1987, Reagan and Gorbachev signed the INF Treaty in Washington, the first time that any nuclear power had reduced rather than simply limited nuclear weapons. At the signing ceremony, Reagan couldn't resist repeating "trust but verify" in both Russian and English. Gorbachev called out "You repeat that at every meeting!" The crowd laughed, and laughed louder when Reagan responded "Well, I like it!"[44] The Treaty was an enormous victory for Reagan's vision of strategic arms reductions and Gorbachev's reform programs. Gorbachev then invited Reagan to visit Moscow in May 1988. Exactly two months after the INF Treaty signing, Gorbachev announced that he would begin withdrawing troops from Afghanistan. On April 4, 1988, the Soviets officially agreed to begin withdrawals on May 15.

Meanwhile, Gorbachev began to implement glasnost, or openness. He started to ease restrictions on press and speech and allow underground samizdat (dissident) writers, actors, and other members of the dissident intelligentsia to produce their works without harassment by the secret police. He also began releasing political prisoners and allowed citizens to openly criticize his policies. When Reagan arrived in Moscow in May, Gorbachev suggested he walk through Red Square, the heart of the Kremlin, and meet ordinary Soviet citizens. Reagan accepted. During their stroll, a Western reporter asked him whether he still considered the Soviet Union an "evil empire." Reagan replied, "No, I was talking about a different time and a different era."[45]

Gorbachev, in a move none of his predecessors would have even considered, also invited the president to speak directly to Soviet students at his alma mater, Moscow State University. Reagan told the audience that the technological and informational revolution that had begun sweeping the world depended on "freedom of thought, freedom of information, freedom of communication," not to mention free markets. He criticized centralized planning and praised political pluralism, religious, and political freedom. Reagan had just explicitly endorsed glasnost, and he praised Gorbachev's attempts to change Soviet society. Human rights, he said, were universal, and the sooner the Soviet Union respected them, the easier it could change.[46]

FIGURE 6.1 *Gorbachev and Reagan walk through Red Square, May 1988. United States Information Agency.*

Reagan's endorsement helped Gorbachev further push glasnost. Only a month later, Gorbachev instituted political reforms by calling for a new legislature, the Congress of People's Deputies, which would be elected by Soviet citizens. He proposed a new executive system would create the position of President as head of state, and began the process of devolving more power from the central government to the Republics. He later extended this to the Eastern European nations. In a memorable December 7, 1988 speech to the UNGA, Gorbachev denounced the Brezhnev Doctrine's "interference in those internal processes with the aim of altering them according to someone else's prescription." Furthermore, he said, "Freedom of choice is a universal principle to which there should be no exceptions," a stunning rejection of the fundamental tenets of Marxism-Leninism. Finally, he announced that he would unilaterally begin to withdraw a half a million Soviet troops and six tank divisions from Eastern Europe in 1989.[47]

That afternoon, Gorbachev officially met for the last time with Reagan, as well as with the newly elected president, George H. W. Bush, at Governor's Island in New York Harbor. Gorbachev and Bush reminisced about how their personal relationship had deepened since their first meeting, and the Soviet leader remarked "that in a rather difficult time they had been able to begin movement toward a better world." Reagan replied that while he was "proud of what they had accomplished together," more needed to be done. Bush said he wanted "to build on what President Reagan had done," because "what had been accomplished could not be reversed." He qualified this statement, however, by saying he needed "a little time to review the issues." Gorbachev, on the other hand, saw "good prospects" for further cooperation with the new administration, and emphasized that his "country had become a different one. It would never go back to what it had been three years before regardless of whether he or someone else were leading it."[48]

Although he had served as Reagan's vice-president for the past eight years, Bush and his new team, which included Secretary of State James Baker and National Security Adviser Brent Scowcroft, wanted to reassess US-Soviet relations. In a February 15, 1989, memorandum called National Security Review-3, Bush noted that while "it would be unwise thoughtlessly to abandon policies that have brought us this far," he worried that the Soviet Union remained "an adversary with awesome military power whose interests conflict in important ways with ours... [m] y own sense is that the Soviet challenge may be even greater than before because it is more varied." Bush therefore tasked his national security team with determining the Soviet Union's domestic and foreign policy objectives, assessing the internal situation in the Soviet Union, and determining what short- and long-term policies toward Moscow would be most effective.[49]

Scowcroft scoffed at what the various agencies recommended to Bush, calling them "bureaucratic exercises" that "said do more of the same." The president dismissed the results as "status quo plus" that could not deal with the "radical change taking place in Eastern Europe." At the same time, Bush admitted that he "wanted to be careful. The traumatic uprisings in East Germany in 1953, Hungary in 1956, and Czechoslovakia in 1968 were constantly on my mind...I did not want to encourage a course of events which might turn violent and get out of hand which we couldn't—or wouldn't—support, leaving people stranded at the barricades." Scowcroft shared this caution. He subsequently ordered an NSC group headed by Soviet expert Condoleezza Rice to draft a shorter "think piece" about Gorbachev rather than a piece of grand strategy. Rice subsequently argued that the United States needed to move "beyond containment" by accelerating Eastern Europe's movement away from the Soviet bloc and convincing Gorbachev to move further toward the West. Scowcroft, Baker, and Bush accepted Rice's argument. Observers, in particular Gorbachev, noticed the so-called "pause" brought about by the Review and began to get impatient.[50]

In a series of speeches in April and May, Bush laid out his new policy. On April 17, he told an audience in Hamtramck, Michigan, a city with a large Polish-American population, that "liberty is an idea whose time has come in Eastern Europe." Furthermore, he stated that "the true source of tension" in the Cold War "is the imposed and unnatural division of Europe." More important, for the first time he publicly endorsed glasnost and perestroika. He praised the recent political agreement in Poland, which broadened the government to include Solidarity, as "a watershed in the postwar history of Eastern Europe." On May 12, he told graduates at Texas A&M University that he would move "beyond containment" by actively promoting "the integration of the Soviet Union into the existing international system" as long as it continued to move "toward greater openness and democratization."[51]

Events in China, meanwhile, convinced Bush that he must encourage political reform in Eastern Europe but not to the point of bloodshed. The economic reforms that Deng Xiaoping had instituted had not been matched by political reform. In the spring, students demonstrating for political liberalization were later joined by a cross-section of Chinese society, to the point where hundreds of thousands began to protest daily in Tiananmen Square in Beijing. In May, the Chinese government declared martial law. On June 3, soldiers began firing on protesters and tanks began to roll in to the Square. Hundreds were killed and thousands wounded in the massacre.

In July Bush and Gorbachev made dueling trips to Europe. Gorbachev was "mobbed by Germans" during his trip to West Germany, and he made more headlines during his July 6 address to the Council of Europe in Strasbourg. He offered immediate cuts in short-range nuclear missiles in return for a NATO pledge to negotiate, the goal being the elimination of those weapons.

Scowcroft said the proposal, as popular as it was, "was clearly designed to create mischief within NATO." This confirmed his contention that the United States should move "cautiously in respect to Gorbachev."

Bush shared Scowcroft's skepticism, and during visits to Poland and Hungary he said he "could support freedom and democracy," but in such a way "that would not make us appear to be gloating over Gorbachev's political problems with Party hard-liners as he moved away from the iron-fisted policies of his predecessors." In Gdansk, after meeting with both Jarulzeski and Walesa, he told a crowd of approximately 250,000 in front of the Solidarity Worker's Monument, "Your time has come...It is Poland's time of possibilities. It is Poland's time of destiny, a time when dreams can live again." In Hungary, he told an audience at Karl Marx University, "For the first time, the Iron Curtain has begun to part. And Hungary, your great country, is leading the way."[52]

Bush then flew from Budapest to a summit of the Group of 7 (G-7) Advanced Economies in Paris. During down times at the meeting, Bush, Baker, and Scowcroft began to believe that "the groundwork had been set for a face-to-face meeting with Gorbachev." Scowcroft recalled that the president believed "that things were moving too fast, that there was too much danger of misunderstanding." Initially he didn't even want to call it a summit, but rather "an exchange of views—not to make agreements, which is what summits usually are." Bush wrote a letter to Gorbachev proposing a meeting. The Soviet leader agreed but wanted the meeting to be held on neutral ground. For weeks various sites were proposed, but when Gorbachev announced a state visit to Italy in November, and Bush's brother "Bucky" spoke favorably of a recent visit to Malta, the administration began to consider the small nation in the Mediterranean as a potential site. When Scowcroft noted that Roosevelt and Churchill had met aboard a ship off Newfoundland during the Second World War, the president's interest in another history-making shipboard summit was piqued. A shipboard Summit off the coast of Malta, he suggested, could create the perfect climate for significant agreements to be reached. Gorbachev agreed to the idea in late summer.[53]

Events in the Soviet Union, meanwhile, showed that perestroika and glasnost had begun to take on lives of their own, and not always with positive results. On the positive side, on March 26, 1989, the Soviets held the first contested elections for the Congress of People's Deputies. Candidates debated on television, and the proceedings were not censored by the government. Even though most of the newly elected deputies were Communist Party members and the election was a far cry from Western standards, the fact that people with different views of socialism could air their differences showed that the Soviet system had begun to reform.

The economy continued to struggle, however, and unrest began to stir in the republics. On April 9, Tbilisi, Georgia, exploded. Tens of thousands of Georgians had rallied and called for Georgian independence. Soviet troops used batons, spades, and gas against the demonstrators. Nineteen people, seventeen of them women, died. The Georgian government, as well as Gorbachev, initially blamed the deaths on the demonstrators, but later admitted that the Soviet troops had overreacted. As Chernyaev noted in his diary: "In general, wherever you look…the country is in torment. The country is unwell. And glasnost is like a sick person's feverish delirium. As of yet, there are no signs of improvement."[54]

Eventually, Gorbachev declared a ban on the use of force against demonstrators, but his popularity started to decline. Nationalist sentiment continued to grow, however, especially after the three Baltic Republics—Estonia, Latvia, and Lithuania—began to make demands that ultimately led to calls for independence. Bush responded with National Security Directive 23 on September 22, which called for the "demilitarization of Soviet foreign policy," the "renunciation of the principle of class conflict," and "self-determination for the countries of East-Central Europe."[55]

The Eastern European nations also continued to liberalize. In March, Hungarian prime minister Miklós Németh had told Gorbachev that he intended to "completely remove the electronic and technological defenses from the Western and Southern borders of Hungary. They have outlived their usefulness." On June 27, Németh and his foreign minister, Gyula Horn, cut sections of the fence on Hungary's border with Austria, and presented Bush and Baker a piece of barbed wire during their July visit. In August, Németh repudiated Hungary's participation in the 1968 Warsaw Pact invasion of Czechoslovakia, and on September 10 he began to allow East Germans and "tourists" to cross the border. Many of these tourists traveled to Austria and ended up in West Germany. Another brain drain like the one that led to the construction of the Berlin Wall in 1961 had begun as approximately 13,000 East Germans escaped to West Germany. Czechoslovakian "tourists," meanwhile, crossed into East Germany.[56]

In September, civil unrest began in East Germany after the government banned travel to Hungary. A wave of popular protests led to the resignation of East German Head of State Erich Honecker, who had organized the construction of the Berlin Wall, on October 18. Replaced by Egon Krenz, the change failed to end the protests. On November 4 a half a million East Germans demonstrated for political change in Alexanderplatz in East Berlin. On November 9, Krenz decided to allow Czechoslovak refugees and East Germans interested in "private travel" to cross the East German border directly into West Germany.

That evening, East Germans began gathering at the Wall and at the six border checkpoints between East and West Germany and demanded that the guards open the gates. The guards appealed to their superiors, but hearing nothing, and overwhelmed by the sheer numbers of people, opened the checkpoints. Thousands began streaming through the checkpoints, climbing the Wall, and some began breaking off pieces of it with sledgehammers. Kohl called Bush to report "I've just arrived from Berlin.

It is like witnessing an enormous fair. It has the atmosphere of a festival. The frontiers are absolutely open. At certain points they are literally taking down the wall and building new checkpoints. At Checkpoint Charlie, thousands of people are crossing both ways."

Bush told Gorbachev "the U.S. will stay calm" and "will not be making exhortations about unification or setting any timetables. We will not exacerbate the problem by having the President of the United States posturing on the Berlin Wall." Hearing the news, Chernyaev wrote, "The Berlin Wall has collapsed. This entire era in the history of the socialist system is over."[57] The following weekend, bulldozers began demolishing the Wall, and within weeks, every communist government had collapsed.

During the night of December 1, aboard the USS *Belknap*, the flagship of the Sixth Fleet off the coast of Malta, Bush wrote in his diary that the Summit "has now taken on worldwide proportions. How do I feel? I feel confident. Our brief is good, and we're going to offer him certain things on the economy." Conceding that he had been "criticized for not doing enough," he now believed "things are coming our way, so why do we have to jump up and down, risk those things turning around and going the wrong direction?"[58]

The following morning, Bush and Gorbachev met for the first time since Governor's Island. Because the seas were so rough, Gorbachev had to host Bush on the *Maxim Gorky*, a Soviet cruise liner that could handle the seas better, rather than the naval cruiser *Slava*. Gorbachev began by welcoming the president and acknowledging that the Summit had occurred thanks to Bush's "initiative." He admitted that he was initially puzzled as to why Bush wanted the meeting, presumably given "the Pause" that Bush had implemented at the beginning of the year. But now he understood that "a lot is happening" and that they now needed "to find a dialogue commensurate with the pace of change. We need more working contacts," Gorbachev contended, because the "changes underway affect fundamental things." He and Bush needed "to be more active in developing personal contacts" so they could handle the new world situation.

Bush replied that he had changed "180 degrees on the need and benefit of such a meeting. That change of heart has been well received in my country for the most part." Acknowledging the changes in the world, he wanted "to be sure how you view them, including in Eastern Europe, and for you to understand the way I see things." He urged that sometime during the Summit that they meet alone with just one note taker. Recognizing that Gorbachev had feared that some in the United States wanted perestroika to fail, Bush assured him that "there are no serious elements" who felt that way, "and most Americans don't feel that way." His administration and most of the Congress "want to see you succeed."

Bush proceeded to lay out an ambitious agenda. After proposing another meeting for May 1990, he declared he wanted to waive Jackson–Vanik. But he needed Gorbachev to change Soviet emigration law, and the two nations would need to complete a trade agreement before he could grant Most-Favored Nation status. He asked that they begin the trade negotiations immediately so they could be completed by the 1990 Summit. He also wanted to "remove statutory restrictions on our ability to provide export credit guarantees." Bush made it clear that "these steps will not be presented as the superiority of one system over another," nor as a bailout. He wanted to implement a program of cooperation, not assistance, because he understood that the Soviet Union was a proud country that didn't need handouts.

Bush also explained that he had changed his mind and would now back the Soviet Union's application to be granted "observer status" at the General Agreement on Tariffs and Trade (GATT), the international organization that sets and administers world trading rules. This would allow Moscow to begin the process of moving its economy to one that was more market-based rather than its Marxist command economy.

After a short discussion about human rights and a list of Soviet citizens who wished to emigrate, Bush raised the "most contentious issue … having two countries identified with the USSR swimming against the tide in Central America is a great dividing wedge between us." The president of Costa Rica, Óscar Arias, had urged him to "ask President Gorbachev to get Fidel Castro to stop exporting revolution into these fragile democracies." Bush wanted a "frank" discussion about Cuba and Nicaragua, "the single most disruptive factor to a relationship that is going in the right direction." Some in the United States, he noted, could not understand why the Soviet Union continued to fund Castro and yet ask for credits from the United States. He understood that Nicaragua had "promised" Shevardnadze "not to ship arms" to rebels in Costa Rica, but nonetheless continued to do so. "Nicaragua," the President argued, "owes you an explanation." Only "honest elections in Nicaragua and a transfer of power" could fix the Central American problem. As for Castro, "t[h]e best thing would be if you gave him a signal that it would no longer be business as usual."

Turning to arms control, Bush said "I want to get rid of chemical weapons. I mean it." He offered "a concession." If Gorbachev agreed to Bush's chemical weapons initiative from the September UNGA session— he had proposed that the United States and Soviet Union destroy their chemical weapons stockpiles in the hopes that this would lead to a global ban on the weapons—he would "terminate the U.S. binary modernization program as soon as a global ban is in force."[59] Next, he wanted to complete a Conventional Forces in Europe (CFE) treaty, but that required "high-level political attention" from both nations, otherwise the negotiations would get "bogged down in the bureaucracies." He wanted to sign a CFE and START treaty in 1990.

In order to accomplish these two goals, they needed to concentrate on Air-Launched Cruise Missiles (ALCMs), non-deployed missiles, and telemetry encryption, and urged they be resolved by January. In another concession, he said he would order his negotiators to "lift the U.S.-proposed ban on mobiles and make acceptance of mobile ICBMs part of the negotiating text." He also asked Gorbachev to "consider ending modernization of the SS-18," the "only 'heavy' missile in either arsenal" and also offer "deeper reductions" in the SS-18 force. As for nuclear testing, he suggested that they sign the TTBT and PNET protocols at the proposed May Summit. Last, he suggested that the Soviet Union, like the United States, publicize "the details of your budget, force posture, and weapons figures" as a "trust-building measure."

Turning to "general points," he suggested they jointly propose that Berlin be the site of the 2004 Olympics, "a fitting symbol of the new era in East-West relations." He also acknowledged that they were both "getting hit hard" on "global climate change" and criticized those who wanted to "shut down the whole world" because of the issue. Still, he offered to host a conference and a separate White House meeting devoted to negotiating "a framework treaty on global climate change." He hoped Gorbachev would join such efforts. Last, he proposed they create a student exchange program so that undergraduates from each nation could study in the other.

Following Bush's lead, Gorbachev began with some general, "philosophic" remarks. He suggested that they "evaluate the period of the Cold War." Though he understood that they could not rewrite history, he claimed that it was "our privilege, even duty, to examine what happened." They had arrived at a "historic watershed" and must "address completely new problems, ones we did not anticipate or expect to become so acute." But they should look to the future, not to the past, and acknowledge that "not everything in the past was totally negative. We have avoided a big war for 45 years."

Still, they should acknowledge the folly of "reliance on force, on military superiority." They should never have confronted each other "based on our different ideologies," because they had "reached a dangerous point, and it is good that we stopped to reach an understanding." He now believed that "strategically and philosophically, the methods of the Cold War were defeated." It had become obvious that "people are having an impact" in each nation. They must "move toward each other." But he did worry about some Americans who still believed that the "policies of the Cold War were right; those policies should not change." He was heartened that Bush did not share these views. "We cannot," he proclaimed, "permit our nations to base their policies on illusions and mistakes regarding each other."

Furthermore, he argued "[t]here is a major regrouping in the world now. We are moving from a bipolar to a multipolar world." A more integrated Europe, Japan, India, and China—he urged that neither "try to exploit" China against the other—had become new and important factors in world affairs. But he warned that this regrouping "can be accompanied by disquieting trends." He noted that Eastern Europe's economy "is not much," yet it was receiving attention from around the world. Limited resources would also affect the world economy. However, he argued that the lingering mistrust between the United States and the Soviet Union remained the biggest disquieting trend. He called for "patterns of cooperation to take into account new realities." Speaking for himself, Gorbachev said he wanted the United States to be "a confident country which tackles its problems confidently: economic, technical, and social." To believe otherwise was "dangerous. It is dangerous to ignore or neglect the interests of the U.S."

But the United States, he warned, "must take into account the interests of others." He again raised the question of whether some Americans had "not entirely abandoned old approaches." While he conceded that "we had not entirely abandoned ours," he claimed that he "feels the U.S. wants to teach, to put pressure on others." He advised Bush to join him in building "bridges across rivers rather than parallel to them. This is very important," and he slapped the table with emphasis.

Bush replied that he hoped Gorbachev had noticed that "as dynamic change has accelerated in recent months, we have not responded with flamboyance or arrogance that would complicate USSR relations." While some had accused him of being "cautious and timid," he admitted to the former but not the latter. Instead "I had conducted myself in ways not to complicate your life. That's why I have not jumped up and down on the Berlin Wall."

Gorbachev recalled how the Reykjavik Summit represented "an intellectual breakthrough" that helped US-Soviet relations, and asked Bush to use "political will to influence U.S. business" to establish economic relations with his country. After essentially agreeing with Bush's points about high-level participation in the CFE and START negotiations, he suggested that they "take the world economy into perestroika." He recognized that "some in the U.S." would worry that we would "politicize" the international financial institutions since "we were ideological." But he argued "So were you. But it is a different time, and we will work on new criteria." He thanked Bush for his determination to help integrate the Soviet Union into the world economy and said "far-reaching laws" such as new emigration, freedom of conscience, and freedom of the press were moving forward in the Supreme Soviet.

Turning to Central America, he believed there had been a "misunderstanding. If we promise something to you, we always want to keep our pledges or you will not have trust in you. We want to convince you we are not engaged in political games." He denied providing weapons to Nicaragua and "appreciate[d]" that Congress had cut off funding to the contras. Moreover, Nicaragua leader Daniel Ortega and Castro insisted they were not sending weapons to El Salvador or Costa Rica. As long as "your position doesn't change," he promised, "ours won't." To call the Nicaraguan government Marxist was "ridiculous." The current government reflected Nicaragua's history, not a political ideology." As for Cuba, he said "no one can really give orders to Cuba," and claimed he didn't want "bridgeheads in Cuba or Central America. We don't need that. You must be convinced of that."

Gorbachev called Bush's proposal to end the production of binary chemical weapons "very important, so we will think it over. It certainly shows movement," but asked whether a ban would be done "through steps." Baker said that was correct and noted that the United States had traditionally supported "an effectively verifiable worldwide global ban" but found that verification was impossible to achieve. The United States would drop "further progress on verification" as long as the Soviets signed on to Bush's proposal. Baker suggested that they could agree on a goal of a worldwide ban of chemical weapons during the Summit, and Gorbachev said, "Let's get our experts together."

Gorbachev claimed that Bush's CFE proposal was "100% the same proposal we have been pushing." As for START, he said, "We need political will," but noted that Bush had not mentioned Submarine-Launched Cruise Missiles (SLCMs). With an agreement that covered SLCMs, they could have a START Treaty by June. But without them, "that would cause significant problems. You have a significant advantage." He noted that Scowcroft and his arms control advisor, Marshal Sergei Akhromeyev, had discussed this issue earlier; Bush suggested they talk more about it. Gorbachev acknowledged that in "all issues we have to be neck and neck. There are differences in the structure of our forces. But nuclear SLCMs are a serious factor if we reduce everything else while those remain without some SLCM constraints." He warned that the Supreme Soviet would not ratify a START Treaty without such constraints. Baker remarked "Come on. That's our argument," referring to Bush's own worries that Congress would not approve a START Treaty. Gorbachev ignored his comment and acknowledged Bush's proposals on nuclear testing and his request to publicize Soviet defense budget information.[60]

Bush recalled that he was "very pleased with this first session," but said that Gorbachev seemed "relieved" when they "spoke in private" for an hour afterward with only Scowcroft, Chernyaev, and their interpreters present.[61] The Soviet leader began by explaining that during his recent visit to Cuba, the talks "weren't simple. Castro expressed caution about our policy," despite Gorbachev's assurances that his "aims were good." Castro also asked him to "help normalize U.S.-Cuban relations." Moreover, he believed that Castro understood "that the world is changing dramatically but he had his own sense of dignity and pride. Raising the possibility" of normalizing relations with the United States "was not easy for him."

Bush replied, "Let's put all our cards on the table about Castro." Despite the feelings of the NATO allies and the United States left, "for the fledgling democracies in Latin America and the U.S. right it is a gut issue. Castro is like a sea anchor as you move forward and the Western Hemisphere moves. He is against all this—Eastern Europe and the Western Hemisphere."

He conceded that publicly, Latin American leaders "will not criticize a colleague." But Arias's "call was a clear indication that Castro is now totally isolated." In addition, Cuban émigrés in Florida "have strong emotions about this last dictator. We have had feelers from Castro," he contended, "but never with an indication of a willingness to change." Regarding Nicaragua, he acknowledged that Ortega was not a Marxist. However, he was "convinced that they are exporting revolution. They are sending weapons. I don't care what they have told you," they were backing the El Salvadoran guerillas. Only free, verifiable elections could fix Nicaragua.

Gorbachev replied that the Soviet government wondered whether there was "no barrier to the U.S. action in independent countries," and claimed that some of his compatriots believed that a "Bush Doctrine" had replaced the Brezhnev Doctrine.[62]

Bush disputed that his actions in the Philippines could be compared to the Soviet invasion of Czechoslovakia. A Colonel had wanted "to shoot his way to power," he said, and Filipino president Corazon Aquino, who had been democratically elected, had asked him to help prevent this rebellion. Gorbachev answered that his government now practiced "non-interference" in other nations' affairs and urged Bush to do so as well.

After the two leaders repeated their positions on Cuba, Gorbachev turned to Eastern Europe. He accused some American politicians of wanting European unity based on "Western values." This sounded like they wanted to "export" American ideology. More importantly, he worried that Kohl was "in too much of a hurry on the German question." This approach, he warned, "could damage things" and call into question whether a united Germany would be part of NATO or move "outside alliances."

Bush replied that he believed Kohl felt "an enormous emotional response to what has happened," but recognized that his allies had "some private reservations about reunification." Gorbachev said he knew of the latter sentiment and suggested they let "history decide the outcome." The president assured him he would "do nothing to recklessly try to speed up reunification," and suggested that Gorbachev ignore Kohl's emotional rhetoric. Gorbachev closed the session by remarking, "[t]he times we live in are of great responsibility—great opportunity but great responsibility."[63]

During a 75-minute lunch session, Gorbachev noted that Chernobyl had cost his government 8–10 billion rubles and a December 1988 earthquake in Soviet Armenia cost him 12–14 billion. When Bush said the United States savings and loan crisis could cost $50 billion, Gorbachev dismissed it as "not much considering the size of your economy." He noted that in Italy he had seen "lots of products and few customers. In our country, it is the opposite." The main problem, he maintained, was the "deformation" of the Soviet economy, and "the great ruble overhang," a phenomenon that occurred when Soviet governments and state enterprises could not accumulate enough rubles to pay wages and pensions. Citizens

FIGURE 6.2 *Bush and Gorbachev lunch aboard the* Maxim Gorky *during the* *Malta Summit. Scowcroft is on Bush's right. To Gorbachev's left is Alexander* *Yakovlev, the Party's chief ideologist, who backed Gorbachev's reforms. George* *H.W. Bush Presidential Library.*

could therefore not pay for goods and services. Soviet workers, Gorbachev further contended, needed "to learn how to work, to depend on themselves. Our society is changing and we must change our thinking."

The president empathized with Gorbachev, and noted that the recent visits to the Soviet Union by the Chair of the Federal Reserve, Alan Greenspan, as well as American businessmen, had been "very helpful." American business wanted increased trade with the Soviet Union, and more exchanges could only strengthen the overall Soviet-American relationship. Gorbachev replied "That is exactly what we favor." As long as Bush provided a "political statement in support of what we are doing," he expected business exchanges to flourish.

Baker recommended that Gorbachev explore gold backed bonds as instruments to contend with the ruble overhang. The Soviet leader said his government had begun "initial measures" to cut their deficit by 60 billion rubles, shift spending from the industrial and military sectors to consumer goods, and initiated an overall move to private property and market mechanisms. Bush extolled these efforts, and returned to the *Belknap* for a rest before their dinner meeting. However, the weather deteriorated, forcing them to cancel the evening meeting.[64]

That night Bush wrote that the meetings "went reasonably well." They had made "some progress on arms control; on what we can do for MFN, etc." But the weather, however, "really broke for the worst." The medical team gave him a patch behind his ear and he noted "the things really work—I'm blessed by not getting seasick." But he lamented "the best laid plans of men: Here we are, the two super power leaders several hundred yards apart, and we can't talk because of the weather."[65]

Overnight the storm weakened, and the second day of the Summit began with an hour-long conversation between the two leaders, Scowcroft, Chernyaev, and their interpreters. After Bush asked whether Gorbachev would use force to quell the unrest in the Baltics, Gorbachev explained that he had originally planned to deal with all the Republics "through greater autonomy." But his first priority was to save perestroika. He claimed that for the past fifty years the Soviet Union had been "integrated" and that in many of the Republics half the population were Russian. "Our country is that way," he argued, "and separatism brings out strong feelings by people." Despite recent "calming down," further unrest would create "all sorts of terrible fires." He warned that if Bush did not understand this dynamic, "it would spoil relations with the U.S. more than anything else."

Bush countered that if "you use force—you don't want to—that would create a firestorm." Gorbachev replied that he wanted "all to get equal treatment." For example, if he withdrew his troops from the Nagarno-Karabakh region in Azerbaijan, "we would have war. We are committed to a democratic process and we hope you understand." He was happy with what they had accomplished so far at Malta. "Destructive forces," he vowed, "should not be allowed to undermine this." Bush agreed that the Summit "is exactly what I hoped," and though he wanted to "move forward" on arms control, he would have to consult NATO on the specifics.[66]

The final meeting of the Malta Summit began with an extraordinary pledge from Gorbachev that "the Soviet Union will under no circumstances start a war—that is very important." Moreover, he no longer considered the United States "as an adversary and is ready to state that our relationship is cooperative." This was an astonishing repudiation of over four decades of Soviet national security policy and a concrete indication that the Cold War had ended. He also said he favored "joint efforts for verifiable limitation on nuclear weapons" and, most crucially, said the United States and the Soviet Union should "go beyond the arms race and renounce the creation of new weapons."

He complained, however, that while his country had switched to "a defensive military doctrine," the United States and NATO maintained a posture that was no longer justifiable." Moscow also remained concerned about the size of the US Navy, which had remained "outside the process of negotiations." Even worse, the US Navy still "surrounded" the Soviet Union with aircraft carriers and submarines. He conceded that the United States faced other "potential problems" that required a two-ocean navy, but he believed "we are entitled to expect that the naval threat should be reduced." He suggested that they begin naval talks after they concluded the CFE and START negotiations.

Regarding the current arms control talks, Gorbachev said he wanted to "get a handle on heavy bombers and ALCMs. If the current US proposal were adopted, the overall aggregate total" would result in a US advantage. He wanted equality, not "an advantage for ourselves." He repeated his call for a reduction in US SLCM arsenals so that they equaled the Soviet Union's. While he accepted that both sides should be able to include submarines in their strategic triads, he wanted to eliminate tactical nuclear forces at sea. He suggested that they could also eventually eliminate all sea-based nuclear forces.

Gorbachev also argued that the "problem is reducing not only weapons but people." He first proposed that each side reduce troop levels by 1 million, especially since "the people will find the decision to reduce weapons and not people unacceptable." Second, they should each reduce the number of troops deployed on foreign territory by 300,000. So far, however, NATO had rejected these proposals.

Shevardnadze raised Bush's earlier chemical weapon offer, and Bush not only reaffirmed the proposal but said he wanted to prevent proliferation of the weapons to countries such as Libya. Chemical weapons, he averred, were the "poor man's atomic bomb—horrible weapons." Gorbachev agreed with this position, said he opposed proliferation of such weapons, and called for more "specific" US-Soviet steps to achieve this goal.

When it was his turn, Bush steered the conversation to Europe. First, he called the suggestions to reduce both weapons and troops "very important." He noted that "Our military has clout with NATO" and could help convince the alliance to continue arms and troop reduction negotiations. Turning to Germany, he acknowledged his surprise at "the rapidity of change," but claimed "We cannot be asked to disapprove of German reunification." Still, he wanted to make sure he did not act "in a provocative way" given that German reunification had been a "highly sensitive" matter for the Soviet Union since 1945.

Gorbachev answered that he wanted changes in Europe to be governed "within the Helsinki context rather than ruining what has been done." He suggested a Helsinki II that could "improve stability and limit the damage and make sure not to ruin the instruments that have maintained the balance." Such a framework would "transform" the Warsaw Pact and NATO into organizations that would "change to a more political than a military nature." Eastern Europe, however, should be allowed to change on its own; it would be "dangerous…to try to force the issues—to push it artificially in order to achieve an advantage." While conceding the process would not be "painless," he nevertheless said "I look at things optimistically," because ultimately "things fall into place." The "deep and historical" changes occurring daily should not be undermined.

Bush replied that he understood Gorbachev's reservations about Western values when they were "presented with arrogance or chauvinistic pride." But the West considered glasnost a Western value, and Gorbachev should accept his support for glasnost in that spirit. When Gorbachev replied that each country had the right "to make its own choices," Bush reassured him "We don't differ. Self-determination is a value we endorse and it is openness that permits self-determination. Western values does not mean the imposition of our system."

After Baker conceded that "great nervousness" about German reunification existed because "no one wants the kind of Germany" from the 1930s and 1940s, Gorbachev pivoted to the Middle East. He asked what should be done about Palestine Liberation Organization (PLO) Chairman Yasser Arafat. Bush replied that he had received "some encouraging news" that Arafat "may be ready to go forward" with Egyptian president Hosni Mubarak's ten-point proposal aimed at achieving peace between Israel and the Palestinians. In the meantime, he believed Gorbachev should restore diplomatic relations with Israel and help the peace process along.

Gorbachev opined, "we have never had more favorable circumstances than now to settle the Middle East conflict" because the United States and the Soviet Union "were involved together." The United States had tried to go it alone for too many years, and he pledged he would "contribute constructively" to the process as a partner. He "welcome[d]" the new US–PLO dialogue, and promised to recognize Israel as soon as he saw "progress in the settlement" of the Arab–Israel dispute.

Bush applauded this, and raised the issue of Syrian interference in Lebanon. He said he supported the Tripartite Plan—an Arab-proposed ceasefire—which had been forestalled after Lebanese president René Moawad had been assassinated on November 22. Gorbachev pledged to support the Plan, and Shevardnadze said that the Syrians told him "they don't want to be in Lebanon permanently and are acting in the Tripartite spirit." Bush acknowledged the comments but noted no one could "dictate an outcome" in the dispute. Gorbachev remarked that they must cooperate in Lebanon, not dictate.

Gorbachev then asked Shevardnadze to talk about Afghanistan. The foreign minister said he wanted to concentrate on "the future instead of bickering about the past." He was interested in setting up elections and an international conference under UN auspices, and hoped that Bush would stop sending weapons to the Mujahideen in exchange for his country stopping weapons to the Afghan government. Gorbachev noted that he had completed the withdrawal of Soviet troops and a political settlement was now necessary.

The president said he wanted the Afghan situation settled, and did not want to see "a hostile regime on your border." Gorbachev countered that he didn't want the regime to be hostile to the United States either. Baker and Gorbachev then debated whether or not they could trust the current Afghan leader, Mohammad Najibullah, and whether Najibullah could successfully reconcile with the Mujahideen. Knowing that they had run out of time, Bush and Gorbachev agreed that they would cover Africa in their press event following this last meeting.[67]

During their joint press conference following the close of the Summit, Bush said "I am convinced that a cooperative U.S.-Soviet relationship can, indeed, make the future safer and brighter. And there is virtually no problem in the world, and certainly no problem in Europe, that improvement in the U.S.-Soviet relationship will not help to ameliorate." More cooperation, he contended, would establish "a lasting peace and transform the East-West relationship to one of enduring cooperation." For his part, Gorbachev praised their "open exchange of views" and remarked "We reaffirmed our former positions that all those acute issues must be resolved by political methods, and I consider that this was a very important statement of fact."[68]

Chernyaev called the joint press conference "extraordinary. Gorbachev appreciated the President's statement about his changed view of perestroika and relations with the Soviet Union." Bush and Baker's "concrete proposals" during the Summit "confirmed their resolve to begin a new stage in U.S.-Soviet relations." The Soviets believed that the Americans had spoken "if not as members of our leadership, then at least experts sincerely interested in our success." Baker said that the Malta Summit allowed Bush and Gorbachev to establish a "personal bond," signified that the "pause" had ended, and showed that the president "was fully engaged in support of perestroika."[69]

Over the next seven months, Bush, Gorbachev, and Kohl haggled over German reunification. Kohl initially said that Germans alone should decide their future. Gorbachev, on the other hand, wanted to internationalize the issue and have the Four Powers settle Germany as they had at Potsdam. Bush suggested a compromise, what he called the "Two Plus Four" plan, that would let the two Germanys decide internal issues of reunification, such as citizenship, currency, and the like, while the Four Powers would handle the external issues, such as diplomatic relations. Gorbachev agreed to the formula but continued to resist a formal reunification plan until the May 1990 Summit in Washington, when he acknowledged the fact that only Germans could determine their own future. In the final agreement, signed in Moscow on September 12, the four powers renounced their rights in Germany and Berlin. The reunified Germany agreed to uphold West Germany's signature of the NPT, declared that the former East Germany and Berlin would become a permanent nuclear-free zone, and reaffirmed the 1945 border with Poland. Reunification occurred on October 3, and on October 14 Germany and Poland signed the German-Polish Border Treaty, which officially acknowledged the border agreed to at Potsdam in 1945.

The May 1990 Washington summit was also notable in that the two leaders signed a trade agreement that included granting MFN status to the Soviet Union, provided that Gorbachev lifted his embargo on Lithuania. If he failed to do so, Bush said he would not forward the agreement to Congress for ratification. They also signed the 1990 Chemical Weapons Accord, which implemented Bush's proposal from Malta. The two nations pledged to halt production of chemical weapons and to begin destroying their respective stockpiles in 1993. More important, the Accord would be verified by OSIs.

On August 3, 1990, Baker and Shevardnadze publicly condemned Iraq's invasion of Kuwait in a joint statement. In his memoirs, Baker described this event as the moment the Cold War ended.[70] Just over forty years after the creation of a US-led UN force to drive North Korea out of South Korea, Bush and Baker convinced Gorbachev to approve a UN resolution approving a similar force to oust Iraq from Kuwait. After the coalition forced the Iraqi military out of Kuwait after four days of fighting in March 1991, Bush honored the resolution by refusing to march on Baghdad to overthrow the Iraqi dictator Saddam Hussein.

Perestroika, however, could not reform the Soviet system. Meanwhile, the Republics demanded further autonomy. In January 1991, Soviet troops fired on protesters in Lithuania, killing 14. The Soviet economy also continued to struggle. While wages and government spending increased, production declined, which led to inflation, which further destabilized the economy.

Many of Gorbachev's supporters began to turn to Boris Yeltsin, formerly the First Secretary of the Moscow Communist Party, whom they believed represented true reform. On June 12, 1991, Yeltsin defeated Gorbachev's candidate and became the first president of the Russian Soviet Republic. On July 23, plans to draft a Union Treaty that would replace the Soviet Union with a confederation that devolved more power to the individual republics began. Bush continued to support Gorbachev and on July 31 they signed the START treaty, another landmark arms control achievement that reduced the number of ICBMs in their respective arsenals.

On August 18, two days before the Union Treaty's scheduled signing, some of his opponents took advantage of the vacationing Gorbachev and staged a brief three-day coup. Television images of Soviet tanks surrounding the Kremlin were beamed around the world. Gorbachev, who had been detained in Crimea, watched his rival Yeltsin rally the anti-coup forces and the hundreds of thousands of demonstrators who turned out and removed the backers of the coup.

Shortly thereafter, Gorbachev, who had briefly returned to power, resigned as General Secretary. On September 2, Bush recognized the independence of the three Baltic states. By the end of October, the three officially declared their independence from the Soviet Union.

Gorbachev tried to hang on and proposed an updated version of the Union Treaty, but Yeltsin wanted an arrangement more like the British Commonwealth, where all the states in the arrangement kept their independence. In December, Yeltsin secretly met with the leaders of Ukraine and Belarus, who decided to dissolve the Soviet Union and create the Commonwealth of Independent States. The three leaders informed Bush, who said he would recognize the new arrangement. On December 21, every republic with the exception of Georgia signed the declaration. Gorbachev resigned five days later, and on December 25, 1991, the Soviet Union dissolved with a whimper.

Conclusion

In this analysis of six twentieth-century summits, I have tried to show the commonalities that bind these meetings that occurred over the course of the Cold War between the East and the West, democracy and capitalism. The Cold War has often been assumed to be a bipolar conflict between the United States and the Soviet Union, and indeed, this book shows that the competition between the two superpowers dominated the four-plus decades between 1945 and 1991. This is partly due to the fact that the Second World War fatally weakened the British, French, and other European empires, which left the United States and the Soviet Union as the only two nations with the desire to and that could afford to assume global responsibilities. No geographic region was immune from either the influence of or the competition between the superpowers. It is also a function of the way that the destructive power of atomic weapons fundamentally altered the international relations of the post–Second World War era. Looming over each and every Summit was the desire to limit and eventually reduce the threat of a global conflagration resulting from a nuclear war.

At the same time, the American and Soviet desire to compete for influence in and the allegiance of the Third or Developing World allowed the newly decolonized and independent nations of these regions to exercise agency in their own development and resist Washington's and Moscow's ability to influence their actions or determine their destinies. At Potsdam, Nationalist China was forced to make territorial concessions to the Soviet Union at the urging of its ostensible allies, the United States and Great Britain. But the People's Republic of China repudiated its "century of humiliation" after 1949 and quickly became an independent actor that made life difficult for both superpowers for the rest of the Cold War. The six Summits examined in this book therefore show both the ambitions and the limits of global power in the second half of the twentieth century.

At Potsdam, the United States and Great Britain clashed with the Soviet Union over competing visions of the postwar era. Truman, Churchill, and Atlee were determined to uphold the Yalta Agreements, but disagreed with Stalin over just what had been promised at the February 1945 meeting.

Stalin believed that he had secured 200 miles of German territory for Poland and expected $20 billion in reparations from Germany, while the Americans and British had assumed that the issues had been left to be decided at Potsdam. In the end, the three leaders compromised: Poland got the extra territory, but because of the humanitarian crisis created by the new land transfer, the Soviets lost the extra reparations they had anticipated. Truman wanted Stalin to uphold his promise to declare war on Japan, but the news of the successful test allowed him to take a tougher line with Stalin over Chinese territorial and political concessions. The three nations expected another "peace conference" to settle all the outstanding issues, which showed that they still expected to cooperate. The Cold War actually began after Potsdam.

The Bandung Summit, on the other hand, demonstrated that the nations of the Third World had become influential actors in the global Cold War. De-colonization and the rebellion against the European empires, embodied by the Korean, Indochina, and Algerian wars, had forced the United States and the Soviet Union to compete for influence in the Third World. The emergence of the People's Republic of China as a "third way" and its willingness to shed its ideological belief in "continuous revolution" in favor of cooperation with India, Burma, and Indonesia lent another dimension to what had become a multipolar Cold War. At the same time, influential nations in the Third World such as the regional SEATO and CENTO served as compelling checks on Jawaharlal Nehru's attempt to steer a neutralist path between the communist and capitalist blocs.

The 1972 Beijing Summit, meanwhile, showed that, despite the isolationism of the Cultural Revolution, Mao's China had become a significant player on the world scene. The United States and the PRC, for different reasons, wanted to improve relations with the other, and when the international atmosphere made it propitious to do so, they acted. Nixon had already made significant concessions regarding Taiwan in his first year in office. Mao, meanwhile, had determined that the Soviet Union had become his main enemy, and interpreted the invasion of Czechoslovakia as an attack on his legitimacy. The Summit, not surprisingly, showed that significant differences remained, especially over the US war in Vietnam, the status of the Korean peninsula, and Taiwan. That the two enemies that had been firing bullets at each other less than twenty years before could now sit down and rationally discuss contentious issues free from the highly charged rhetoric of the past showed that cooperation among the nuclear powers was possible.

The other summits follow the more traditional, bipolar model of Cold War summitry. Leaders of the United States and the Soviet Union grappled with the issue of nuclear weapons, whether or not superpower cooperation was possible in the nuclear age, and significant events in the Third World that threatened to drag the superpowers into armed conflict. The Glassboro Summit occurred in the immediate aftermath of the Six Day War between

Israel and its Arab neighbors, but Johnson and Kosygin had wanted to meet for some time to discuss the American war in Vietnam, the threat from China, and nuclear non-proliferation, and strategic arms limitations. The relationship between the two had been strained ever since the Cuban Missile Crisis, and although the Summit did not solve any of the critical issues—which were not truly solvable, but rather needed to be managed given the deep divides between the two adversaries—it served as a launching point for the process of détente that defined the 1970s. Johnson and Kosygin also made it clear that neither wanted war, an important point that the two nations often seemed to forget in their diplomatic encounters.

The Summit in Vienna in 1979, however, showed the limits of détente. An ailing yet still powerful Brezhnev and his American counterpart, Jimmy Carter, agreed that neither wanted war with the other—an important point, to be sure. But each leader defined détente differently. Brezhnev considered it a means for continued competition (and the fomenting of revolution) in the Third World, while Carter, ironically like his predecessors Nixon and Ford, believed it meant that the Soviets would behave like responsible members of a rational, cooperative international order. Although they signed the SALT II Treaty in Vienna, the two nations were really headed in different directions. Carter preferred to emphasize human rights, while Brezhnev wanted to reestablish the cozy relationship he had enjoyed with Nixon and Ford. The Soviet leader upbraided Carter for extending diplomatic recognition to China and criticized the Camp David Accords. Most important, he refused to move beyond mutually assured destruction (MAD) and dismissed the idea of reducing nuclear stockpiles as a non-starter.

Ten years later, however, the Cold War ended at the Malta Summit when Gorbachev, who had become Soviet General Secretary six years after Vienna, declared that he no longer considered the United States an adversary. Instead, he argued that the two superpowers should cooperate on a global basis. Events of the previous four years, of course, had made Malta possible. Reagan and Gorbachev's repudiation of MAD, embodied in START, the INF treaty, and the success of glasnost in the Soviet Union and liberalization in the Warsaw Pact countries, had led to the peaceful fall of the Berlin Wall just a few weeks earlier. Bush's desire to move "beyond containment" and encourage liberalization and his desire to help Moscow to become truly integrated in the international system in ways that Nixon and Kissinger could have only dreamed of—such as his support for the repeal of the Jackson–Vanik Act and his advice on how Gorbachev could contend with the ruble overhang—showed that he had overcome his earlier skepticism and embraced the idea of superpower cooperation.

What, then, can be said about summitry and the Cold War? Why did these meetings receive so much attention from the public and later, historians? Summits mattered because in the nuclear age—yes, even at Potsdam, when the atomic weapon had only been tested in a remote desert and not been used in warfare, the nuclear age had arrived—the public understood that their leaders possessed, as Truman said, weapons of "unusual destructive force." Nuclear weapons, and the rapid development of new, more destructive, and more accurate weapons, made diplomacy even more important. The risks associated with mistakes, miscalculations, belligerency, and being allied with nations that seemed almost determined to drag the superpowers into proxy wars that could escalate into direct confrontation made the idea of summits after Hiroshima and Nagasaki not only more attractive but crucial to the survival of the world.

Although ideology remained important—democracy and communism remained compelling philosophies—survival became paramount. Control of nuclear weapons and limitation of stockpiles, even after both sides had accumulated thousands of weapons, made non-proliferation and the idea of arms limitations seem attractive. At the same time, the idea of MAD seemed to make sense. The fact that both sides could destroy each other many times over compelled them to step back from the nuclear brink whenever such a confrontation seemed either imminent or possible. The nations of the developing world, meanwhile, understood the danger of nuclear weapons, and feared that they would suffer from a direct attack or from the fallout associated with nuclear explosions.

These summits also demonstrate the importance of personal interaction between world leaders. No matter how many letters or telegrams leaders exchanged, or how many times a leader met with the adversary's ambassador; nor the number of secret "back channel" meetings that occurred between ambassadors and other representatives, there was no substitute for personal meetings between leaders. The commitment of leaders to high-level, personal diplomacy signaled the seriousness with which leaders took summitry and helped to overcome mistrust and misunderstanding, and ultimately create the safest world possible. By 1989, the Cold War ended without a nuclear war, to a large measure due to the summits convened by world leaders in the preceding decades.

NOTES

Introduction

1   David Reynolds, *Summits: Six Meetings that Shaped the Twentieth Century* (New York: Basic Books, 2007), pp. 1–2. Reynolds analyzes the following summits: Munich 1938, Yalta 1945, Vienna 1961, Moscow 1972, Camp David 1979, and Geneva 1985.

2   George W. Ball, *Diplomacy for a Crowded World: An American Foreign Policy* (Boston: Little Brown and Co., 1976), pp. 31–39. That Ball does not consider that Soviet, Chinese, and other non-English speaking leaders would be concerned about the accuracy of American interpreters is telling.

3   G.R. Berridge, *Diplomacy: Theory and Practice* (New York: Prentice Hall, 1995), pp. 79–83.

4   Elmer Plischke, *Diplomat in Chief: The President at the Summit* (New York: Praeger Publishers), pp. 456–65.

5   David H. Dunn, "How Useful is Summitry?" in David H. Dunn, ed., *Diplomacy at the Highest Level: The Evolution of International Summitry* (New York: St. Martin's Press, 1996), pp. 247–60.

6   Keith Hamilton and Richard Langhorne, *The Practice of Diplomacy: Its Evolution, Theory and Administration* (London: Routledge, 1995), pp. 222–24.

7   Odd Arne Westad, *The Global Cold War* (New York: Cambridge University Press, 2007).

Chapter 1

1   William Manchester, *Last Lion: Winston Spencer Churchill; Alone: 1932–1940* (New York: Dell Publishing, 1988), pp. 333–79, 674–84.

2   Reynolds, *Summits*, pp. 122–44.

3   Michael Dobbs, *Six Months in 1945: FDR, Stalin, Churchill and Truman, From World War to Cold War* (New York: Vintage Books, 2012), pp. 63–64, 84–85.

4   Ibid., pp. 158–65.

5   Geoffrey Roberts, *Stalin's Wars: From World War to Cold War, 1939–1953* (New Haven: Yale University Press, 2006), p. 267.

6   Truman quoted in David McCullough, *Truman* (New York: Simon and Schuster, 1992), pp. 362–77.

7   Albert Resis, ed., *Molotov Remembers: Inside Kremlin Politics: Conversations with Felix Chuev* (Chicago: Ivan R. Dee, 1993), p. 55 and Roberts, *Stalin's Wars*, pp. 269–70.

8   "Telegram from Churchill to Truman," May 6, 1945 and "Telegram from Truman to Churchill," May 9, 1945, in *Foreign Relations of the United States 1945*, Vol. I, Conference of Berlin (The Potsdam Conference) (Washington: Government Printing Office, 1960), pp. 3–4. (hereafter *FRUS*, Year, Vol.)

9   "Telegram 40 from Churchill to Truman," May 11, 1945, "Telegram 41 from Churchill to Truman," May 11, 1945, and "Telegram 39 from Truman to Churchill," May 14, 1945, in ibid., pp. 5–8, 11.

10 "Memoranda of Conversation between Hopkins, Stalin, Harriman, Bohlen, Molotov, and Nikolai Pavlov [Stalin's Personal Secretary and Interpreter]," May 26 and May 28, 1945, ibid., pp. 31, 41–52. After the Hopkins visits, Truman wrote in his diary "I'm not afraid of Russia. They've always been our friends and I can't see why they shouldn't always be." Robert H. Ferrell, ed., *Off the Record: The Private Papers of Harry S Truman* (New York: Harper & Row, 1980), p. 44.

11 Davies and Eden quoted in Dobbs, *Six Months in 1945*, p. 219.

12 "Davies's Report to Truman," June 12, 1945, *FRUS*, Vol. I, Conference of Berlin, pp. 177–78.

13 "Telegram from Grew to Harriman," June 23, 1945, "Telegram 83 from Truman to Churchill," July 2, 1945, "Telegram 101 from Churchill to Truman," July 3, 1945, and "Telegram 85 from Truman to Churchill," July 3, 1945, in ibid., pp. 724, 733–34.

14 "Telegram from Murphy to Grew," July 7, 1945, ibid., pp. 755–56.

15 "Telegram from Grew to Murphy," July 9, 1945, ibid., pp. 756–57.

16 "Telegram from Churchill to Halifax," July 6, 1945, "Telegram from Churchill to Halifax," July 6, 1945, "Telegram from Lord Halifax to Eden," July 7, 1945, and "Telegram from Eden to Halifax," July 10, 1945, in Foreign and Commonwealth Office, *Documents on British Policy Overseas* Vol. I, Conference at Potsdam July–August 1945 (London: Her Majesty's Stationery Office, 1984), pp. 2–7, 31–33, 124 (hereafter *DBPO*).

17 "Joint Intelligence Committee Political Intelligence Report," July 9, 1945, and "Telegram from Kerr to Eden," July 10, 1945, ibid., pp. 93–98, 141–48.

18 Byrnes, Truman, and Stimson, quoted in Dobbs, *Six Months in 1945*, pp. 237–40.

19 "Minutes of a Combined Policy Committee Meeting," July 4, 1945 and "Minutes of Combined Committee Meeting," July 4, 1945, *FRUS* 1945, Vol. I, Conference of Berlin, p. 221, "Minute from [British Science Advisor] Lord Cherwell to Churchill," July 12, 1945, *DBPO* Vol. I, Conference at Potsdam July–August 1945, p. 211.

20 David Holloway, *Stalin and the Bomb: The Soviet Union and Atomic Energy, 1939–1956* (New Haven: Yale University Press, 1994), pp. 103–7.

21 "Minutes of Meeting Held at the White House," June 18, 1945 and "Memorandum from Stimson to Truman," July 2, 1945, *FRUS* 1945, Vol. I, Conference of Berlin, pp. 889–92, 903–10.

22 "Briefing Book Paper: "Special Manchurian Problems," undated and "Telegram from Harriman to Truman and Byrnes," July 12, 1945, ibid., pp. 858–60. It is important to note, however, that Soong told Kerr "he was sore about the terms of the Yalta Agreement on the Far East and about China's not having been consulted," and claimed that he had "only learned about Yalta from Truman in June." Still, "they were realists enough

to recognise that it had been done and signed by the three Heads of Governments, and that China would have to face it or, at any rate, some form of it." The concessions "touched China very painfully." See "Minute from Kerr to Eden," July 18, 1945 in *DBPO* Vol. I, Conference at Potsdam July–August 1945, pp. 364–66.

23 Truman, quoted in McCullough, *Truman*, p. 403.

24 Dobbs, *Six Months in 1945*, pp. 292–93.

25 Ibid., pp. 293–94.

26 McCullough, *Truman*, pp. 414–15 and Gromyko, *Memoirs*, pp. 105–06.

27 "Memorandum of Conversation between Truman and Stalin," July 17, 1945, in *FRUS 1945*, Vol. II, Conference of Berlin, pp. 1582–87, "Diary," July 17, 1945, in Ferrell, *Off the Record*, p. 53, and "Letter from Truman to Bess Truman," July 18, 1945, in Robert Ferrell, ed., *Dear Bess: The Letters from Harry to Bess Truman, 1910–1959* (Columbia: University of Missouri Press, 1998), p. 519.

28 Dobbs, *Six Months in 1945*, pp. 297–98 and McCullough, *Truman*, pp. 418–19.

29 "Memorandum of Conversation, First Plenary Meeting between Truman, Churchill, and Stalin," July 17, 1945, in *FRUS 1945*, Vol. II, Conference of Berlin, pp. 52–59 . For the Soviet record, see "Memorandum of Conversation, First Plenary Meeting between Truman, Churchill, and Stalin," July 17, 1945, in *Tehran, Yalta, and Potsdam Conferences* (Moscow: Progress Publishers, 1969), p. 147. (hereafter *TYP*)

30 "Record of a Private Talk between Churchill and Stalin," after plenary, July 17, 1945, in *DBPO* Vol. I, Conference at Potsdam July–August 1945, pp. 348–50. Eden, however, argued that "The truth is that on any and every point, Russia tries to seize all that she can and she uses these meetings to grab as much as she can…To meet this situation we have not many cards in our hand. One of them, however, is the possession of the German Fleet. I agree with the Admiralty view that it would be best if this Fleet were sunk." If they chose not to sink it, he argued that Britain should still not "yield a single German ship in our possession until we have obtained satisfaction for our interests, which the Russians are treating with contempt in all the countries where their authority holds sway." See "Minute from Eden to Churchill," July 17, 1945, ibid., pp. 352–54.

31 "Summarized Note of Churchill-Truman Conversation," July 18, 1945, ibid., pp. 367–71.

32 "Memorandum of Conversation between Truman and Stalin," July 18, 1945, 3:04 p.m., *FRUS 1945*, Vol. II, The Conference of Berlin (The Potsdam Conference), pp. 1587–88.

33 "Memorandum of Conversation, Second Plenary Meeting between Truman, Churchill, and Stalin," July 18, 1945, ibid., pp. 88–94. For the Soviet version, see "Memorandum of Conversation, First Plenary Meeting between Truman, Churchill, and Stalin," July 18, 1945, in *TYP*, p. 162.

34 "Letter from Truman to Bess Truman," July 20, 1945, in Ferrell, ed., *Dear Bess*, p. 520.

35 Stimson quoted in Holloway, *Stalin and the Bomb*, p. 116 and "Diary Entry," July 18, 1945, in Ferrell, ed., *Off the Record*, pp. 55–56.

36 "Memorandum of Conversation, Fifth Plenary Meeting between Truman, Churchill, and Stalin," July 21, 1945, in *FRUS 1945*, Vol. II, Conference of Berlin, pp. 203–15.

37   Dobbs, *Six Months in 1945*, pp. 239–41.

38   "Memorandum of Conversation, Sixth Plenary Meeting between Truman, Churchill, and Stalin," July 22, 1945, in *FRUS* 1945, Vol. II, Conference of Berlin, pp. 244–60.

39   "Memorandum of Conversation, Seventh Plenary Meeting between Truman, Churchill, and Stalin," July 23, 1945, ibid., pp. 299–311.

40   Stimson quoted in McCullough, *Truman*, pp. 436–37 and Truman quoted in Dobbs, *Six Months in 1945*, p. 327.

41   "Memorandum of Conversation, Eighth Plenary Meeting between Truman, Churchill, and Stalin," July 24, 1945, in *FRUS* 1945, Vol. II, Conference of Berlin, pp. 357–68.

42   Truman, Churchill, and Stalin, quoted in Dobbs, *Six Months in 1945*, pp. 329–31 and Resis, ed., *Molotov Remembers*, pp. 55–57.

43   See "Minute from Atlee to Churchill," and "Memorandum by the United States Delegation," July 23, 1945, in *DBPO* Vol. I, Conference at Potsdam July–August 1945, pp. 573–74, 598.

44   "Memorandum of Conversation, Ninth Plenary Meeting between Truman, Churchill, and Stalin," July 25, 1945, in *FRUS* 1945, Vol. II, Conference of Berlin, pp. 381–88.

45   For more on Atlee and Bevin, see Wilson D. Miscamble, *From Roosevelt to Truman: Potsdam, Hiroshima, and the Cold War* (New York: Cambridge University Press, 2007), p. 204.

46   "Memorandum of Conversation between Byrnes and Molotov," July 27, 1945, in *FRUS* 1945, Vol. II, Conference of Berlin, pp. 449–52.

47   "Memorandum of Conversation, Tenth Plenary Meeting between Truman, Atlee, and Stalin," July 28, 1945, ibid., pp. 459–65.

48   "Memorandum of Conversation between Truman, Byrnes, and Molotov," July 29, 1945 and "Memorandum of Conversation between Byrnes and Molotov," July 30, 1945, ibid., pp. 471–76, 480–83. Stalin, Tsuyoshi Hasegawa has convincingly argued, "was tormented by the possibility that the war might be over before the Soviet troops crossed the Manchurian border." Truman, on the other hand, now "saw Stalin not as an ally committed to the common cause of defeating Japan, but as a competitor in the race to see who could force Japan to surrender." See Hasegawa, *Racing the Enemy: Stalin, Truman, and the Surrender of Japan* (Cambridge: Harvard University Press, 2005), pp. 132–33, 39.

49   "Tenth Meeting of the Foreign Ministers," July 30, 1945, in *FRUS* 1945, Vol. II, Conference of Berlin, pp. 483–97.

50   Memorandum of Conversation, Eleventh Plenary Meeting between Truman, Atlee, and Stalin," July 31, 1945, ibid., pp. 510–28.

51   Dobbs, *Six Months in 1945*, p. 343.

52   Miscamble, *From Roosevelt to Truman*, pp. 172–73, Dobbs, *Six Months in 1945*, pp. 342–44, McCullough, *Truman*, 451, and Memorandum of Conversation, Twelfth Plenary Meeting between Truman, Atlee, and Stalin," August 1, 1945, in *FRUS* 1945, Vol. II, Conference of Berlin, pp. 565–78.

53   Memorandum of Conversation, Thirteenth Plenary Meeting between Truman, Atlee, and Stalin," August 1, 1945, in *FRUS* 1945, Vol. II, Conference of Berlin, pp. 586–96.

54   "Protocol of Proceedings of the Berlin Conference," August 1, 1945, ibid., pp. 1477–98.

55 "Letter from Atlee to Churchill," August 1, 1945, in *DBPO* Vol. I, The Conference at Potsdam July–August 1945, pp. 1143–44, Molotov quoted in Roberts, *Stalin's Wars*, p. 279, and Truman quoted in McCullough, *Truman*, p. 451.
56 McCullough, *Truman*, pp. 454–61 and Chen Jian, *Mao's China and the Cold War* (Chapel Hill: The University of North Carolina Press, 2001), p. 27.
57 Roberts, *Stalin's Wars*, pp. 271–72.
58 Dobbs, *Six Months in 1945*, pp. 310–19, 346–48 and Norman M. Naimark, *The Russians in Germany, 1945–1949* (Cambridge: Harvard University Press, 1995).
59 John Lewis Gaddis, *George F. Kennan: An American Life* (New York: Penguin Books, 2011), pp. 218–22.
60 Truman and Kennan quoted in ibid., pp. 253–62, 280–87.

Chapter 2

1 Westad, *Global Cold War*, p. 99.
2 NSC 68, "United States Objectives and Programs for National Security", April 14, 1950, in *FRUS 1950*, National Security Affairs; Foreign Economic Policy, pp. 234–96.
3 Jian, *Mao's China and the Cold War*, p. 7.
4 Chen Jian, "The Sino-Soviet Alliance and China's Entry into the Korean War," Cold War International History Project Working Paper 1 (Washington, DC: Woodrow Wilson International Center for Scholars, 1992), pp. 21–25. (hereafter CWIHP)
5 Jian, *Mao's China and the Cold War*, pp. 91–96.
6 Ibid., pp. 118–27.
7 William I. Hitchcock, *France Restored: Cold War Diplomacy and the Quest for Leadership in Europe, 1944–1954* (Chapel Hill: The University of North Carolina Press, 1998), pp. 116–17.
8 See Chris Tudda, *Truth is our Weapon: The Rhetorical Diplomacy of Dwight D. Eisenhower and John Foster Dulles* (Baton Rouge: Louisiana State University Press, 2006), p. 57.
9 Jian, *Mao's China and the Cold War*, pp. 165–67.
10 Eisenhower, quoted in Frederik Logevall, *Embers of War: The Fall of an Empire and the Making of America's Vietnam* (New York: Random House, 2012), pp. 338–58.
11 "United States Delegation Record of the Fifth Restricted Meeting of the Berlin Conference," February 17, 1954, in *FRUS 1952–1954*, Vol. VII, Germany and Austria, Part 1, 1142–48 and "Department of State Press Release," February 18, 1954, in *FRUS 1952–1954*, Vol. XIII, Indochina, Part 1, pp. 1057–58.
12 Logevall, *Embers of War*, pp. 383–94.
13 Bidault, quoted in Jian, *Mao's China and the Cold War*, p. 135.
14 "Memorandum of Discussion at the 190th Meeting of the National Security Council," March 25, 1954, "Telegram from Dulles to the Embassy in London," April 4, 1954 (which contains Eisenhower's letter to Churchill), in *FRUS 1952–1954*, Vol. XIII, Indochina, Part 1, pp. 1163–68, and Churchill, quoted in Logevall, *Embers of War*, p. 505.

15 Qiang Zhai, *China and the Vietnam Wars, 1950–1975* (Chapel Hill: The University of North Carolina Press, 2000), p. 53.

16 Ronald C. Keith, *The Diplomacy of Zhou Enlai* (New York: St. Martin's Press, 1989), 117–19. The text of the Sino-Indian Agreement is available on the journalist Claude Arpi's website at http://www.claudearpi.net/maintenance/ uploaded_pics/ThePancheelAgreement.pdf (accessed July 17, 2014) (hereafter Arpi website).

17 Xu Jingli, *Jiemi Zhongguo Waijiao Dangan* [Declassifying Chinese Diplomatic Files] (Beijing: Zhongguo Dangan Chubanshe, 2005), pp. 276–79 and Ji Chaozhu, *The Man on Mao's Right: From Harvard Yard to Tiananmen Square: My Life Inside China's Foreign Ministry* (New York: Random House, 2008), pp. 126–27. I am grateful to Yafeng Xia for alerting me about Xu Jingli's work.

18 "Memorandum of Conversation between Dulles and Eden," April 25, 1954, and "Telegram from Dulles to the Department of State," April 26, 1954, in *FRUS 1952–1954*, Vol. XVI, The Geneva Conference, pp. 553–57, 570–71.

19 Logevall, *Embers of War*, pp. 524–58.

20 Nehru and Ali, quoted in Disha Jani, "On-Stage, Off-Stage: Jawaharlal Nehru, Diplomacy, and the Indochina Conflict, 1954–1955," December 4, 2013, https://www.academia.edu/6532548/On-Stage_Off-Stage_Jawaharlal_Nehru_ Diplomacy_and_the_Indochina_Conflict_1954-1955 (accessed July 13, 2014) and Ali, quoted in "Telegram from Colombo to the Department of State," April 29, 1954, in *FRUS 1952–1954*, Vol. XVI, The Geneva Conference, pp. 610–11.

21 Logevall, *Embers of War*, p. 563 and Zhai, *China and the Vietnam Wars, 1950–1975*, pp. 52–55.

22 "Memorandum of Discussion at the 202d Meeting of the National Security Council," June 17, 1954, in *FRUS 1952–1954*, Vol. XIII, Indochina, Part 2, pp. 1713–18.

23 Dulles, quoted in Logevall, *Embers of War*, p. 593.

24 "Memorandum of Conversation between Nehru and Zhou," first meeting, June 25, 1954, Arpi website. In their fifth meeting on June 28, Nehru said the "United States are occupying an extreme position and they do not want to change that position either by themselves or by others. They would like surrender and not a settlement. Other countries like the UK and France are more realistic and want a settlement."

25 "Memorandum of Conversation between Nehru and Zhou," fourth meeting, June 26, 1954, ibid. and Keith, *The Diplomacy of Zhou Enlai*, p. 76.

26 "Minutes of the First Meeting between Premier Zhou Enlai and Prime Minister of Burma U Nu," June 28, 1954, in Chen Jian, ed., *Bandung as a Turning Point in Chinese and Cold War History*, CWIHP, forthcoming publication.

27 "Minutes of the Second Meeting between Premier Zhou Enlai and Prime Minister of Burma U Nu," June 29, 1954, ibid. Zhou also stated "We are not willing to see our neighbors allow foreign interventionists to establish military bases. Burma, India and Indonesia do not agree with the United States organizing an invasive bloc in Southeast Asia and oppose the United States' establishment of military bases."

28 Logevall, *Embers of War*, pp. 569–612.

29 Mao, quoted in Jian, *Mao's China and the Cold War*, pp. 168–69.

30 "Memorandum of Discussion at the 195th Meeting of the National Security Council," May 6, 1954, in *FRUS, 1952–1954*, Vol. XII, East Asia and the Pacific Part 1, pp. 452–59. In 1951, Australia, the United States, and New Zealand signed a similar security treaty, ANZUS.

31 Jawaharlal Nehru, "Speech before Parliament," September 29, 1954, in Nehru, *Selected Works of Jawaharlal Nehru, Second Series, Volume 26: 1 June 1954–30 September 1954* (New Delhi: Oxford University Press, 2002), pp. 318–332. (hereafter *SWJN*)

32 "Memorandum from Acting Secretary of Defense Robert Anderson to Eisenhower," September 3, 1954, "Memorandum of Discussion at the 214th Meeting of the National Security Council," September 12 and "Telegram from Dulles to the Department of State," September 4, 1954, in *FRUS 1952–1954*, Vol. XIV, Part 1, China and Japan, pp. 556–57, 560, 613–24.

33 "Memorandum of Conference between Dulles and Eisenhower," October 18, 1954," and "Telegram from Dulles to the Department of State," October 21, 1954, ibid., pp. 770–71.

34 "Minutes of Chairman Mao Zedong's First Meeting with Nehru," October 19, 1954, 11:15 am–12:30 pm, in Jian, ed., *Bandung as a Turning Point in Chinese and Cold War History.*

35 "Minutes of the First Meeting between Premier Zhou Enlai and Nehru," October 19, 1954, 7–11:30 p.m., ibid.

36 "Minutes of Premier Zhou Enlai's Second Meeting with Nehru," October 20, 1954, ibid.

37 Ang Cheng Guan, "The Bandung Conference and the Cold War International History of Southeast Asia," in See Seng Tan and Amitav Acharya, eds., *Bandung Revisited: The Legacy of the 1955 Asian-African Conference for International Order* (Singapore: National University of Singapore, 2008), pp. 28–29 and Roeslan Abdulgani, *Bandung Connection: The Asia-Africa Conference in Bandung in 1955* (Jakarta: Gunung Agung, 1981), pp. 33–35.

38 Carlos P. Romulo, *Meaning of Bandung* (Chapel Hill: The University of North Carolina Press, 1956), p. 5.

39 On Nehru's motives for inviting Japan, see Kweku Ampiah, *Political and Moral Imperatives of the Bandung Conference of 1955: The Reactions of the US, UK and Japan* (Kent: Global Oriental, 2007), p. 32.

40 "Memorandum from G.E. Crombie to Eden," November 18, 1954, Dominions Office and Commonwealth Relations Office: Original Correspondence. Far East and Pacific Department. Afro-Asian Conference 1955, Bandung, DO 35/6096, The National Archives, United Kingdom (hereafter UKNA).

41 "Telegram from the British Embassy in Washington to the Foreign and Commonwealth Office," January 27, 1955, ibid. and "Circular Telegram From the Department of State to Certain Diplomatic Missions," February 25, 1955, in *FRUS 1955–1957*, Vol. XXI, East Asian Security; Cambodia; Laos, pp. 50–54.

42 Richard Wright, *Color Curtain: A Report on the Bandung Conference* (Jackson: University of Mississippi Press, 1995), reprint of 1956 edition published by World Press, p. 12.

43 Abdulgani, *Bandung Connection*, p. 48.

44 Ibid., pp. 71–72 and Keith, *The Diplomacy of Zhou Enlai*, pp. 81–82.

45 "Summary of the Talks between Premier Zhou and Nehru and U Nu," April 16, 1955, in Jian, ed., *Bandung as a Turning Point in Chinese and Cold War History*.

46 Abdulgani, *Bandung Connection*, pp. 77–79.

47 Wright, *Color Curtain*, pp. 133–34.

48 "Let a New Asia and a New Africa be Born," Opening Address by President Sukarno, April 18, 1955, in Centre for the Study of Asian-African and Developing Countries, *Collected Documents of the Asian-African Conference, April 18–24, 1955* (Jakarta: Agency for Research and Development, The Department of Foreign Affairs, 1983), pp. 3–10.

49 "Address by Ali Sastroamidjojo," April 18, 1955, ibid., pp. 15–19.

50 Romulo, *Meaning of Bandung*, p. 11.

51 "Main Speech by Premier Chou En-Lai" and "Supplementary Speech by Chou En-Lai," April 19, 1955, in Foreign Ministry of the People's Republic of China, *China and the Asian-African Conference (Documents)* (Beijing: Foreign Languages Press, 1955), pp. 9–27.

52 Abdulgani, *Bandung Connection*, pp. 108–10.

53 Romulo, *Meaning of Bandung*, pp. 9–10 and Abdulgani, *Bandung Connection*, pp. 115–19.

54 Nehru, "Problems of Dependent Peoples," April 22, 1955, in *SWJN* Second Series, Vol. 28, February 1–May 31, 1955, pp. 100–06.

55 Abdulgani, *Bandung Connection*, pp. 137–40.

56 Nehru, "World Peace and Cooperation," April 22, 1955, in *SWJN* Second Series, Vol. 28, February 1–May 31, 1955, pp. 106–13.

57 Abdulgani, *Bandung Connection*, pp. 144–45.

58 Romulo, *Meaning of Bandung*, p. 33 and Abdulgani, *Bandung Connection*, pp. 144–45.

59 "PRC Delegation Head Premier Zhou Enlai's Speech at the Political Committee of the Afro-Asian Conference," April 23, 1955, in Jian, ed., *Bandung as a Turning Point in Chinese and Cold War History*, and Romulo, *Meaning of Bandung*, pp. 18–19.

60 Nehru, "The Policy of Friendly Coexistence," April 23, 1955, in *SWJN* Second Series, Vol. 28, February 1–May 31, 1955, pp. 114–24.

61 Abdulgani, *Bandung Connection*, pp. 151–52.

62 Nehru, "A Historic Milestone in Cooperation," April 24, 1955, in *SWJN* Second Series, Vol. 28, February 1–May 31, 1955, pp. 125–28.

63 "Final Communiqué of the Asian-African conference of Bandung," April 24, 1955, in Ministry of Foreign Affairs, Republic of Indonesia, ed., *Asia-Africa Speak from Bandung* (Djakarta: Ministry of Foreign Affairs, 1955), pp. 161–169.

64 For more on the Suez crisis and its aftermath, see Keith Kyle, *Suez: Britain's End of Empire in the Middle East*, 2nd ed. (New York: I.B. Tauris, 2002) and Michael B. Oren, *Six Days of War: June 1967 and the Making of the Modern Middle East* (New York: Presidio Press, 2002), pp. 10–12.

65 For Kennedy's and MacMillan's speeches, see Philip E. Muehlenbeck, *Betting on the Africans: John F. Kennedy's Courting of African Nationalist Leaders* (New York: Oxford University Press, 2012), pp. 36, 178.

Chapter 3

1 Günter Bischof and Saki Dockrill, eds., *Cold War Respite: The Geneva Summit of 1955* (Baton Rouge: Louisiana State University Press, 2000).

2 Philip Nash, *The Other Missiles of October: Eisenhower, Kennedy, and the Jupiters 1957–1964* (Chapel Hill: The University of North Carolina Press, 1997).

3 KennethOsgood, *Total Cold War: Eisenhower's Secret Propaganda Battle at Home and Abroad* (Lawrence: The University Press of Kansas, 2006).

4 For a discussion of the U-2 crisis, see Michael Beschloss, *Mayday: Eisenhower, Khrushchev and the U-2 Affair* (New York: Harper and Row, 1988).

5 See Howard Jones, *Bay of Pigs* (New York: Oxford University Press, 2008).

6 For the Vienna Summit, see Reynolds, *Summits*, 163–221. For the construction of the Berlin Wall, see Frederick Kempe, *Berlin 1961: Kennedy, Khrushchev, and the Most Dangerous Place on Earth* (New York: Berkeley Books, 2011).

7 For more on Cuba, see Aleksandr Fursenko and Timothy Naftali, "*One Hell of a Gamble*": *Khrushchev, Castro, and Kennedy 1958–1964—The Secret History of the Cuban Missile Crisis* (New York: W.W. Norton & Co., 1997).

8 Johnson, quoted in Randall B. Woods, *LBJ: Architect of American Ambition* (New York: Free Press, 2006), pp. 483–84.

9 Vladislav Zubok, *A Failed Empire: The Soviet Union in the Cold War from Stalin to Gorbachev* (Chapel Hill: The University of North Carolina Press, 2007), pp. 153, 193–94 and Warren I. Cohen, "Introduction," in Warren I. Cohen and Nancy Bernkopf Tucker, eds., *Lyndon Johnson Confronts the World: American Foreign Policy, 1963–1968* (New York: Cambridge University Press, 1994), p. 2.

10 "Memorandum of Conversation between Bundy and Dobrynin," September 25, 1964, *FRUS 1964–1968*, Volume XIV, Soviet Union, pp. 107–8 and Hal Brands, Non-Proliferation and the Dynamics of the Middle Cold War: The Superpowers, the MLF, and the NPT," *Cold War History* 7:3 (August 2007), pp. 389–423.

11 "Memorandum of Conversation between Johnson and Dobrynin," October 14, 1964, and "Message from the Soviet Government," November 3, 1964, *FRUS 1964–1968* Volume XIV, Soviet Union, pp. 127–30, 165–68.

12 "Message from Johnson to the Soviet Government," January 14, 1965, ibid., pp. 210–12.

13 Anatoly Dobrynin, *In Confidence: Moscow's Ambassador to America's Six Cold War Presidents* (Seattle: University of Washington Press, 1995), pp. 133–34 and "Memorandum from Thompson to Bundy," February 1, 1965, in *FRUS 1964–1968* Volume XIV, Soviet Union, pp. 227–28.

14 "Summary Notes of the 545th Meeting of the NSC," February 6, 1965, 7:45–9 pm," *FRUS 1964–68* Vol. II, Vietnam, January–June 1965, pp. 155–57.

15 Dobrynin, *In Confidence*, p. 136 and "Telegram from Moscow to the State Department," February 9, 1965, both in *FRUS 1964–1968* Volume XIV, Soviet Union, pp. 233–38.

16 "Memorandum of Conversation between Humphrey and Dobrynin," February 12, 1965, *FRUS 1964–1968*, Vol. XIV, Soviet Union, pp. 257–62.

17 "Memorandum of Conversation between Kohler and Dobrynin," September 9, 1965, in ibid., pp. 325–26.

18 For Kosygin's "madman" quote, see Thomas Alan Schwartz, *Lyndon Johnson and Europe: In the Shadow of Vietnam* (Cambridge: Harvard University Press, 2003), p. 136. Wilson's discussion of his visit to Moscow is in "Circular Telegram 18817 from the Department of State to Posts in NATO Capitals," July 30, 1966, *FRUS 1964–1968*, Vol. XII, Western Europe, pp. 558–60.

19 Dobrynin, *In Confidence*, pp. 147–48.

20 "Memorandum of Conversation between Rusk and Gromyko," September 22, 1966, *FRUS, 1964–1968*, Vol. XI, Arms Control and Disarmament, pp. 368–74, Frank Costigliola, "Lyndon B. Johnson, Germany, and 'the End of the Cold War'," in Cohen and Tucker, eds., *Lyndon Johnson Confronts the World*, 196, and Schwartz, *Lyndon Johnson and Europe*, p. 181.

21 "Letter from Johnson to Koysgin," January 21, 1967, *Foreign Relations, 1964–1968*, Vol. XI, Arms Control and Disarmament, pp. 431–32.

22 Dobrynin, *In Confidence*, pp. 150–51.

23 "Conversations between Wilson and Kosygin," February 6–13, 1967, PREM 13, Office Papers, Prime Minister's Office: Correspondence and Papers, 1964–1970, PREM 13/1715 PRIME MINISTER, Visit of Mr. Kosygin to UK: Record of Talks, UKNA.

24 Johnson to Wilson, quoted in Lyndon Johnson, *Vantage Point: Perspectives on the Presidency 1963–1969* (New York: Holt, Rinehart and Winston, 1971), pp. 480–81 and "Recording of a Telephone Conversation between Lyndon B. Johnson and Walt Rostow," February 11, 1967, 9:15 a.m., Citation #11526, Recordings and Transcripts of Conversations and Meetings, LBJ Library. Audio available on the Miller Center website at http://millercenter.org/scripps/archive/presidentialrecordings/johnson/1967/02_1967 (accessed June 5, 2014). Rostow also estimated that there was only a "5%" chance that Kosygin and Wilson would "develop anything" constructive to bring the North Vietnamese to the bargaining table.

25 "Telegram from Rusk to Thompson," March 6, 1967 and "Oral Statement from the Soviet Leadership," March 23, 1967, *FRUS 1964–1968*, Vol. XIV, Soviet Union, pp. 462–63, 476–77.

26 "Transcript, Robert S. McNamara Oral History Interview I, January 8, 1975" by Walt W. Rostow, Internet Copy, LBJ Library and Dobrynin, *In Confidence*, pp. 151–52.

27 Johnson, *Vantage Point*, pp. 252–54.

28 Dobrynin, *In Confidence*, pp. 160–61.

29 Oren, *Six Days of War*, pp. 14–16.

30 Ibid., 21–22, pp. 46–55, 111–12.

31 "Message from Kosygin to Johnson," June 5, 1967, 7:47 a.m. and "Message from Johnson to Kosygin," June 5, 1967, 8:15 a.m., in *FRUS 1964–1968* Vol. XIX, Arab-Israeli Crisis and War, 1967, pp. 300–1.

32 "Memorandum of Conversation between Thompson and Dobrynin," June 16, 1967, *FRUS 1964–1968*, Vol. XIV, Soviet Union, pp. 492–94.

33 Dobrynin, *In Confidence*, pp. 162–63, and "Memorandum by Zbigniew Brzezinski," June 16, 1967, ibid., pp. 494–95. Rusk told Johnson "there would be enormous political loss to you if Kosygin were to go home without a conversation between the two of you." See "Memorandum from Rusk to Johnson," June 17, 1967, ibid., pp. 495–97 .

34 "Address at the State Department's Foreign Policy Conference for Educators," June 19, 1967, *Public Papers of the Presidents: Lyndon B. Johnson Volume I* (Washington: Government Printing Office, 1968, pp. 651–52. (hereafter *PPP*)

35 "Text of Kosygin Address to General Assembly and Excerpts from Eban Speech," June 19, 1967 and J. Anthony Lukas, "Kosygin Hears Johnson's Policy Speech on TV," *The New York Times*, June 20, 1967, pp. 16–17, 19.

36 "Recording of a Telephone Conversation between Lyndon B. Johnson and J. William Fulbright," June 19, 1967, 10:57 p.m., Citation #11909, Recordings and Transcripts of Conversations and Meetings, LBJ Library. Audio available on the Miller Center website at http://millercenter.org/scripps/archive/presidentialrecordings/johnson/1967/06_1967 (accessed June 4, 2014).

37 "Recording of a Telephone Conversation between Lyndon B. Johnson and Julian Goodman," June 21, 1967, 9:50 a.m., Citation #11910, Recordings and Transcripts of Conversations and Meetings, LBJ Library. Audio available on the Miller Center website at http://millercenter.org/scripps/archive/presidentialrecordings/johnson/1967/06_1967 (accessed June 1, 2014).

38 "Transcript, Robert S. McNamara Oral History Interview I, January 8, 1975," Internet Copy, LBJ Library, Dobrynin, *In Confidence*, pp. 162–63, and Johnson, *Vantage Point*, pp. 481–83.

39 Dobrynin, *In Confidence*, p. 163.

40 Johnson, *Vantage Point*, pp. 483–84.

41 "Memorandum of Conversation between Johnson and Kosygin," June 23, 1967, 11:30 a.m.–1:30 p.m., *FRUS 1964–1968*, Vol. XIV, Soviet Union, pp. 514–25 and Dobrynin, *In Confidence*, pp. 163–64.

42 "Memorandum of Conversation between Johnson and Kosygin," June 23, 1967, 1:30 p.m.–3:10 p.m., *FRUS 1964–1968*, Vol. XIV, Soviet Union, pp. 528–31, Dobrynin, *In Confidence*, pp. 165–66, and "Transcript, Robert S. McNamara Oral History Interview I, January 8, 1975," Internet Copy, LBJ Library.

43 "Memorandum of Conversation between Johnson and Kosygin," June 23, 1967, 3:44 p.m.–4:45 p.m., ibid., pp. 531–36. In his memoirs, Johnson wrote that "I tried repeatedly to bring the talks back to limiting the missile race" and told Kosygin he wanted to put offensive and defensive systems on the table, but "the point did not get across clearly—or Kosygin chose not to understand." Johnson, *Vantage Point*, p. 484.

44 Max Frankel, "A Cordial Session: But There is No Sign of Gains on Substantive Issues," *The New York Times*, June 24, 1967, pp. 1, 6.

45 "Memorandum of Conversation between Johnson and Kosygin," June 25, 1967, 1:05 p.m.–3:05 p.m.," *FRUS 1964–1968*, Vol. XIV, Soviet Union, pp. 538–43.

46 "Oral Message from President Johnson to Chairman Kosygin," undated, ibid., p. 537.

47 This message is included in "Memorandum from Rusk to Johnson," June 24, 1967, ibid., p. 536.

48 "Memorandum of Conversation between Johnson and Kosygin," June 25, 1967, 3:20–6:09 p.m., ibid., pp. 544–56.

49 "The President's Remarks upon Arrival at the White House Following the Glassboro Meetings with Chairman Kosygin," June 25, 1967, *PPP Johnson Vol. I*, pp. 651–52.

50 Mutual concern about the Chinese remained, however. In September, McNamara announced the United States would begin building a "light" ABM system, "Sentinel," that would be deployed against Chinese missiles.

51 "United Nations Security Council Resolution 242," November 22, 1967,
    available at the UN Security Council website at http://unispal.un.org/unispal.
    nsf/0/7D35E1F729DF491C85256EE700686136 (accessed October 15, 2014).

52 Walter Cronkite, "Who, What, When, Where, Why: Report from Vietnam,"
    CBS News Broadcast, February 27, 1968. Video available at http://www.
    youtube.com/watch?v=Nn4w-ud-TyE (accessed August 12, 2014).

53 "Letter from Johnson to Kosygin," June 22, 1967 and "Letter from Kosygin,"
    June 27, 1967, in *FRUS, 1964–1968*, Vol. XI, Arms Control and Disarmament,
    pp. 623–24.

54 "Memorandum of Conversation between Johnson and Dobrynin," July 1,
    1967, in *FRUS 1964–1968*, Vol. XIV, Soviet Union, pp. 655–57.

Chapter 4

1 "Memorandum of Conversation between Dulles and Bulganin," July 21,
   1955 and "Memorandum of Conversation between Eisenhower and Zhukov,"
   July 23, 1955, in *FRUS 1955–1957*, Vol. II, China, pp. 670–74.

2 The text of the Announcement is published as footnote 2 of "Telegram 58
   from U.S. to the Embassy in Taiwan," July 24, 1955," ibid., p. 677. Zhou's
   speech is printed in part as "Editorial Note" in ibid., pp. 688–89. For the
   Chinese release of the American agents, see Gong Li, "Tension Across the
   Taiwan Strait in the 1950s: Chinese Strategy and Tactics" in Robert S. Ross
   and Jiang Changbin, eds., *Re-examining the Cold War: U.S.-China Diplomacy,
   1954–1973* (Cambridge: Harvard University Asia Center/Harvard University
   Press, 2001), p. 153.

3 Yafeng Xia, *Negotiating with the Enemy: U.S.-China Talks during the Cold
   War, 1949–1972* (Bloomington: Indiana University Press, 2006), p. 97.

4 Gong Li, "Tension Across the Taiwan Strait in the 1950s, in Ross and Jiang
   Changbin, eds., *Re-examining the Cold War*, pp. 156–62.

5 Lorenz Lüthi, *The Sino-Soviet Split: Cold War in the Communist World*
   (Princeton: Princeton University Press, 2008), pp. 80–83. Chinese journalist
   Yang Jisheng argues that the famines caused by the Great Leap Forward killed
   an estimated 36 million Chinese. See *Tombstone: The Great Chinese Famine
   1958–1962* (New York: Farrar, Straus and Giroux, 2012, originally published
   in Chinese in 2008). Historian Frank Dikötter, on the other hand, believes
   that at least 45 million died. See *Mao's Great Famine: The History of China's
   Most Devastating Catastrophe, 1958–1862* (New York: Walker Publishing
   Company, 2010).

6 Sergey Radchenko, *Two Suns in the Heavens: The Sino-Soviet Struggle for
   Supremacy, 1962–1967* (Washington: Woodrow Wilson Center Press, 2009),
   pp. 12–13. For more on Camp David and the Khrushchev-Mao meetings, see
   Lüthi, *The Sino-Soviet Split*, pp. 144–52.

7 Lüthi, *The Sino-Soviet Split*, pp. 157–93. War eventually broke out between
   China and India in 1962.

8 "Memorandum of Conversation between Kennedy and Prime Minister
   Holyoake of New Zealand," March 3, 1961, in *FRUS 1961–1963*, Vol. XXII,
   Northeast Asia, pp. 20–22.

9   Memorandum of Conversation between Kennedy and Prime Minister
    Holyoake of New Zealand," March 3, 1961, in *FRUS 1961–1963*, Vol. XXII,
    Northeast Asia, pp. 20–22. Xia, *Negotiating with the Enemy*, p. 116.

10 "Memorandum of Conversation between Kennedy and Khrushchev," June 3,
    1961, in *FRUS 1961–1963*, Vol. V, Soviet Union, pp. 182–97.

11 "Editorial Note, including Kennedy's remarks to McCone and Bundy,"
    January 1, 1963, "Editorial Note," including Kennedy's remarks to the
    NSC of January 22, 1963, in *FRUS 1961–1963*, Vol. XXII, Northeast Asia,
    pp. 339–42, and Lüthi, *The Sino-Soviet Split*, pp. 247–67.

12 Lüthi, *The Sino-Soviet Split*, pp. 305–08 and James G. Hershberg and Chen
    Jian, "Informing the Enemy: Sino-American 'Signaling' and the Vietnam War,
    1965," in Priscilla Roberts, ed., *Behind the Bamboo Curtain: China, Vietnam,
    and the World Beyond Asia* (Washington: Woodrow Wilson Center Press,
    2006), pp. 194–95.

13 Xiaoming Zhang, "The Vietnam War, 1965–1969: A Chinese Perspective," *The
    Journal of Military History* 60.4 (October 1996), pp. 731–62 and Radchenko,
    Two Suns in the Heavens, p. 171.

14 See Ilya V. Gaiduk, *The Soviet Union and the Vietnam War* (Chicago: Ivan R.
    Dee, 1996), pp. 65–66 and Yang Kuisong, "Mao Zedong and the Indochina
    Wars," in Roberts, ed., *Behind the Bamboo Curtain*, pp. 80–81.

15 Lüthi, *The Sino-Soviet Split*, pp. 296–99 and Sultan M. Khan, *Memories and
    Reflections of a Pakistani Diplomat* (London: The Centre for Pakistan Studies,
    1997), pp. 206–07.

16 Xiaohong Liu, *Chinese Ambassadors: The Rise of Diplomatic Professionalism
    since 1949* (Seattle: University of Washington Press, 1999), pp. 110–14,
    Kuo-Kang Shao, *Zhou Enlai and the Foundations of Chinese Foreign Policy*
    (NY: St. Martin's Press, 1996), p. 148, and Hoxha, quoted in Lüthi, *The Sino-
    Soviet Split*, p. 299.

17 "Report from Paye to Maurice Couve de Murville," January 10, 1968 and
    "Telegram from Beijing to the Ministère des Affaire Etrangères," March 11,
    1968, Politique Extérieure, 724, 10-23-1, January 1968–February 1969.
    Archives Diplomatiques, Direction Des Affaires Politique, Series Asie-Oceanie,
    Etate de Politique Extérieure, Sous-Séries—Chine, 1968–1972.

18 Zhang Baiji and Jia Quingguo, "Steering Wheel, Shock Absorber, and
    Diplomatic Probe in Confrontation: Sino-American Ambassadorial Talks
    Seen from the Chinese Perspective," in Ross and Jiang Changbin, eds.,
    Re-examining the Cold War, p. 193.

19 "Memorandum of Conversation between Johnson and Maurer," June 26,
    1967, in *FRUS 1964–1968*, Vol. XVII, Eastern Europe, pp. 430–35.

20 "Annual Message to the Congress on the State of the Union," January 17,
    1968, *PPP: Lyndon B. Johnson 1968–1969*, pp. 25–33.

21 "Paper Prepared by Alfred Jenkins," October 9, 1968, *FRUS 1964–1968*,
    Vol. XXX, China, pp. 709–18.

22 Chen Jian and David L. Wilson, "All under Heaven is Great Chaos: Beijing,
    the Sino-Soviet Border Clashes, and the Turn toward Sino-American
    Rapprochement, 1968–1969," *CWIHP Bulletin* 11 (Winter 1998), p. 155.

23 Yang Kuisong, "The Sino-Soviet Border Clash of 1969: From Zhenbao Island
    to Sino-American Rapprochement." *Cold War History* 1.1 (August 2000):
    35–37 and Xia, *Negotiating with the Enemy*, p. 138–39.

24   Richard M. Nixon, "Asia after Vietnam," reprinted in *FRUS 1969–1976*, Vol. I, Foundations of Foreign Policy, 1969–1972, pp. 10–21.

25   "Acceptance Speech at the Republican National Convention," August 8, 1968, 4 President website, http://www.4president.org/speeches/nixon1968acceptance. htm. See also Evelyn Goh, *Constructing the U.S. Rapprochement with China, 1961–1974: From "Red Menace" to "Tacit Ally* (New York: Cambridge University Press, 2005), pp. 103–09.

26   Chris Tudda, *A Cold War Turning Point: Nixon and Mao, 1969–1972* (Baton Rouge, 2012), p. 17.

27   Rockefeller, quoted in Walter Isaacson, *Kissinger: A Biography* (New York: Simon & Schuster, 1992), pp. 125–26, 334.

28   Yang Kuisong, "The Sino-Soviet Border Clash of 1969," pp. 24–29. Qiao Guanhua, the Vice Foreign Minister, supervised "intelligence reports concerning international reactions to the battle" and reported to Zhou Enlai. "All important decisions," meanwhile, "were made by Zhou himself."

29   "Memorandum of Conversation between Dobrynin and Kissinger," March 11, 1969, in Department of State, *Soviet-American Relations: The Détente Years* (Washington: Government Printing Office, 2007), pp. 35–38.

30   "Report by Four Chinese Marshals to the Central Committee: 'A Preliminary Evaluation of the War Situation'," July 11, 1969, in Chen Jian and David L. Wilson, "All Under Heaven is Great Chaos," pp. 166–68.

31   Henry Kissinger, *White House Years* (Boston: Little, Brown and Co., 1979), pp. 180–81.

32   "Restrictions Eased on U.S. Travel to Communist China," July 21, 1969, in Department of State *Bulletin Vol. LXI, No. 1573*, p. 126 and "Memorandum of Private Conversation between President Nixon and President Ceausescu," August 2, 1969, in *FRUS 1969–1976*, Vol. XXIX, Eastern Europe; Eastern Mediterranean, 1969–1972, pp. 438–47.

33   William S. Rogers, "Address Before the National Press Club, Canberra, Australia," August 8, 1969, Department of State *Bulletin LXI, No. 1575*, pp. 178–81.

34   "Minutes of Meeting of the National Security Council," August 14, 1969, in *FRUS 1969–1976*, Vol. XII, Soviet Union, January 1969 to October 1970, pp. 225–26 and "Memorandum of Conversation between Boris Davydov and William Stearman," August 18, 1969, Record Group 59, Department of State Files, Central Files, DEF 12 CHICOM, National Archives (hereafter DOSCF, NA).

35   Eliot Richardson, "The Foreign Policy of the Nixon Administration: Its Aims and Strategy," September 5, 1969, in Department of State *Bulletin* Vol. LXI, No. 1578, pp. 257–60.

36   "The CCP Central Committee's Order for General Mobilization in Border Provinces and Regions," August 28, 1969," in Chen Jian and Wilson, "All Under Heaven is Great Chaos," pp. 168–69.

37   "Report by Four Chinese Marshals to the Central Committee: 'Our Views of the Current Situation'," September 17, 1969, "Further Thoughts by Chen Yi on Sino-American Relations," September 17, 1969, in Chen Jian and Wilson, "All Under Heaven is Great Chaos," pp. 170–71, and Yang Kuisong and Yafeng Xia, "Vacillating between Revolution and Détente: Mao's Changing Psyche and Policy toward the United States," *Diplomatic History* 34.2 (April 2010), pp. 399–401.

38   "Memorandum of Conversation between Nixon and Stoessel," September 9, 1969," DOSCF, POL CHICOM–US, Box 1963, NA, "Telegram 161648 from

the Department of State to the Embassy in Taiwan and Commander, U. S. Taiwan Defense Command," September 23, 1969, DOSCF, DEF 6–2 US, NA, and "Memorandum from Sher Ali to Yahya," October 10, 1969, quoted in F.S. Aijazuddin, *From a Head, Through a Head, to a Head: The Secret Channel between the US and China through Pakistan.* Oxford: Oxford University Press, 2000, p. 27 (hereafter *FAH*).

39 Stoessel, quoted in Yafeng Xia, *Negotiating with the Enemy: U.S.-China Talks during the Cold War, 1949–1972* (Bloomington: Indiana University Press, 2006), pp. 146–48 and Mao, quoted in Yafeng Xia "China's Elite Politics and Sino-American Rapprochement, January 1969–February 1972," *Journal of Cold War Studies* 8.4 (Fall 2006), pp. 10–11. Xia argues that this episode "convinced Mao and Zhou that the United States was genuinely interested in" rapprochement.

40 "Telegram 3724 from the Embassy in Warsaw to the Department of State," December 7, 1969, NSC Country Files—Europe, Poland, Box 700, Warsaw Talks, Vol. 1, Richard Nixon Presidential Library and Museum, Yorba Linda, California (hereafter NPL).

41 Nixon Interview, "I Did Not Want the Hot Words of TV," *Time*, October 5, 1970 and "Memorandum of Conversation between the President and Yahya Khan," October 25, 1970, Record Group 59, Records of the Department of State, Winston Lord Files, Box 334, Winston Lord–Chrons, November 1970, NA.

42 "Letter from Yahya Khan to Hilaly," November 23, 1970, quoted in Aijazuddin, *FAH*, pp. 42–45 (emphasis Yahya's).

43 "Note Verbale from the U.S. Government to the PRC Government," undated, printed as Tab A, attached to "Memorandum from Kissinger to Nixon," undated, "Record of Discussion between Kissinger and Hilaly," December 16, 1970, both in *FRUS 1969–1976*, Vol. XVII, China, 1969–1972, pp. 248–52, "Telegram from Hilaly to Yayha," December 16, 1970, quoted in Aijazuddin, *FAH*, 50–52, and "Second Annual Report to the Congress on United States Foreign Policy," February 25, 1971, *PPP: Richard M. Nixon, 1971*, pp. 219, 277–78.

44 "Transcript of Conversation between Mao Zedong and Edgar Snow," December 18, 1970, in Chen Jian, ed., *Chinese Materials on the Sino-American Rapprochement (1969–1972)*, Compiled for the George Washington's University Cold War Group Conference on the Sino-American Opening and the Cold War, February 8–9, 2002, pp. 2–19.

45 Chen Jian, *Mao's China and the Cold War*, pp. 258–62.

46 "Conversation between Nixon and Kissinger," April 14, 1971, White House Tapes, Executive Office Building Conversation 28–16, NPL and "Diary Entry," April 12, 1971, in H.R. Haldeman ed., *The Haldeman Diaries* CD-Rom version (New York: Putnam, 1994) (hereafter *HD*).

47 "Message from Zhou Enlai to President Nixon," April 21, 1971, *FRUS 1969–1976*, Vol. XVII, China 1969–1972, pp. 300–01 and "Note from the U.S. Government to the Government of the People's Republic of China," May 10, 1971, NSC, Files for the President–China Materials, Exchanges Leading up to HAK's Trip to China, December 1969–July 1971, Box 1031, NPL.

48 "Politburo's Meeting's Decisions on the Principles of Improving Relations with the United States," May 26, 1971, in Chen Jian, ed., *Chinese Materials on the Sino-American Rapprochement*, pp. 25–28.

49 Khan, *Memories and Reflections of a Pakistani Diplomat*, pp. 261–65 and "Oral Interview with Winston Lord," Frontline Diplomacy: The Foreign Affairs Oral History Collection for the Association for Diplomatic Studies and Training, Library of Congress, http://memory.loc.gov/ammem/collections/diplomacy (accessed August 6, 2014) (hereafter *FD*, LOC).

50 John Holdridge, *Crossing the Divide: An Insider's Account of Normalization of U.S.-China Relations* (Lanham: Rowman and Littlefield, 1997), p. 56.

51 Henry Kissinger, *On China* (New York: The Penguin Press, 2011), pp. 238–39.

52 Ji Chaozhu, *The Man on Mao's Right*, p. 246.

53 "Memorandum of Conversation between Kissinger and Zhou Enlai," July 7, 1971, NSC Files, Files for the President, China Materials, Box 1032, POLO I Record, NPL.

54 "Memorandum of Conversation between Kissinger and Chou En-lai," July 10, 1971, 12:10–6:00 p.m., ibid. and Xia, *Negotiating with the Enemy*, pp. 170–71.

55 "Oral Interview with Winston Lord," FD, LOC.

56 "Backchannel Message TOSIT 26 from Kissinger to General Haig," July 11, 1971 and "Backchannel Message SITTO 88 from Haig to Kissinger," July 11, 1971, NSC Files, Files for the President, China Materials, Box 1032, POLO I Record, NPL.

57 "Remarks to the Nation Announcing Acceptance of an Invitation To Visit the People's Republic of China," July 15, 1971, *PPP: Richard M. Nixon 1971*, p. 121.

58 "Conversation between Nixon, Rogers, and Kissinger," July 22, 1971, White House Tapes, Oval Office Conversation 543–1, NPL.

59 Xia, "China's Elite Politics and Sino-American Rapprochement," pp. 3–28.

60 "Memorandum from Kissinger to the President," September 22, 1971, *FRUS 1969–1976*, Vol. XVII, China, 1969–1972, pp. 476–79, "Telegram from the Department of State to All Diplomatic Posts," September 24, 1971, DOSCF, POL-CHICOM, Box 1574, NA, and "Telegram from the American Consul in Hong Kong to the State Department," NSC, Kissinger Office Files, CF-Far East, Box 87, China Reports-Sensitive, Folder 2, NPL.

61 Kissinger, *White House Years*, 776–77, Yafeng Xia, *Negotiating with the Enemy*, p. 177, and Oral Interview with John H. Holdridge, December 1989, FD, LOC.

62 "Oral Interview with Winston Lord," April 29, 1998, FD, and "Memorandum of Conversation between Kissinger and Zhou Enlai," October 20, 1971, NSC Files, Box 1034, Files for the President, China Materials, Polo II, HAK China Trip, Transcripts of Meetings, NPL.

63 "Memorandum of Conversation between Kissinger and Zhou Enlai," October 21, 1971, 4:42 p.m.–7:17 p.m., NSC Files, Box 1034, Files for the President, China Materials, Polo II, HAK China Trip, NPL.

64 Kissinger, *White House Years*, p. 782 and Kissinger, *On China*, p. 269.

65 "Memorandum of Conversation between Nixon, Rogers, Haig, and Bush," October 22, 1971, *FRUS 1969–1976*, Vol. V, United Nations, 1969–1972, pp. 844–46.

66 Haig, Alexander M. with Charles McCarry, *Inner Circles: How America Changed the World, A Memoir* (New York: Warner Books, 1992), pp. 258–59.

67 "Conversation between Nixon and Kissinger," February 15, 1972, White House Tapes, Oval Office Conversation 672–2, NPL (emphasis Kissinger's).

68 Nixon's "Handwritten Notes," undated, President's Personal Files, Name/Subject File, Box 7, China Notes, NPL.

69 Kissinger, *White House Years*, pp. 1053–55 and Richard M. Nixon, *RN: The Memoirs of Richard M. Nixon* (New York: Grosset and Dunlap, 1978), pp. 559–60.

70 Li Zhisui, *The Private Life of Chairman Mao* (New York: Random House, 1994), pp. 553–65.

71 Kissinger, *White House Years*, pp. 1057–59 and Nixon, *RN*, pp. 560–61.

72 "Memorandum of Conversation between Nixon, Kissinger, Mao Zedong, and Zhou Enlai," February 21, 1972, 2:50–3:55 p.m., *FRUS 1969–1976*, Vol. XVII, China 1969–1972, pp. 677–84.

73 "Diary Entry," Sunday, February 21, 1972, *HD*.

74 "Memorandum of Conversation between President Nixon and Zhou Enlai," February 22, 1972, 2:10–6:00 p.m., ibid., pp. 693–719.

75 "Memorandum of Conversation between President Nixon and Zhou Enlai," February 23, 1972, 2:00–6:00 p.m., ibid., pp. 719–52.

76 "Memorandum of Conversation between President Nixon and Zhou Enlai," February 24, 1972, 5:15–8:00 p.m., ibid., pp. 761–85.

77 "Memorandum of Conversation between Rogers and Ji Pengfei," February 22, 1972, Document #91, *FRUS* Volume E-13, Documents on China, 1969–1972, http://history.state.gov/historicaldocuments/frus1969-76ve13/d91 (accessed July 29, 2014).

78 "Memorandum of Conversation between Rogers and Ji Pengfei," February 23, 1972, in *FRUS 1969–1976*, Vol. XVII, China, 1969–1972, pp. 753–61.

79 "Memorandum of Conversation between Kissinger and Qiao Guanhua," February 22, 1972, 10:05 a.m.–11:55 p.m., Document #90, *FRUS* Volume E-13, Documents on China, 1969–1972.

80 "Memorandum of Conversation between Kissinger and Qiao Guanhua," February 24, 1972, 9:59 a.m.–12:42 p.m., Document #93, ibid. For a more detailed discussion of the final communiqué negotiations, see Tudda, *Cold War Turning Point*, pp. 194–97.

81 "Memorandum of Conversation between President Nixon and Zhou Enlai," February 25, 1972, 5:45–6:45 p.m., *FRUS 1969–1976*, Vol. XVII, China 1969–1972, pp. 785–94.

82 Ji Chaozhu, *The Man on Mao's Right*, pp. 259–60 and "Memorandum of Conversation between President Nixon and Zhou Enlai," February 26, 1972, 9:20–10:05 a.m., *FRUS 1969–1976*, Vol. XVII, China 1969–1972, pp. 794–801.

83 Marshall Green, "*Evolution of US-China Policy, 1956–1973: Memoirs of an Insider*," *FD*, LOC and "News Conference of Dr. Kissinger and Mr. Green," February 27, 1972, *Bulletin LXVI, No. 1708*, pp. 426–31.

84 "Toast by President Nixon," February 27, 1972, *Bulletin LXVI, No. 1708*, pp. 432–33.

85 "CCP Central Committee: 'Notice on the Joint Sino-American Communiqué'," March 7, 1972, in Chen Jian, ed., *Chinese Materials on the Sino-American Rapprochement*, pp. 31–51.

86 Kissinger then placed US forces on a worldwide military and nuclear alert and the Chair of the Joint Chiefs of Staff, Admiral William Moorer, ordered all military commands to DefCon (Defense Condition) 3, the highest stage of readiness during peacetime. Fortunately, the Israelis pulled back after massive American pressure and neither the US nor the Soviet Union intervened. See Asaf Siniver, *Nixon, Kissinger, and U.S. Foreign Policy Making: The Machinery of Crisis* (New York: Cambridge University Press, 2011), pp. 202–7.

Chapter 5

1   James Mann, *Rise of the Vulcans: The History of Bush's War Cabinet* (New York: Penguin Books, 2004), p. 34.

2   Nelson, Anna Kasten. "Senator Henry Jackson and the Demise of Détente," in Nelson, ed., *The Policymakers: Shaping American Foreign Policy from 1947 to the Present* (Lanham: Rowman & Littlefield Publishers, Inc., 2009), pp. 95–102.

3   "Memorandum from Cheney to Rumsfeld," July 8, 1975, in *FRUS* 1969–1976, Vol. XVI, Soviet Union, August 1974–December 1976, pp. 612–13.

4   Mann, *Rise of the Vulcans*, pp. 72–73.

5   Jimmy Carter, "Inaugural Address," January 20, 1977, *PPP: Jimmy Carter 1977*, pp. 1–4.

6   Zbigniew Brzezinski, *Power and Principle: Memoirs of the National Security Adviser 1977–1981* (New York: Farrar Strauss Giroux, 1983), p. 48.

7   Jimmy Carter, *Keeping Faith: Memoirs of a President* (New York: Bantam Books, 1982), pp. 212–14, 218.

8   Zubok, *A Failed Empire*, pp. 239, 254–57.

9   Dobrynin, *In Confidence*, pp. 385–86.

10   "Memorandum of Conversation between Carter and Dobrynin," February 1, 1977, *FRUS 1977–1980* Vol. VI, Soviet Union, pp. 6–12.

11   "Letter from Carter to Brezhnev," March 3, 1977, and "Letter from Brezhnev to Carter," March 15, 1977, ibid., pp. 39–44. Brezhnev, Vladislav Zubok has argued, "was enraged" because he "felt had paid with his own health for the Vladivostok agreement," *A Failed Empire*, p. 255.

12   Dobrynin, *In Confidence*, pp. 393–94.

13   "Memorandum of Conversation between Vance and Gromyko," March 28, 1977, *FRUS 1977–1980* Vol. VI, Soviet Union, pp. 60–72 and Cyrus Vance, *Hard Choices: Critical Years in America's Foreign Policy* (New York: Simon and Schuster, 1983), pp. 53–54.

14   Jimmy Carter, "Address at Commencement Exercises at the University of Notre Dame," May 22, 1977, *PPP: Jimmy Carter 1977*, pp. 954–62.

15   For an excellent analysis of the Camp David peace process, see Reynolds, *Summits*, pp. 283–342.

16   For more on the Soviet desire for parity, see Betty Glad, *An Outsider in the White House: Jimmy Carter, His Advisors, and the Making of American Foreign Policy* (Ithaca: Cornell University Press, 2009), p. 55 and Zubok, *A Failed Empire*, p. 243.

17   "Speech by Brezhnev at the Political Consultative Committee Meeting in Moscow," November 22, 1978, Document #84, in Vojtech Mastny and Malcolm Byrne, eds., *A Cardboard Castle? An Inside History of the Warsaw Pact 1955–1991* (Budapest: Central European University Press, 2005), pp. 418–21.

18   "Telephone Conversation between Brzezinski and Dobrynin," December 19, 1978, in *FRUS 1977–1980* Vol. VI, Soviet Union, pp. 494–96.

19   "Telegram from the State Department to Vance in Mexico, Kabul, and Moscow," February 15, 1979, ibid., pp. 512–14. Dobrynin said he had known Dubs well from his time at the Moscow embassy, and admitted that an

investigation ultimately determined that the Soviet advisors "failed to control" the Afghani police properly. See *In Confidence*, pp. 435–36.

20 "Letter from Carter to Brezhnev," February 17, 1979 and "Backchannel Message from Brzezinski to Carter," February 18, 1979 [containing Brezhnev's letter], ibid., pp. 514–17, and Vance, *Hard Choices*, pp. 121–22.

21 "Memorandum of Conversation," February 27, 1979, ibid., pp. 523–24. Dobrynin said he left the White House "with the impression that Carter was beginning to show real interest in a shift in our relations. Remarkably, it was the first time that he did not touch on his favorite subject of human rights." See *In Confidence*, pp. 418–19.

22 "Letter from Carter to Brezhnev," March 7, 1979 and "Letter from Brezhnev to Carter," March 11, 1979, in *FRUS 1977–1980* Vol. VI, Soviet Union, pp. 529–31.

23 "Letter from Carter to Brezhnev," March 27, 1979, ibid., pp. 538–39.

24 "Letter from Brezhnev to Carter," April 25, 1979, ibid., pp. 545–47.

25 Zubok, *A Failed Empire*, pp. 241–42, 245–46 and "Memorandum from Scowcroft to Ford," December 14, 1974, *FRUS 1969–1976*, Vol. XVI, Soviet Union, August 1974–December 1976, pp. 382–84.

26 Vance, *Hard Choices*, 134–37.

27 Carter, *Keeping Faith*, pp. 243–45.

28 "Memorandum of Conversation between Carter, Brezhnev, and Kirchschlaeger," June 15, 1979, *FRUS 1977–1980* Vol. VI, Soviet Union, pp. 576–78 and Carter, *Keeping Faith*, pp. 243–45.

29 Memorandum of Conversation between Carter and Brezhnev," June 16, 1979, 11 a.m.–12:30 p.m., ibid., pp. 579–88. Carter recalled: "As the first morning session adjourned, all of us were impressed with the vigor of Brezhnev as compared with the reports we had heard, with his ability to make extemporaneous remarks, and his obvious though heavy-handed attempt at humor. He moves around with difficulty. At first his speech is slurred, but as he talks more and more and becomes animated, this speech defect seems to go away." See Carter, *Keeping Faith*, pp. 249.

30 "Memorandum of Conversation between Carter and Brezhnev," June 16, 1979, 5:35–7:20 p.m., *FRUS SALT II, 1972–1980*, pp. 943–52.

31 Carter, *Keeping Faith*, p. 251.

32 "Memorandum of Conversation between Carter and Brezhnev," June 17, 1979, 11 a.m.–1 p.m., *FRUS 1977–1980*, Soviet Union, pp. 591–603.

33 Dobrynin, *In Confidence*, pp. 428–29.

34 "Memorandum of Conversation between Carter and Brezhnev," June 17, 1979, 5:30.–7:20 p.m., *FRUS 1977–80*, Soviet Union, pp. 603–13.

35 The "Basic Principles of Soviet-American Relations" essentially accepted the principle of détente. See Reynolds, *Summits*, pp. 270–71.

36 "Joint Declaration between the United States and Soviet Union," June 17, 1979, *FRUS 1977–80*, Soviet Union, pp. 613–15.

37 Carter, *Keeping Faith*, p. 257.

38 "Memorandum of Conversation between Carter and Brezhnev," June 18, 1979, 10–11:30 a.m., *FRUS 1977–80*, Soviet Union, pp. 615–23.

39 "Memorandum of Conversation between Carter and Brezhnev," June 18, 1979, 10–11:30 a.m., ibid., pp. 624–28 and Carter, *Keeping Faith*, pp. 260–61.

40 Brzezinski, *Power and Principle*, pp. 342–43 and Dobrynin, *In Confidence*, pp. 425–26.

41 Dobrynin, *In Confidence*, pp. 422–25, Brzezinski, *Power and Principle*, pp. 343–44, and Carter, *Keeping Faith*, pp. 260–61.

42 Vance, *Hard Choices*, pp. 349–53.

43 Dobrynin, *In Confidence*, pp. 428–29 and Vance, *Hard Choices*, pp. 358–59.

44 "Letter from Nineteen Senators to Carter," December 17, 1979, in *FRUS* Vol. XXXIII, SALT II 1972–1980, pp. 968–71.

45 Betty Glad notes that Carter had actually begun secretly funding the *mujahideen* in the summer of 1979. See *An Outsider in the White House*, pp. 197–99.

46 "Telegram 68654 from the State Department to Moscow," March 15, 1980, *FRUS* 1977–1980, Vol. VI, Soviet Union, pp. 769–71.

47 Brezhnev, quoted in Zubok, *A Failed Empire*, p. 267.

Chapter 6

1 Ronald Reagan, *An American Life: The Autobiography* (New York: Simon and Schuster, 1990), pp. 266–68.

2 "The President's News Conference," January 29, 1981, *PPP: Ronald Reagan 1981*, pp. 55–62.

3 Alexander M. Haig, Jr., *Caveat: Realism, Reagan, and Foreign Policy* (New York: MacMillan Publishing Company, 1984), pp. 100–5.

4 Dobrynin, *In Confidence*, pp. 484–86.

5 Reagan, "Remarks to Members of the National Press Club on Arms Reduction and Nuclear Weapons," November 18, 1981, *PPP: Ronald Reagan, 1981*, pp. 1062–67.

6 Zubok, *A Failed Empire*, pp. 267–70.

7 "Diary Entry," December 21, 1981, in Ronald Reagan, *Reagan Diaries*, ed. Douglas Brinkley (New York: Harper Perennial, 2007), p. 57 (hereafter *RD*), Reagan, "Address to the Nation about Christmas and the Situation in Poland," December 23, 1981, *PPP: Ronald Reagan, 1981*, pp. 1185–88, and "Diary Entry," *RD*, December 25, 1981, p. 58.

8 Reagan, "Address at Commencement Exercises at Eureka College in Illinois," May 9, 1982, in *PPP: Reagan 1982*, pp. 580–86.

9 Reagan, "Address to Members of the British Parliament," June 8, 1982, ibid., pp. 742–48.

10 James Graham Wilson, *Triumph of Improvisation: Gorbachev's Adaptability, Reagan's Engagement, and the End of the Cold War* (Ithaca: Cornell University Press, 2014), p. 63 and George Shultz, *Turmoil and Triumph: My Years as Secretary of State* (New York: Charles Scribner and Sons, 1993), pp. 6, 19.

11 Zubok, *A Failed Empire*, p. 272.

12 Dobrynin, *In Confidence*, p. 478.

13 "Cable from Bush to Reagan," November 15, 1982, in George Bush, *All the Best: My Life in Letters and Other Writings* (New York: Simon & Schuster, 1999), pp. 321–22.

14 Shultz, *Turmoil and Triumph*, pp. 125–27.

15 "National Security Decision Directive-75," January 17, 1983, available at the Ronald Reagan Presidential Library and Museum website, http://www.reagan. utexas.edu/archives/reference/NSDDs.html#.U_vSq-l0xjo. (accessed August 25, 2014) and Reed, quoted in James Mann, *Rebellion of Ronald Reagan: A History of the End of the Cold War* (New York: Penguin Books, 2009), p. 31.

16 Reagan, "Remarks at the Annual Convention of the National Association of Evangelicals in Orlando, Florida," March 8, 1983, in *PPP: Reagan 1983*, pp. 359–64 and Zubok, *A Failed Empire*, p. 272.

17 Reagan, "Address to the Nation on Defense and National Security," March 23, 1983, ibid., pp. 437–43.

18 Dobrynin, *In Confidence*, p. 528.

19 Benjamin B. Fischer, "A Cold War Conundrum: The 1983 Soviet War Scare," *Center for the Study of Intelligence* (Central Intelligence Agency, 2007). Available at https://www.cia.gov/library/center-for-the-study-of-intelligence/ csi-publications/books-and-monographs/a-cold-war-conundrum/source. htm#HEADING1-13 (accessed August 25, 2014).

20 Reagan, "Diary Entry," November 18, 1985," *RD*, pp. 198–99.

21 Jack F. Matlock, Jr., *Reagan and Gorbachev: How the Cold War Ended* (New York: Random House, 2004), pp. 75–77 and Reagan, "Address to the Nation and Other Countries on United States-Soviet Relations," January 16, 1984, in *PPP: Reagan 1984*, pp. 40–44.

22 "Cable from Bush to Reagan," February 15, 1984, in Bush, *All the Best*, pp. 331–32.

23 Zubok, *A Failed Empire*, p. 276.

24 Shultz, *Turmoil and Triumph*, pp. 473–77.

25 Dobrynin, *In Confidence*, p. 479.

26 "Memorandum of Conversation between Thatcher and Reagan," December 28, 1985, The Margaret Thatcher Foundation website, http://www. margaretthatcher.org/document/IilYl85 (accessed August 26, 2014).

27 Shultz, *Turmoil and Triumph*, pp. 528–33 and "Cable from Bush to Reagan," March 13, 1985, in Bush, *All the Best*, pp. 342–44.

28 Archie Brown, *Seven Years That Changed the World: Perestroika in Perspective* (New York: Oxford University Press, 2007).

29 Matlock, *Reagan and Gorbachev*, pp. 115–17 and Andrei Grachev, *Gorbachev's Gamble: Soviet Foreign Policy & the End of the Cold War* (London: Polity Press, 2008), pp. 56–57.

30 "Diary Entry," September 27, 1985, *RD*, p. 356, Matlock, *Reagan and Gorbachev*, pp. 140–42, and Shultz, *Turmoil and Triumph*, pp. 576–77.

31 "Memorandum of First Private Meeting between Reagan and Gorbachev," November 19, 1985, Document #15, "Briefing Book: To the Geneva Summit," National Security Archive website, http://www2.gwu.edu/~nsarchiv/NSAEBB/ NSAEBB172/index.htm. (accessed August 28, 2014) (hereafter NSA)

32 "Memorandum of Third Plenary Meeting between Reagan and Gorbachev," November 20, 1985, Document #21, NSA.

33 Shultz, *Turmoil and Triumph*, pp. 606–7.

34 "Diary Entry," November 24, 1985, in The Diary of Anatoly Chernyaev, 1985, NSA (hereafter DAC, NSA) and Pavel Palazchenko, *My Years with Gorbachev and Shevardnadze: The Memoirs of a Soviet Interpreter* (University Park: Pennsylvania State University Press, 1997), p. 45.

35   "Diary Entry," January 15, 1986, in *RD*, pp. 383–84.

36   The first quote is from Zubok, *A Failed Empire*, p. 289; the second is from Grachev, *Gorbachev's Gamble*, p. 81.

37   Grachev, *Gorbachev's Gamble*, pp. 82–84 and Ken Adelman, *Reagan at Reykjavik: Forty-Eight Hours That Ended the Cold War* (New York: Broadside Books, 2014), pp. 74–76.

38   Mann, *Rebellion of Ronald Reagan*, pp. 97–100 and Shultz, *Turmoil and Triumph*, pp. 728–50.

39   Adelman, *Reagan at Reykjavik*, pp. 83–85.

40   Reagan, *An American Life*, pp. 676–79 and Shultz, *Turmoil and Triumph*, pp. 773–74. The Summit's memoranda of conversation are available on the NSA website as "The Reykjavik File" at http://www2.gwu.edu/~nsarchiv/NSAEBB/NSAEBB203/index.htm.

41   Shultz, *Turmoil and Triumph*, p. 790.

42   Adelman, *Reagan at Reykjavik*, pp. 230–31.

43   Reagan quoted in Mann, *Rebellion of Ronald Reagan*, p. 202.

44   Reagan and Gorbachev, quoted in Adelman, *Reagan at Reykjavik*, p. 249.

45   Reagan, quoted in Mann, *Rebellion of Ronald Reagan*, p. 304.

46   Reagan, "Remarks and a Question-and-Answer Session with the Students and Faculty at Moscow State University," May 31, 1988, *PPP: Reagan 1988*, pp. 683–92.

47   "Excerpts from Address by Mikhail Gorbachev, 43rd U.N. General Assembly Session," December 7, 1988, available at http://www.nytimes.com/1988/12/08/world/the-gorbachev-visit-excerpts-from-speech-to-un-on-major-soviet-military-cuts.html. (accessed October 7, 2014)

48   "Memorandum of Conversation between Reagan, Bush, and Gorbachev," December 7, 1988, Document #8, Reagan, Bush, and Gorbachev at Governor's Island, NSA Website, http://www2.gwu.edu/~nsarchiv/NSAEBB/NSAEBB261/index.htm. (accessed September 2, 2014)

49   "National Security Review 3," February 15, 1989, George H.W. Bush Library website, http://bushlibrary.tamu.edu/research/nsr.php. (accessed September 2, 2014)

50   Scowcroft and Bush, quoted in Christopher Maynard, *Out of the Shadow: George H.W. Bush and the End of the Cold War* (College Station: Texas A&M University Press, 2008), pp. 16–18 and George Bush and Brent Scowcroft, *A World Transformed* (New York: Vintage Books, 1998), p. 39.

51   Bush, "Remarks to Citizens of Hamtramck, Michigan," April 17, 1989 and "Remarks at the Texas A&M University Commencement Ceremony in College Station," May 12, 1989, in *PPP: George Bush, 1989*, pp. 430–33, 540–43.

52   Bush and Scowcroft, *A World Transformed*, pp. 114–25.

53   James A. Baker, III with Thomas M. DeFrank, *Politics of Diplomacy: Revolution, War & Peace, 1989–1992* (New York: G.P. Putnam's Sons, 1995), p. 168, Scowcroft, quoted in Maynard, *Out of the Shadow*, 39–40, and Bush and Scowcroft, *A World Transformed*, pp. 132–33.

54   "Diary Entry," April 23, 1989, DAC 1989, NSA.

55   "National Security Directive 23," September 22, 1989, George H.W. Bush Library Website, http://bushlibrary.tamu.edu/research/nsd.php. (accessed September 2, 2014)

56   "Record of Conversation between Gorbachev and Németh," March 3, 1989, in Svetlana Savranskaya, Thomas Blanton, and Vladislav Zubok, eds., *Masterpieces*

of History: The Peaceful End of the Cold War in Europe, 1989 (Budapest: Central European University Press, 2010), pp. 412–13, Baker, *Politics of Diplomacy*, p. 160, and Wilson, *Triumph of Improvisation*, pp. 146, 165–66.

57 "Record of Telephone Conversation between Bush and Kohl," "Record of Telephone Conversation between Bush and Gorbachev," and "Diary of Anatoly Chernyaev," all November 10, 1989, in Savranskaya et al., *Masterpieces of History*, pp. 586–89, 595–97.

58 "Diary Entry," December 1, 1989, in Bush, *All the Best*, pp. 445–46.

59 The toxin in a binary chemical weapon is separated into two chemical precursors. When the weapon is fired, the barrier between the two precursors is removed, and the toxin is activated.

60 "Memorandum of First Expanded Conversation between Bush and Gorbachev," December 2, 1989, 10:00–11:55 a.m., National Security Council, Condoleeza Rice Files, Soviet Union/USSR Subject Files, Summit at Malta December 1989: Malta Memcons, George H.W. Bush Presidential Library.

61 Bush and Scowcroft, *A World Transformed*, p. 165.

62 In the Soviet transcript of this meeting, Gorbachev accused Bush of taking "steps with regard to such countries as, for instance, Panama, Colombia and, most recently, the Philippines. In the Soviet Union people ask: The fact that these are sovereign countries—is this not a barrier for the United States? Why does the U.S. arrange a trial, reach a verdict and carry it out by itself?" See "Soviet Transcript of the Malta Meeting, December 2–3, 1989, in "Bush and Gorbachev at Malta: Previously Secret Documents from Soviet and U.S. Files on the 1989 Meeting, 20 Years Later," NSA.

63 "Memorandum of First Restricted Bilateral Conversation between Bush and Gorbachev," December 2, 1989, 12:00–1:00 p.m., National Security Council, Arnold Kanter Files, Soviet Union/USSR Subject Files, Summit at Malta December 1989: Malta Memcons, George H.W. Bush Presidential Library.

64 "Memorandum of Luncheon Conversation between Bush and Gorbachev," December 2, 1989, 1:30–2:45 p.m., National Security Council, Condoleeza Rice Files, Soviet Union/USSR Subject Files, Summit at Malta December 1989: Malta Memcons, George H.W. Bush Presidential Library.

65 "Diary Entry," December 2, 1989, in Bush, *All the Best*, pp. 446–48.

66 "Memorandum of Second Restricted Bilateral Conversation between Bush and Gorbachev," December 3, 1989, 11:45 a.m.–12:45 p.m., National Security Council, Condoleeza Rice Files, Soviet Union/USSR Subject Files, Summit at Malta December 1989: Malta Memcons, George H.W. Bush Presidential Library.

67 "Memorandum of Second Expanded Bilateral Conversation between Bush and Gorbachev," December 3, 1989, 4:35 p.m.–6:45 p.m., ibid.

68 Bush and Gorbachev, "Remarks of the President and Soviet Chairman Gorbachev and a Question-and-Answer Session with Reporters in Malta," December 3, 1989, in *PPP: Bush 1989, Vol. II*, pp. 1625–34.

69 Anatoly S. Chernyaev, *My Six Years with Gorbachev* (University Park: The Pennsylvania State University Press, 2000), pp. 233–34 and Baker, *Politics of Diplomacy*, pp. 169–70.

70 Baker, *Politics of Diplomacy*, p. 16.

BIBLIOGRAPHY

Unpublished Sources

Archival sources

National Archives II, College Park, Md.
Department of State, Record Group 59:
Department of State Central Files, 1967–1969 and 1970–1973:
DEF 6–2 US
DEF 12 CHICOM
POL CHICOM
POL CHICOM–US
Records of the Policy Planning Director Winston Lord (1969–1977), Lot 77 D 112.
George H.W. Bush Presidential Library:
National Security Council, Condoleeza Rice Files, Soviet Union/USSR Subject Files, Summit at Malta December 1989: Malta Memcons.
Arnold Kanter Files, Soviet Union/USSR Subject Files, Summit at Malta December 1989: Malta Memcons.
Richard Nixon Presidential Library and Museum, Yorba Linda, California:
Henry A. Kissinger Office Files:
Country Files-Far East
National Security Council:
Country Files—Europe, Poland
Files for the President, China Materials, Exchanges Leading up to HAK's Trip to China.
Files for the President, China Materials, POLO I Record.
Files for the President, China Materials, Polo II, HAK China Trip, Transcripts of Meetings.
White House Special Files:
President's Personal Files, Name/Subject Files
Lyndon Baines Johnson Presidential Library:
Oral Histories Collection
Recordings and Transcripts of Conversations and Meetings
Archives Diplomatiques, Direction Des Affaires Politique, Ministère des Affaires étrangères et européennes, Direction des Archives, [Diplomatic Archive Center of the French Ministry of Foreign and European Affairs]:
Series Asie-Oceanie, Etate de Politique Extérieure, Sous-Séries—Chine, 1968–1972
The National Archives, United Kingdom:

Dominions Office and Commonwealth Relations Office: Original Correspondence. Far East and Pacific Department. Afro-Asian Conference 1955, Bandung, DO 35/6096.

Office Papers, Prime Minister's Office: Correspondence and Papers, 1964–1970, PREM 13/1715 PRIME MINISTER, Visit of Mr. Kosygin to UK: Record of Talks.

Other unpublished material

Jian, Chen, ed. *Chinese Materials on the Sino-American Rapprochement (1969–1972)*, Compiled for the George Washington's University Cold War Group Conference on the Sino-American Opening and the Cold War, February 8–9, 2002.

Jian, Chen, ed. *Bandung as a Turning Point in Chinese and Cold War History*, Cold War International History Project, forthcoming publication.

Published Sources

Aijazuddin, Fakir Syed. *From a Head, Through a Head, to a Head: The Secret Channel between the US and China through Pakistan*. Oxford: Oxford University Press, 2000.

Bush, George. *All the Best: My Life in Letters and Other Writings*. New York: Simon & Schuster, 1999.

Centre for the Study of Asian-African and Developing Countries. *Collected Documents of the Asian-African Conference, April 18–24, 1955*. Jakarta: Agency for Research and Development, the Department of Foreign Affairs, 1983.

Ferrell, Robert H., ed. *Off the Record: The Private Papers of Harry S Truman*. New York: Harper & Row, 1980.

Ferrell, Robert H., ed. *Dear Bess: The Letters from Harry to Bess Truman, 1910–1959*. Columbia: University of Missouri Press, 1998.

Foreign and Commonwealth Office. *Documents on British Policy Overseas*, Vol. I, The Conference at Potsdam July–August 1945. London: Her Majesty's Stationery Office, 1984.

Foreign Ministry of the People's Republic of China. *China and the Asian-African Conference (Documents)*. Beijing: Foreign Languages Press, 1955.

Foreign Ministry of the Soviet Union. *Tehran, Yalta, and Potsdam Conferences*. Moscow: Progress Publishers, 1969.

Haldeman, Harry R., ed. *The Haldeman Diaries*. New York: Putnam, 1994.

Jian, Chen and David L. Wilson, "All Under Heaven is Great Chaos": Beijing, the Sino-Soviet Border Clashes, and the Turn Toward Sino-American Rapprochement, 1968–1969." Cold War International History Project *Bulletin 11*, Winter 1998.

Ministry of Foreign Affairs, Republic of Indonesia, ed. *Asia-Africa Speak from Bandung*. Djakarta: Ministry of Foreign Affairs, 1955.

Nehru, Jawaharlal. *Selected Works of Jawaharlal Nehru, Second Series, Volume 26: June 1, 1954–September 30, 1954*. New Delhi: Oxford University Press, 2002.

Nehru, Jawaharlal. *Second Series, Vol. 28, February 1-May 31, 1955*. New Delhi: Oxford University Press, 2002.

Public Papers of the President. Washington: Government Printing Office.
Lyndon Baines Johnson
Richard M. Nixon
Jimmy Carter
Ronald Reagan
George Bush

Reagan, Ronald. *Reagan Diaries*, ed. Douglas Brinkley. New York: Harper Perennial, 2007.

Savranskaya, Svetlana, Thomas Blanton, and Vladislav Zubok, eds. *Masterpieces of History: The Peaceful End of the Cold War in Europe, 1989*. Budapest: Central European University Press, 2010.

U.S. Department of State. *Department of State Bulletin*. Washington: United States Government Printing Office.

U.S. Department of State. *Foreign Relations of the United States*. Washington: United States Government Printing Office:
1945, Vol. I, The Conference of Berlin (The Potsdam Conference)
1950, National Security Affairs; Foreign Economic Policy
1952–1954, Vol. VII, Germany and Austria, Part 1
1952, 1954, Vol. XII, East Asia and the Pacific Part 1
1952–1954, Vol. XIII, Indochina, Part 1
1952–1954, Vol. XIII, Indochina, Part 2
1952–1954, Vol. XIV, China and Japan, Part 1
1952–1954, Vol. XVI, Geneva Conference
1955–1957, Vol. II, China
1955–1957, Vol. XXI, East Asian Security; Cambodia; Laos
1961–1963, Vol. XXII, Northeast Asia
1961–1963, Vol. V, Soviet Union
1964–1968, Vol. II, Vietnam, January-June 1965
1964–1968, Vol. XI, Arms Control and Disarmament
1964–1968, Vol. XII, Western Europe
1964–1968 Volume XIV, Soviet Union
1964–1968, Vol. XVII, Eastern Europe
1964–1968, Vol. XIX, Arab-Israeli Crisis and War, 1967
1964–1968, Vol. XXX, China
1969–1976, Vol. I, Foundations of Foreign Policy, 1969–1972
1969–1976, Vol. V, United Nations, 1969–1972
1969–1976, Vol. XII, Soviet Union, January 1969–October 1970
1969–1976, Vol. XVI, Soviet Union, August 1974–December 1976
1969–1976, Vol. XVII, China, 1969–1972
1969–1976, Vol. XXIX, Eastern Europe; Eastern Mediterranean, 1969–1972
1969–1976, Vol. XXXIII, SALT II 1972–1980
1977–1980 Vol. VI, Soviet Union

U.S. Department of State. *Soviet-American Relations: The Détente Years*. Washington: Government Printing Office, 2007.

Vojtech, Mastny and Malcolm Byrne, eds. *A Cardboard Castle? An Inside History of the Warsaw Pact 1955–1991*. Budapest: Central European University Press, 2005.

Internet websites

4 President, http://www.4president.org

American Presidency Project, http://www.presidency.ucsb.edu

Claude Arpi, http://www.claudearpi.net/maintenance/uploaded_pics/
ThePancheelAgreement.pdf

Frontline Diplomacy: The Foreign Affairs Oral History Collection for the
Association for Diplomatic Studies and Training, Library of Congress, http://
memory.loc.gov/ammem/collections/diplomacy

George, H.W. Bush Presidential Library, http://bushlibrary.tamu.edu/research

Margaret Thatcher Foundation, http://www.margaretthatcher.org

Miller Center, University of Virginia, Johnson Tapes: http://millercenter.org/scripps/
archive/presidentialrecordings/johnson/1967/02_1967

National Security Archive http://www2.gwu.edu/~nsarchiv

The *New York Times*, http://www.nytimes.com

Nixon Tapes.Org, http://nixontapes.org/cab.htm, White House Tapes: Executive
Office Building Conversations; and Oval Office Conversations

Office of the Historian, Department of State, *Foreign Relations of the United
States*: Vol. E-13, Documents on China, 1969–1972, http://www.state.gov/r/pa/
ho/frus/nixon/e13/c18861.htm

Ronald Reagan Presidential Library and Museum, http://www.reagan.utexas.edu/
archives

United Nations Security Council, http://unispal.un.org/unispal.nsf/0/7D35E1F729
DF491C85256EE700686136

YouTube, http://www.youtube.com

Memoirs

Abdulgani, Roeslan. *Bandung Connection: The Asia-Africa Conference in Bandung
in 1955*. Jakarta: Gunung Agung, 1981.

Adelman, Ken. *Reagan at Reykjavik: Forty-Eight Hours That Ended the Cold War*.
New York: Broadside Books, 2014.

Baker, James A., III with Thomas M. DeFrank, *Politics of Diplomacy: Revolution,
War & Peace, 1989–1992*. New York: G.P. Putnam's Sons, 1995.

Brzezinski, Zbigniew. *Power and Principle: Memoirs of the National Security
Adviser 1977–1981*. New York: Farrar Strauss Giroux, 1983.

Bush, George and Brent Scowcroft. *A World Transformed*. New York: Vintage
Books, 1998.

Carter, Jimmy. *Keeping Faith: Memoirs of a President*. New York: Bantam Books, 1982.

Chaozhu, Ji. *The Man on Mao's Right: From Harvard Yard to Tiananmen Square,
My Life inside China's Foreign Ministry*. New York: Random House, 2008.

Chernyaev, Anatoly S. *My Six Years with Gorbachev*. University Park: The
Pennsylvania State University Press, 2000.

Dobrynin, Anatoly. *In Confidence: Moscow's Ambassador to America's Six Cold
War Presidents*. New York: Times Books, 1995.

Grachev, Andrei. *Gorbachev's Gamble: Soviet Foreign Policy & the End of the
Cold War*. London: Polity Press, 2008.

Green, Marshall. *Evolution of US-China Policy, 1956–1973: Memoirs of an Insider*. Washington: The Association for Diplomatic Studies and Training, 1998.

Haig, Alexander M., Jr. *Caveat: Realism, Reagan, and Foreign Policy*. New York: MacMillan Publishing Company, 1984.

Haig, Alexander M., Jr. with Charles McCarry. *Inner Circles: How America Changed the World, A Memoir*. New York: Warner Books, 1992.

Holdridge, John H. *Crossing the Divide: An Insider's Account of Normalization of U.S.–China Relations*. Lanham: Rowman and Littlefield, 1997.

Hua, Huang. *Memoirs*. Beijing: Foreign Languages Press, 2008.

Johnson, Lyndon. *Vantage Point: Perspectives on the Presidency 1963–1969*. New York: Holt, Rinehart and Winston, 1971.

Khan, Sultan M. *Memories and Reflections of a Pakistani Diplomat*. London: The Centre for Pakistan Studies, 1997.

Kissinger, Henry A. *White House Years*. Boston: Little, Brown and Co., 1979.

Matlock, Jr., Jack F. *Reagan and Gorbachev: How the Cold War Ended*. New York: Random House, 2004.

Molotov, Vyacheslav. *Molotov Remembers: Inside Kremlin Politics: Conversations with Felix Chuev*, ed. by Albert Resis. Chicago: Ivan R. Dee, 1993.

Nixon, Richard M. *RN: The Memoirs of Richard M. Nixon*. New York: Grosset and Dunlap, 1978.

Palazchenko, Pavel. *My Years with Gorbachev and Shevardnadze: The Memoirs of a Soviet Interpreter*. University Park: Pennsylvania State University Press, 1997.

Reagan, Ronald. *An American Life: The Autobiography*. New York: Simon and Schuster, 1990.

Romulo, Carlos P. *Meaning of Bandung*. Chapel Hill: The University of North Carolina Press, 1956.

Shultz, George. *Turmoil and Triumph: My Years as Secretary of State*. New York: Charles Scribner and Sons, 1993.

Vance, Cyrus. *Hard Choices: Critical Years in America's Foreign Policy*. New York: Simon and Schuster, 1983.

Articles

Brands, Hal. "Non-Proliferation and the Dynamics of the Middle Cold War: The Superpowers, the MLF, and the NPT," *Cold War History* 7.3 (August 2007).

Fischer, Benjamin B. "A Cold War Conundrum: The 1983 Soviet War Scare" *Center for the Study of Intelligence*. Central Intelligence Agency, 2007.

Jani, Disha. "On-Stage, Off-Stage: Jawaharlal Nehru, Diplomacy, and the Indochina Conflict, 1954–1955," December 4, 2013, https://www.academia.edu/6532548/On-Stage_Off-Stage_Jawaharlal_Nehru_Diplomacy_and_the_Indochina_Conflict_1954-1955.

Jian, Chen. "The Sino-Soviet Alliance and China's Entry into the Korean War," Cold War International History Project Working Paper 1 (Washington, DC: Woodrow Wilson International Center for Scholars, 1992).

Kuisong, Yang. "The Sino-Soviet Border Clash of 1969: From Zhenbao Island to Sino-American Rapprochement," *Cold War History* 1.1 (2000).

Kuisong, Yang and Yafeng Xia. "Vacillating between Revolution and Détente: Mao's Changing Psyche and Policy toward the United States," *Diplomatic History* 34.2 (April 2010).

Xia, Yafeng. "China's Elite Politics and Sino-American Rapprochement, January 1969–February 1972," *Journal of Cold War Studies* 8.4 (Fall 2006).

Zhang, Xiaoming. "The Vietnam War, 1965-1969: A Chinese Perspective," *The Journal of Military History* 60.4 (October 1996).

Books

Ampiah, Kweku. *Political and Moral Imperatives of the Bandung Conference of 1955: The Reactions of the US, UK and Japan.* Kent: Global Oriental, 2007.

Beschloss, Michael. *Mayday: Eisenhower, Khrushchev and the U-2 Affair.* New York: Harper and Row, 1988.

Bischof, Günter and Saki Dockrill, eds. *Cold War Respite: The Geneva Summit of 1955.* Baton Rouge: Louisiana State University Press, 2000.

Brown, Archie. *Seven Years that Changed the World: Perestroika in Perspective.* New York: Oxford University Press, 2007.

Cohen, Warren I. and Nancy Bernkopf Tucker, eds. *Lyndon Johnson Confronts the World: American Foreign Policy, 1963–1968.* New York: Cambridge University Press, 1994.

Dikötter, Frank. *Mao's Great Famine: The History of China's Most Devastating Catastrophe, 1958–1862.* New York: Walker Publishing Company, 2010.

Dobbs, Michael. *Six Months in 1945: FDR, Stalin, Churchill and Truman, From World War to Cold War.* New York: Vintage Books, 2012.

Fursenko, Aleksandr and Timothy Naftali. *"One Hell of a Gamble": Khrushchev, Castro, and Kennedy 1958-1964—The Secret History of the Cuban Missile Crisis.* New York: W.W. Norton & Co., 1997.

Gaddis, John Lewis. *George F. Kennan: An American Life.* New York: Penguin Books, 2011.

Gaiduk, Ilya V. *The Soviet Union and the Vietnam War.* Chicago: Ivan R. Dee, 1996.

Glad, Betty. *An Outsider in the White House: Jimmy Carter, His Advisors, and the Making of American Foreign Policy.* Ithaca: Cornell University Press, 2009.

Goh, Evelyn. *Constructing the U.S. Rapprochement with China, 1961-1974: From "Red Menace" to "Tacit Ally".* New York: Cambridge University Press, 2005.

Guan, Ang Cheng. "The Bandung Conference and the Cold War International History of Southeast Asia," in See Seng Tan and Amitav Acharya, eds., *Bandung Revisited: The Legacy of the 1955 Asian-African Conference for International Order.* Singapore: National University of Singapore, 2008.

Hasegawa, Tsuyoshi. *Racing the Enemy: Stalin, Truman, and the Surrender of Japan.* Cambridge: Harvard University Press, 2005.

Hitchcock, William I. *France Restored: Cold War Diplomacy and the Quest for Leadership in Europe, 1944–1954.* Chapel Hill: The University of North Carolina Press, 1998.

Holloway, David. *Stalin and the Bomb: The Soviet Union and Atomic Energy, 1939–1956.* New Haven: Yale University Press, 1994.

Isaacson, Walter. *Kissinger: A Biography*. New York: Simon & Schuster, 1992.

Jian, Chen *Mao's China and the Cold War*. Chapel Hill: The University of North Carolina Press, 2001.

Jingli, Xu. *Jiemi Zhongguo Waijiao Dangan*. [Declassifying Chinese Diplomatic Files] Beijing: Zhongguo Dangan Chubanshe, 2005.

Jisheng, Yang. *Tombstone: The Great Chinese Famine 1958–1962*. New York: Farrar, Straus and Giroux, 2012.

Jones, Howard. *The Bay of Pigs*. New York: Oxford University Press, 2008.

Keith, Ronald C. *The Diplomacy of Zhou Enlai*. New York: St. Martin's Press, 1989.

Kempe, Frederick. *Berlin 1961: Kennedy, Khrushchev, and the Most Dangerous Place on Earth*. New York: Berkeley Books, 2011.

Kissinger, Henry. *On China*. New York: The Penguin Press, 2011.

Kyle, Keith. *Suez: Britain's End of Empire in the Middle East, 2nd ed*. New York: I.B. Tauris, 2002.

Liu, Xiaohong. *Chinese Ambassadors: The Rise of Diplomatic Professionalism since 1949*. Seattle: University of Washington Press, 1999.

Logevall, Frederik. *Embers of War: The Fall of an Empire and the Making of America's Vietnam*. New York: Random House, 2012.

Luthi, Lorenz. *The Sino-Soviet Split: Cold War in the Communist World*. Princeton: Princeton University Press, 2008.

Manchester, William. *Last Lion: Winston Spencer Churchill; Alone: 1932–1940*. New York: Dell Publishing, 1988.

Mann, James. *Rise of the Vulcans: The History of Bush's War Cabinet*. New York: Penguin Books, 2004.

Mann, James. *Rebellion of Ronald Reagan: A History of the End of the Cold War*. New York: Penguin Books, 2009.

Maynard, Christopher. *Out of the Shadow: George H.W. Bush and the End of the Cold War*. College Station: Texas A&M University Press, 2008.

McCullough, David. *Truman*. New York: Simon and Schuster, 1992.

Miscamble, Wilson D. *From Roosevelt to Truman: Potsdam, Hiroshima, and the Cold War*. New York: Cambridge University Press, 2007.

Muehlenbeck, Philip E. *Betting on the Africans: John F. Kennedy's Courting of African Nationalist Leaders*. New York: Oxford University Press, 2012.

Naimark, Norman M. *The Russians in Germany, 1945–1949*. Cambridge: Harvard University Press, 1995.

Nash, Philip. *The Other Missiles of October: Eisenhower, Kennedy, and the Jupiters 1957–1964*. Chapel Hill: The University of North Carolina Press, 1997.

Nelson, Anna Kasten, ed. "Senator Henry Jackson and the Demise of Détente," in *The Policymakers: Shaping American Foreign Policy From 1947 to the Present*. Lanham: Rowman & Littlefield Publishers, Inc., 2009.

Oren, Michael B. *Six Days of War: June 1967 and the Making of the Modern Middle East*. New York: Presidio Press, 2002.

Osgood, Kenneth. *Total Cold War: Eisenhower's Secret Propaganda Battle at Home and Abroad*. Lawrence: The University Press of Kansas, 2006.

Radchenko, Sergey. *Two Suns in the Heavens: The Sino-Soviet Struggle for Supremacy, 1962–1967*. Washington: Woodrow Wilson Center Press, 2009.

Reynolds, David. *Summits: Six Meetings That Shaped the Twentieth Century*. New York: Basic Books, 2007.

Roberts, Geoffrey. *Stalin's Wars: From World War to Cold War, 1939–1953*.
New Haven: Yale University Press, 2006.
Roberts, Priscilla, ed. *Behind the Bamboo Curtain: China, Vietnam, and the World
Beyond Asia*. Washington: Woodrow Wilson Center Press, 2006.
Ross, Robert S. and Jiang Changbin, eds. *Re-examining the Cold War: U.S.–China
Diplomacy, 1954–1973*. Cambridge: Harvard University Press, 2001.
Schwartz, Thomas Alan. *Lyndon Johnson and Europe: In the Shadow of Vietnam*.
Cambridge: Harvard University Press, 2003.
Shao, Kuo-Kang. *Zhou Enlai and the Foundations of Chinese Foreign Policy*.
New York: St. Martin's Press, 1996.
Siniver, Asaf. *Nixon, Kissinger, and U.S. Foreign Policy Making: The Machinery of
Crisis*. New York: Cambridge University Press, 2011.
Tudda, Chris. *A Cold War Turning Point: Nixon and Mao, 1969–1972*. Baton
Rouge: Louisiana State University Press, 2012.
Tudda, Chris. *Truth Is Our Weapon: The Rhetorical Diplomacy of Dwight
D. Eisenhower and John Foster Dulles*. Baton Rouge: Louisiana State University
Press, 2006.
Westad, Odd Arne. *Global Cold War*. New York: Cambridge University Press,
2007.
Woods, Randall B. *LBJ: Architect of American Ambition*. New York: Free Press,
2006.
Wright, Richard. *Color Curtain: A Report on the Bandung Conference*. Jackson:
University of Mississippi Press, 1995, reprint of 1956 edition published by
World Press.
Zhai, Qiang. *China and the Vietnam Wars, 1950–1975*. Chapel Hill: The University
of North Carolina Press, 2000.
Zhisui, Li. *The Private Life of Chairman Mao*. New York: Random House, 1994.
Xia, Yafeng. *Negotiating with the Enemy: U.S.–China Talks during the Cold War,
1949–1972*. Bloomington: Indiana University Press, 2006.
Zubok, Vladislav. *A Failed Empire: The Soviet Union in the Cold War from Stalin
to Gorbachev*. Chapel Hill: The University of North Carolina Press, 2007.

INDEX

CPSIA information can be obtained
at www.ICGtesting.com
Printed in the USA
LVOW13s0610080618

580065LV00009B/226/P